THE ENCYCLOPEDIA OF DIETARY INTERVENTIONS FOR THE TREATMENT OF AUTISM AND RELATED DISORDERS

BY LISA LEWIS

Special Diets For Special Kids
Special Diets For Special Kids II

BY KARYN SEROUSSI

Unraveling the Mystery of Autism and Pervasive Developmental Disorder:
A Mother's Story of Research and Recovery

The Encyclopedia of
Dietary Interventions

for the Treatment of
Autism and Related Disorders

The Essential Reference Guide
for Parents and Physicians

KARYN SEROUSSI
LISA S. LEWIS, PH.D.

Sarpsborg Press
Pennington, NJ

The Encyclopedia of Dietary Interventions

An ANDI Publication

Published by Sarpsborg Press

PO Box 335

Pennington, NJ 08534-0335

www.sarpsborgpress.com

First Edition - Second Printing

Copyright © 2008 by Sarpsborg Press, Pennington, NJ

Seroussi, Karyn

The Encyclopedia of Dietary Interventions for the Treatment of Autism and Related Disorders

/ Karyn Seroussi and Lisa S. Lewis

p. cm.

Includes bibliographical references.

ISBN: 978-0-615-20169-6

Cover and book design by Karyn Seroussi

Photography by Linda Henriksen

Printed in the United States of America

To our children, Sam, Jacob, Laura, and James,
for inspiration,

To our husbands, Serge and Jørgen,
for their love, support, and patience,

To the thousands of families
who have become our family,

And to the late Dr. Bernard Rimland,
to whom we are all immensely grateful.

ACKNOWLEDGMENTS

We would like to acknowledge every caregiver and professional who has contacted us in the past thirteen years. This book is our way of "paying forward" the knowledge that you have worked so hard to pass along, so that the next generation of caregivers and professionals will have an easier path to follow.

A great deal of credit for this book belongs to the "Defeat Autism Now!" group, who have become a constant source of knowledge and support, and to the "Defeat Autism Now! Doctors" and other medical professionals who have repeatedly stuck their necks out for their patients.

We greatly appreciate the input we have received from Susan Owens, Donna Gates, Ginger Houston-Ludlam, Pam Ferro, RN, Arthur Krigsman, MD, Liz Mumper, MD, Bruce Semon, MD, Stuart Freedenfeld, MD, and Jon Pangborn, Ph.D.

Karyn especially wishes to acknowledge Mette Johansen and Jørgen Klaveness for taking over so many of her responsibilities so she could write, and to Cecilie Klaveness, for lending her a place in which to write.

We would also like to thank Elaine Boby, Paula Hashmall, Julie Matthews, Peg Tipton, Serge Goldstein, Shelley Lewis and Jørgen Klaveness for their careful reading and proofreading. Their efforts were invaluable but any errors remain solely our responsibility.

Contents

Foreword

To the Physician or Medical Professional

Special diets will not change a child's chromosomes or reverse a true genetic disorder, any more than avoiding foods with phenylalanine will cure a patient of PKU. But autism is now understood to be most likely caused by a genetic susceptibility, combined with a pre-natal or post-natal environmental trigger. It is increasingly evident that autism is a complex medical condition with physical as well as behavioral symptoms, and may respond well to one or more biomedical interventions.

Dietary intervention is quickly losing its status as an "alternative" therapy for autistic disorders. It is supported by several peer-reviewed studies, thousands of documented case studies, and a number of new, well-funded research projects.

But why would autistic patients need special diets?

- Dr. Derrick MacCabe and his colleagues at the University of Western Ontario concluded that certain gut and dietary factors may worsen symptoms transiently in autism spectrum disorders, epilepsy, and some inheritable metabolic disorders, relating to a dysregulation of propionic acid, a short chain fatty acid and an important intermediate of cellular metabolism.[1]

- Research by Dr. H. Jyanouchi of the Autism Center at the New Jersey Medical School found that, relative to a control group, children on the autism spectrum have an abnormal immune response to cow's milk protein, wheat protein and soy protein. The reaction in the autistic population was strongest to milk; in many cases, the reaction to soy was even more pronounced than the reaction to wheat.[2][3][4]

---

[1] MacCabe DF, et al. "Neurobiological effects of intraventricular propionic acid in rats: possible role of short chain fatty acids on the pathogenesis and characteristics of autism spectrum disorders." *Behav Brain Res.* 2007 Jan 10;176(1):149-69.

[2] Jyonouchi H, Geng L, Ruby A, Zimmerman-Bier B. "Dysregulated innate immune responses in young children with autism spectrum disorders: their relationship to gastrointestinal symptoms and dietary intervention." *Neuropsychobiology.* 2005;51(2):77-85.

[3] Jyonouchi H, Geng L, Ruby A, Reddy C, Zimmerman-Bier B. "Evaluation of an association between gastrointestinal symptoms and cytokine production against common dietary proteins in children with autism spectrum disorders." *J Pediatr.* 2005 May;146(5):605-10.

[4] Vojdani A, O'Bryan T, Green JA, Mccandless J, Woeller KN, Vojdani E, Nourian AA, Cooper EL. "Immune response to dietary proteins, gliadin and cerebellar peptides in children with autism." *Nutr Neurosci.* 2004 Jun;7(3): 151-61.

- Dr. Kalle Reichelt at the University of Oslo/Rikshospitalet found opioid peptides derived from food proteins (exorphins) in urine of autistic patients.[5] These peptides, primarily casomorphin and gluteomorphin (gliadorphin), are close enough in structure to drugs in the morphine class that they have been long suspected of causing some of the more inexplicable symptoms of autism, such as self-absorption, self-stimulatory behaviors, sensory disturbances, bowel irregularities, and insensitivity to pain.

- Dr. Timothy Buie, a pediatric gastroenterologist at Harvard/Mass General Hospital, has performed over 400 gastrointestinal endoscopies with biopsies on autistic children. In a preliminary study in 2002, he noted the frequent presence of chronic inflammation of the digestive tract, including esophagitis, gastritis and enterocolitis. He found that 55% of the autistic children he examined showed disaccharide/glucoamylase, lactase, and sucrase enzyme levels below normal. These children were thus far more likely to suffer from impaired starch metabolism, carbohydrate malabsorption and undiagnosed bowel disorders than their neurotypical peers. He concluded that more than 50% of autistic children appear to have symptoms of gastrointestinal illness, including abdominal pain, gas, bloating, and chronic diarrhea or loose stools, food allergies, and maldigestion or malabsorption issues.[6] This helps to explain why so many well-fed autistic children, upon medical examination, are sometimes found to be severely deficient in several essential vitamins and minerals.

Regardless of the complex cause, or causes, of these food intolerances, the outcome is simple. When you put these children on special diets, many of them will get better. Dr. Ted Kniker of the San Antonio Autistic Treatment Center in Texas, Dr. Anne-Marie Knivsberg at the Stavanger University College in Norway, Dr. S. Lucarelli at the University of Rome, Italy, and other researchers around the world have published studies demonstrating that some children and adults with autism show improvement after elimination of dairy products and wheat gluten from their diets.[7][8][9][10]

Unfortunately, autistic children are rarely tested for gastrointestinal illnesses, even when they present with symptoms that would raise alarm bells if seen in a typical child. Unusual test results may be disregarded, possibly because there already is a diagnosis: *autism*. Sometimes it is difficult, even for physicians, to remember that children with autism are also children. They may suffer silently from

> *"These children are ill, and they are in distress and pain. They are not just mentally, neurologically dysfunctional."*
>
> *-Timothy Buie, MD*

[5] Reichelt KL, Knivsberg. "Can the pathophysiology of autism be explained by the nature of the discovered urine peptides?" *AM. Nutr Neurosci*. 2003 Feb;6(1):19-28. Review.

[6] Buie T, Winter H, Kushak, R. "Preliminary findings in gastrointestinal investigation of autistic patients." 2002. Harvard University and Mass General Hospital.

[7] Millward C, Ferriter M, Calver S, Connell-Jones G. "Gluten- and casein-free diets for autism spectrum disorder." *Cochrane Database Syst Rev*. 2004;(2):CD003498.

[8] Garvey J. "Diet in autism and associated disorders." *J Fam Health Care* 2002;12(2):34-8.

[9] Knivsberg AM, Reichelt KL, Hoien T, Nodland M. "A randomised, controlled study of dietary intervention in autistic syndromes." *Nutr Neurosci* 2002 Sep;5(4):251-61.

[10] Lucarelli S et al. "Food allergy and infantile autism." *Panminerva Med*. 1995 Sep;37(3):137-41.

diseases or disorders that may, or may not, be related to their "primary complaint."

Some high-functioning people on the autism spectrum attest to the fact that dietary restriction relieves a great deal of pain or physical discomfort, as well as the "noise" that makes it hard for them to learn and to perform socially. It is impossible to judge the level of silent suffering that is going on in the autism population as a whole, because so many of these children cannot tell us how they feel. However, those of us who have experienced severe diarrhea, constipation or intestinal disease will greatly sympathize with those in this group who are known or suspected to have these problems, and cannot express their pain to their caregivers.

Children with autism as a group have notoriously poor nutrition coupled with vitamin and mineral deficiencies. This may be due, in part, to extreme eating habits (they are notoriously picky). Deficiencies are also likely due to the above-mentioned tendency toward malabsorption. This is why physicians who specialize in the biomedical treatment of autism start out by addressing malabsorption issues, adding digestive enzymes to the diet, eliminating problematic foods (usually including gluten and casein), stabilizing the condition of the gastrointestinal tract by removing allergens and harmful organisms, and introducing nutrients not being properly absorbed and utilized by the body. This approach has resulted in significant improvement in cognitive function, and in some cases, a full recovery from many of the symptoms of autism, if not the underlying disorder.

It is our hope that you will find this book to be an excellent resource for yourself and your patients, and that you will join the hundreds of medical practitioners who are knowledgeable and dedicated to exploring effective treatments for this devastating disorder.

To the Parent or Caregiver

NOTE: Throughout this book, we have chosen to use the pronoun "he," with apologies to the thousands of little girls who are affected. We also refer to these interventions in the context of children with autism, even though they may apply to older people or those with other health problems or related disorders. In addition, when we refer to "parents," we include all family members, caregivers, and others with the responsibility of meal planning and preparation. Although many people prefer the term "child/ren) with autism" rather than "autistic child/ren," we have used both these terms in this book. We intend no disrespect to any child or adult on the autism spectrum and use the latter term only when the longer label is cumbersome or awkward.

Please also note that the biomedical interventions mentioned in this book, while meant to alleviate the underlying factors contributing to these disorders, should be used in combination with behavioral programs to help your child progress on social, self-help, and academic skills. There are several excellent books on those subjects. This book is intended only to address dietary and related biomedical treatments for autism.

Remember: Always consult your doctor or nutritionist when making changes to your child's diet.

Most people caring for an autistic child will agree that they have experienced the same dreadful feeling: a vague and persistent worry that they are missing something. What if a magic bullet is out there waiting for your child, and you just didn't know about it, or you ignored the information because you were feeling confused or overwhelmed?

You may have heard about children who never responded to any treatment, and then suddenly "took off" after methyl-B12 injections, or a "GF/CF diet," or intravenous immunoglobulin, or some other biomedical approach. You might hear about children who were having terrible tantrums until they were tested and treated for parasites, or who didn't sleep through the night until they starting taking epsom salt baths or melatonin.

But how can you possibly try everything? How can you narrow down your choices to the treatments that will most likely benefit your child?

The obvious answer is to try to get your child to a physician who is experienced with biomedical interventions, charges reasonable fees and has good references from other parents. Such doctors can be hard to find locally and often have waiting lists. While you search for the right doctor, or wait for an appointment, there is something important you can do for your child. Dietary intervention can be done at home, with little cost and a good chance for success.

> *Because so many children have responded well to changes in their diet, it has become the first-line protocol for nearly all physicians who support biomedical interventions. Some doctors will not even accept a new patient until the child has been on a gluten and dairy free diet for at least six weeks.*

There has recently been a movement among adults with Aspergers and high-functioning autism to raise public awareness to the idea that autism shouldn't be seen as a disability, or a disorder that needs to be "cured." If these adults believe themselves to be physically healthy, then they may have a very different syndrome than the new wave of young autistic children presenting with sensory distress, pain, and/or bowel disease. Our goal is to address what we think is an epidemic of "induced" autism, likely triggered by environmental factors. Autism can bring giftedness and a unique way of perceiving and contributing to the world, but it often results in confusion, social isolation, and sensory discomfort. Adults with autism who have been successful with dietary interventions tell us that it makes the world a far more comfortable place in which to live. Now, let's get your child on a healthy, appropriate diet!

HOW TO USE THIS BOOK:

Although it may be tempting to skip over to the Encyclopedia, try to take some time to read the first part of this book. Even those experienced with dietary interventions need a solid understanding of the current research, and the reasons for commonly-used food restrictions.

Any words or phrases in CAPITAL LETTERS refer to an entry in the Encyclopedia. When you see an unfamiliar term, topic or abbreviation, you can also check the Encyclopedia for an entry with that title.

This book includes many references to online resources. We apologize to those who do not have Internet access, but strongly recommend that anyone caring for a child with a disability should take advantage of that tremendous resource, or get some help from someone who can. If this is impossible for financial or other reasons, most public libraries have Internet-connected computers available for public use.

From 1999 through 2005, we published a quarterly newsletter called The ANDI News. During that time we received thousands of letters and emails from parents. These letters shared ideas, recipes, common questions and personal successes and failures. Throughout this book we have tried to include many of these stories, choosing ones that were informative and, in many cases, inspirational.

Please keep in mind that we have included a selection of letters describing positive results with dietary interventions, which are mostly what we receive. Presumably, people who do not get good results are less likely to write and tell us their stories. Note that the inclusion of a diet in this book does not imply our endorsement or recommendation; this book is for informational purposes only.

Knowledge is increasing so fast that it's a challenge to keep up with it. If you have corrections or suggestions for future editions of this book, please send an email to info@sarpsborgpress.com.

Introduction

There is some debate as to the changes in autism prevalence in the past twenty years, but it has been suggested that there has been a startling increase.[11] According to the CDC (Centers for Disease Control), the prevalence of autism in the United States is estimated at 1 in 150 children.[12]

Scientists have concluded that the disorder is caused by a combination of genetic predisposition and an environmental trigger (either before or after birth). This leads one to question whether autism is, and has always been, a medical illness, masked as a behavioral disorder. If it's a medical illness, is it treatable? How? And for which children?

The movement toward biomedical intervention has been driven largely by the parents of children with autism, who have seen its effectiveness first-hand. Most no longer believe that autism is solely a disorder of the mind. The Autism Research Institute, founded by the late Dr. Bernard Rimland, spawned a large movement of parents, researchers and physicians into an organization called "Defeat Autism Now!" This movement has led to an unprecedented collaboration between parents and professionals, all working to unravel the biochemical, genetic and nutritional factors responsible for the shifts in behavior, language and cognition we presently call autism or Pervasive Developmental Disorder.

There can be no "one size fits all" approach to treating autistic patients because there is no intervention that will make them all better. Some have a major yeast overgrowth (possibly the result of antibiotics taken as infants or toddlers, or a result of an impaired immune system), while others do not. Some parents report a negative reaction and regression in development following a virus or vaccine, perhaps also associated with immune dysfunction. Some children are severely deficient in one or more minerals (such as zinc and/or magnesium) while other children are not. Some test positive for wheat and dairy in the IgG blood work or urinary peptide tests, while some do not. What most of these children do have in common is evidence that they are are physically ill as well as developmentally abnormal. Treating their physical illnesses makes them feel better, act better, and learn better.

Here are some of the common treatment priorities on the medical checklist:

•Improve the quality of the diet, reducing sugars, additives, and environmental pesticides and impurities

•Remove gluten, casein and other proteins that likely cause physical and behavioral symptoms and/or distress

•Identify and address any food allergies and intolerances

---

[11] Wazana A, Bresnahan M, Kline J. "The autism epidemic: fact or artifact?" *J Am Acad Child Adolesc Psychiatry.* 2007 Jun,46(6).721-30.

[12] www.cdc.gov/ncbddd/autism/faq_prevalence.htm

•Identify and correct deficiencies or poor utilization of nutrients with vitamin/mineral supplements, such as vitamin B6 and magnesium, glutathione, selenium, zinc, essential fatty acids, and amino acids

•Check for signs of gastrointestinal distress, and investigate and treat any illness

•Use antifungal and/or antibacterial medications, in conjunction with probiotics to correct gut dysbiosis

Depending on test results, other recommendations might include digestive enzyme tablets, melatonin, thyroid medication, sulfation support, heavy metal detoxification, and immune system regulation.[13]

Whenever possible, parents should find a knowledgeable medical practitioner to help them map out the best sequence of treatments for their child, because the history and physical examination of the child will determine the tests ordered, and ultimately, the course of treatment to be followed. Some of the commonly used tests will not be covered by insurance, even though they may yield potentially useful results. Some parents choose to do an initial consultation with a doctor experienced in biomedical approaches, and then have him/her follow up with the family physician. It is often possible to find a local doctor who is willing to order these tests, although many parents will need to continue working with a specialist, even if they are located elsewhere. Fortunately, most will do phone consultations after a preliminary examination and work-up.

This approach can be challenging for parents. Changes in diet and supplementation are not usually expensive, but can be hard to implement. There are no guarantees, but thousands of parents will tell you that it is worth the effort. Changes in behavior, improvements in bowel function, increased language, and decreased self-stimulation are common responses to biomedical interventions.

---

[13] *Summary of Biomedical Treatments for Autism* by James B. Adams, Ph.D., April 2007, published online at http://autism.asu.edu.

Part I:
Implementing Dietary Interventions

"On our fourth dairy-free day I woke up to silence at 8 a.m. Usually Jay awakened me by 5 a.m., hooting and howling for 30 minutes or more (until the Ritalin took effect). On that day, I walked into our living room to discover all Jay's Legos® disassembled and reassembled into a four foot long space ship with fifteen men sitting in a row. I was stunned and said, 'Jay, look what you did!' He answered, 'Mom, I remember how to play this way.'

We immediately eliminated wheat and gluten products. It's been a year since that wonderful day, and everyone who knows our son is awed by his progress. In the past, a simple request to read or write evoked instant rage and aggression; now it is an activity that he chooses to do in his spare time."

"It is now almost eight months since we started the GF/CF diet with our son. In the first two weeks we saw classic withdrawal—crying and irritability in a previously even-tempered child. Within a month, however, Travis could have served as the "poster child" for a GF/CF diet. He began to eat normal portions of food, and the third week he told me he was "full" after eating— a first.

His stools firmed up, the cradle cap began to disappear, and his weight stabilized. He does not "space out" anymore; he is playing with his sister. He had been lethargic, but now has the energy and attention for many activities he could not sustain in the past. Most telling is that he will not touch wheat or dairy products. It does not bother him if we eat forbidden foods in front of him; he is happy with his special foods. We are thrilled for Travis and send our thanks to you for your observations and research."

Implementing Dietary Interventions

Please be advised that we are not giving medical advice. We have gathered this information so that you can make an informed decision in partnership with your medical practitioner.

A Single Step: Dietary intervention often begins the moment that the first glass of potato, nut or rice milk is poured. However, we all know that it actually begins earlier, when parents or caregivers make a commitment, sometimes against great odds, to give biomedical interventions a try. Changing diet may change your life, but then, so will autism and related illnesses. With any luck, you'll end up with a healthier lifestyle and a well-functioning child.

Most newcomers fear that dietary intervention will be an uphill battle. However, the ground does level off much sooner than you might expect. The diet will get much, much easier, and once improvement is evident, the support you receive from those around you — including spouses, doctors, and educators, will also increase.

Our friend Jenn decided to put her daughter Alix on a gluten free diet after reading about it online. Alix had been milk-free since she was a baby, but this seemed so much more complicated. Jenn postponed it for weeks, feeling guilty and inadequate whenever she thought about getting started. "I know I'm going to have to try this diet," she told us, "but we have three other children, my husband and I work full-time, and I haven't made time to think about it. So many of our family favorites will have to be modified, I'm a terrible cook, and I don't want to add any stress to my life right now."

There were no guarantees that the diet would help Alix. "I guess I'm afraid of being disappointed if it doesn't work," said Jenn, "and yet, in a way, I'm hoping it won't. I know that sounds a little crazy, since of course I want to help my daughter in whatever way I can."

Time management experts tell us that in a situation like this, we need to set a date to begin our project, commit to that date, and tell others of our commitment. Jenn vowed to begin the diet on the first of the upcoming month, come what may. She told all of her family members and Alix's caregivers of the plan.

> *"A year from now you may wish you had started today."*
>
> *-author Robert Schuller, quoted in "The Low Oxalate Cookbook II"*

On the night before the diet was to start, Jenn panicked. She was not prepared, but didn't want to give up the idea. So she sat down and came up with a list of gluten-free meals that her child liked, just for the following day: rice cakes with almond butter for breakfast, baked potato for lunch, and beef vegetable stir-fry with rice for dinner.

The following night, Jenn did the same thing, planning only one day's meals. She did the same thing the next night, and the next. Suddenly, Alix had been on the diet for a week, and then two. Jenn looked for some new recipes online, and began networking with other parents, asking questions and making observations. Before she knew it, the transition had been made. When Alix began making impressive gains, that in itself became the motivation Jenn and her husband needed to carry on.

We know of other families who have approached dietary change in a more organized manner. For example, some parents find childcare and then spend an entire day shopping, preparing the kitchen and cooking food to serve and to freeze. Some make a party of it, inviting friends to help with the cooking. The point is to figure out what strategy fits best with your personality and lifestyle, to best ensure an easy and successful transition.

One should never make an important decision without having as much information as possible, and an informed decision cannot be properly made without a good trial. Some children will respond quickly and noticeably within days, but many will take longer. Give dietary intervention a good chance before making up your mind that it will or won't help your child.

The 'Three Stages' of Dietary Intervention

It is always less daunting to attempt a complicated task if it has been broken down into manageable stages. The following three stages will remove the mystery and difficulty of starting dietary intervention.

Stage 1: Getting Started

Identify the Pre-Diet Diet: Make a list of all the foods your child likes and eats. What do they have in common? Perhaps they are all starchy, sweet, salty, dairy-based or wheat-based. Perhaps they are all the same types of foods. A child eating ice cream, bananas, grapes, chocolate pudding, sweetened yogurt, apple juice, and ketchup is not eating a varied diet – he is eating milk and sugar. A child who only eats bagels, crackers, cereal, pretzels, and waffles is not eating a varied diet; he is mostly eating one food: wheat. Foods that are craved are highly suspect, especially dairy and wheat foods (see OPIOID EXCESS).

> "It's hard work, as you know better than we do. But when you see the results, it's truly incredible. And to think, our pediatrician scoffed at the idea, saying, 'that diet doesn't do a thing.'" –Garth Stein

Next, make a list of your child's physical symptoms. Does he get rashes? Does he get red cheeks or red ears after meals? Is his stomach bloated? Does he have diarrhea or constipation? Is he insensitive to pain? Note how these symptoms are associated with food, for example, does your child get red cheeks shortly after eating a particular food? Are bowel problems associated with any particular types of food? Are his behaviors worse at certain times of day, before or after meals?

Since you are going to further limit the diet of a child who may already be on a limited diet, begin giving a multi-vitamin and mineral formula that is both low allergen and free of gluten and casein (common additives in vitamins). There are several available that are appropriate for children with autism made by specializing companies (see APPENDIX).

If possible, ask your pediatrician to do a blood test for celiac disease (CD) *before* removing gluten. To be thorough, they should check total IgA, gliadin IgA and IgG, and tissue transglutaminase IgA (see CELIAC DISEASE).

It is likely to come back negative, since the blood test for CD is targeting only one specific type of gluten allergy. It is unclear whether celiac disease is actually more common in this group than in the general population. It is now known that celiac disease is far more common than previously believed, so statistically, there will be a number of autistic people with celiac. Due to other GI problems, they are probably more likely to be tested and diagnosed.

Commit to a three-month trial of dietary intervention. Join an online support group such as the one at www.gfcfdiet.com. Choose a date, planning a day or two's meals at a time. Start keeping a food diary—this will turn out to be an important tool and should not be overlooked. Include a column for observing physical symptoms (see RECORD-KEEPING).

A negative result on a celiac blood test does not mean that your child tolerates gluten. It simply means that your child does not qualify for a diagnosis of celiac disease based on those test results. However, if possible, ask to have it done before removing gluten. *The results will not be meaningful after gluten has been removed from the diet.*

Remove all dairy products from the diet, and within a week or two, all gluten. Using sugars, rice, potatoes and other starchy foods to achieve this transition may be necessary, but keep in mind that they will probably need to be reduced or even removed later on. A sugar and starch-based diet has shown to be problematic for many of our children, such as those with abnormal gut pathologies and/or immune abnormalities. Consider removing soy and corn at the same time gluten is removed. Many parents have given up on the gluten free diet because they saw no change or a regression in their children, after having substituted soy for milk or corn for gluten. These two foods are almost universally problematic when starting the diet. They can always be added back later on a trial basis.

It is common to see crankiness, regression, or withdrawal symptoms during these first few days. Stay the course, and let your child know that you mean business.

Keep it Simple: Instead of providing homemade or commercially available chicken nuggets, teach your children to eat plain chicken that has been baked or broiled. Cut the chicken into child-friendly strips and serve with a simple dipping sauce that you can make from scratch quickly and cheaply. Teach your children to eat fruits and vegetables that are raw or gently steamed, again, using a simple sauce at first if they won't even try them plain, or blending them into pasta sauce or soup.

Find the recipes that work for you, create shortcuts so that they can be made in a snap, make large batches, and freeze portions for later use (see COOKING & BAKING).

Time and Money: Some parents worry that dietary intervention will be very expensive, and worry that it won't be worth the trouble and expense. It is true that if you rely on convenience foods like frozen waffles, dietary changes will cost more than buying "regular" food. Although many parents are short on time and energy, making these from scratch is easy and inexpensive. For those who are accustomed to using lots of pre-packaged snack foods and baked goods, and who try to replace these with store-bought alternatives, dietary changes will be relatively costly and will probably contain more starches than is generally optimal. For those who are willing to learn to follow some simple recipes at home, dietary intervention shouldn't increase your family's food bill by very much. In fact, it may save you quite a bit of money, since you are far more likely to pack healthy, safe foods before leaving the house, and far less likely to grab a meal at fast-food restaurants.

Get support: Order free copies of "Your Life: Focus on Autism" for articles on diet that you can give family members, teachers, and other caregivers.[14] Tell them what you are doing, and why. Ask for their support.

Stage 2: Testing and Record Keeping

After the diet is underway, some simple testing could yield some good results. An IgG multiple food allergy ELISA panel could provide a guideline for other foods that may be causing inflammation, and a blood or skin test could identify "regular" IgE-mediated food and environmental allergies. An organic acids test can check for yeast and bacteria, and metabolic abnormalities. Ask your doctor to do a stool test to check for parasites, since this has proven to be a surprisingly common problem. If indicated, treat the child with anti-fungal or anti-bacterial medication, and remove any offending foods (see TESTING). *Remember: just because the child does not test positive for wheat and dairy allergy does not mean that these foods are tolerated.* Only re-introduction of the foods can give you that answer, but try not to do a deliberate challenge at this stage. It is important to give the diet a fair trial first.

When your child appears to be stabilized after the initial withdrawal, introduce bottled probiotics and/or probiotic foods (see the Encyclopedia).

Start a food diary. Get a spiral pad or notebook, and list each food your child eats on the left side of the page. On the right side of the page, list any changes you observe. Make a note of things like aggression, crying, whining, red ears, itchiness, bowel changes, or sleep problems.

Your food diary will help you see patterns, e.g. if your child has a delayed reaction to a food. This can help you determine why your child is experiencing a roller-coaster of good and bad days. You can also use your diary to note the impact of soy, corn, eggs, nuts, starches, citrus, fruits, sugars and brightly colored foods; these foods are often poorly tolerated.

Stage 3: Evaluating the Response

After your child has been on the diet for a few weeks, you should have a good idea of whether or not it will be an important tool in your fight. If there has been improvement, you will want to continue. Although it may seem paradoxical, you will also want to continue if your child's behavioral or physical symptoms have worsened. A regression is very common when offending foods are removed from the diet, and generally indicates that the child will benefit from dietary intervention. If you see no change at all after several weeks or months, it is possible that diet will not be a significant intervention for your child (see STOPPING DIETARY INTERVENTION IN A NON-RESPONDER). After your child has stabilized, you may want to tweak the diet he is on or go further, exploring some of the "advanced" dietary interventions. Detailed information about all of these approaches can be found in the Encyclopedia section of this book.

---

[14] Go to www.vancesfoods.com and click on Online Store, or call 1-800-497-4834.

What To Expect, When to Move On

Most of the overall gains seen in children using these diets are in improved health and GI (gastrointestinal) function, and in cognitive and learning abilities. Some will begin to experience normal feelings of hunger or fullness. Some will begin to react normally to pain, or respond to the feeling of having to use the bathroom.

Sometimes changing the diet can lead to striking results within a short period of time. Younger children who are drinking large quantities of milk or eating primarily dairy or wheat-based foods may exhibit changes within a week. But for most, the change won't be apparent until a few weeks later (often after accidental ingestion, when there is a noticeable regression). You may notice changes within a few days, but if not, be patient.

Keep in mind that if a regression lasts more than three weeks, it may be the result of an increased quantity of an unknown allergen (for example, when corn is heavily substituted for wheat, or dairy is replaced by soy). If you need to rely heavily on starchy foods just to get your child off gluten and casein, a yeast overgrowth may have occurred or been made worse (another reason to keep it simple). For some children, it may be necessary to simultaneously remove other foods, especially soy, corn and even rice. Some children will require the elimination of all complex carbohydrates and others will need to reduce oxalates (see Encyclopedia).

For children who do not show immediate or rapid improvement, it is tempting to slip or go back to the old diet entirely. In most cases, this is a mistake, especially for the children who self-limited their diets or had bowel problems. Although this subgroup is not the only one to benefit from dietary intervention, it describes children who ultimately respond well. Frequently, children with bowel problems are sicker than they appear, and dietary changes, while necessary, are just the tip of the iceberg: see BOWEL DISEASE & AUTISM.

Often parents who report no improvement have not really eliminated all the sources of gluten or casein from the diet. There are many hidden sources; for example, most cheese substitutes contain some form of casein. It can even be found in tuna fish and other canned foods. Many wheat free cereals contain malt (from barley) and thus are not gluten free. Chewing gum, stickers, play clay—all of these can be sources of gluten and casein. In short, you need to be a detective and investigate everything that goes into your child's mouth. Remember that, especially with small children, non-food items often end up there too. Just a trace can make a world of difference in your results.

Parents who have given dietary intervention a trial of at least three months, and who are certain that no hidden ingredients have been missed, may reasonably consider that food is not affecting their children. For those whose children's autism is not coming from these foods, do not give up your search for answers. Test immune function, look at issues like yeast and bacteria in the gut, and look into some of the other treatments that have proved useful to Defeat Autism Now! and other experienced and qualified professionals. There are some safe, inexpensive treatments that seem to be helping many autistic children for reasons that are only beginning to be understood. Remember, autistic behaviors are not a disease; they are a symptom, and there is no such thing as a symptom without a cause.

Different Approaches: "The Diets"

As stated above, some of the children who improve on a basic gluten and casein free diet still have a long way to go. The underlying problems in autism spectrum disorders usually have many layers. Opioid peptides from dairy and gluten may be just part of what is affecting your child. You may not see much improvement until all of the offenders have been addressed.

What to Remove?

Dietary intervention in autism is usually referred to as "the GF/CF diet," but most children seem to need modifications that go well beyond gluten and casein free regimens. It is not unusual to hear a parent in the online support groups say that their child is on a "GF/CF/soy-free/corn-free/egg-free low-oxalate diet, with probiotic foods and limited sugars."

> ### The Two-Tack Rule:
>
> *If you are sitting on a tack, it will take a lot of aspirin to make you feel better. If you are sitting on two tacks, removal of one tack will not result in a 50% improvement.*
>
> *- Dr. Sidney M. Baker, Defeat Autism Now! Co-founder; Author, Detoxification & Healing*

Therefore, it's no wonder that people have begun to refer to most of these dietary interventions simply as "GF/CF diets" or "gluten-free and restricted diets." As public awareness of celiac disease and gluten intolerance increases, this is probably the easiest explanation one can give.

There is much conflicting information on the Internet and on various support lists about which diets are "best." When one child does extremely well on a specific regimen, caregivers may become convinced that his diet will work just as well for other children, sometimes to the point of fanaticism. This can serve to inspire others, but it can also result in pressing for inappropriate adherence to one regimen when another might actually be more suitable.

Experience has shown that most people on the autism spectrum will benefit from a diet that is strictly free of gluten and dairy; therefore, the removal of these should be considered the foundation for dietary interventions. Additional changes are almost always needed for optimum improvement, but one size does not fit all. Every parent's goal is to find the ideal removal or rotation of foods for their child that will provide maximum benefit without being unnecessarily restrictive.

The most commonly restricted foods include gluten, dairy, corn, soy, yeast, oxalates, sugars, and starches. Other principles may apply, such as the use of probiotic foods, healthy fats, organic foods, and the restriction of food additives and artificial colors.

The most common dietary principles currently in use come from "the Specific Carbohydrate Diet,™" developed by Elaine Gottschall, "the Low Oxalate Diet," introduced to the autism community by Susan Owens, and "the Body Ecology Diet," developed by Donna Gates. None of these diets were originally developed to address autism spectrum disorders, so they usually must be modified to suit a child's individual needs. Detailed descriptions can be found under their own entries in the ENCYCLOPEDIA. See APPENDIX A for a comparison chart.

Part II: The Encyclopedia of Dietary Interventions

The Encyclopedia of Dietary Interventions

> **Please Note:** *Although you may be using this book primarily as a quick reference guide, you will probably benefit from reading Part I. This will give you an overview of dietary interventions, and help you avoid common mistakes that will confuse your results and delay your child's progress.*

ACACIA GUM (GUM ARABIC)

Used as an emulsifier (to prevent separation of liquids) and food thickener, this product is found in candy, soft drinks and chewing gum. Because it is a soluble fiber, acacia powder can be a good supplement for those who suffer from alternating constipation or diarrhea, since it helps maintain an even consistency in the stools when taken with plenty of water. Gluten free, but not allowed on SCD™. High-quality acacia powder can be purchased online, at www.helpforibs.com/shop.

ACESULFAME POTASSIUM (AKA SUNETTE®) See SUGAR SUBSTITUTES

ACETIC ACID

Acetic acid is the main ingredient of vinegar, and found naturally in many foods. It is used to aid in processing, enhance flavor, and as a curing agent for stabilizing flavor and color. It is usually considered safe on special diets.

ALKALINE SALTS

Is your child's body too acidic or too alkaline? And is this a problem? The premise behind giving alkaline salts (sodium and potassium bicarbonate) to autistic children is that their presence in the digestive tract stimulates the formation of a hormone called secretin, which may be deficient in some people with impaired digestion. Raising the body's alkalinity has been linked with overall health by some alternative health practitioners. When naturally-occurring digestive enzymes are deficient, alkaline salts are believed to aid digestion.

Reducing the amount of acid in the stomach could theoretically impair digestion and make matters worse, so if you decide to try these salts, look for enteric coated pills that will allow the active ingredient to be released in the duodenum and jejunum, not the stomach. They should be taken with food, and swallowed whole.

ACIDOPHILUS

One of a group of beneficial bacteria called PROBIOTICS, *Lactobacillus acidophilus* is normally present in our bodies, although it is vulnerable to attack by antibiotics and competing organisms (see DYSBIOSIS). It can be found in certain cultured dairy products and in dairy or non-dairy based supplements.

ACTIVATED CHARCOAL

Some people filter tap water through activated charcoal to remove pollutants. More notably, activated charcoal is known for its usefulness as a fast remedy for poisoning, because it absorbs toxins and renders them inert as they pass through the body. When a diet infringement has taken place (for example, the ingestion of milk or gluten), it is possible that an immediate dose could help to reduce the amount of the offending food that is absorbed. It has also been reported that it can be useful as a treatment for yeast die-off, or increased levels of ammonia in the body. While there may be certain benefits to the occasional use of activated charcoal, be aware that it can also absorb food nutrients or components necessary for digestion. Care should be taken not to overuse it, and to avoid taking it for two hours before or after meals.

ADDITIVES (See FOOD ADDITIVES)

ADI DISCUSSION GROUP (See also SUPPORT GROUPS)

The ANDI-ADI Yahoo group is an online forum for parents and professionals, moderated by Karyn Seroussi and Lisa Lewis of the Autism Network for Dietary Interventions. The purpose of the ANDI-ADI list is to discuss "Advanced Dietary Interventions" for the treatment of autism and related disorders, including:

- Theories and hypotheses, modifications and variations on dietary interventions
- Co-existing issues (such as multiple food allergies, yeast, etc.)
- The use of antifungals, and pro-biotic foods and supplements
- Food-combining or food rotation
- Tips, ideas, and advanced support for maintaining restricted diets
- Other discussions of interest to those following dietary interventions, not typically covered on beginner lists

This list is not restricted to the discussion of any single combination of food restrictions. Most of the members are using a gluten-free diet in combination with a diet free of dairy, soy, corn, egg, grains, nuts, rice, sugars, polysaccharides, food dyes, and/or other restrictions, depending on individual needs. To join the group go to: www.yahoogroups.com/group/ANDI-ADI

ADIPIC ACID

A synthetic additive used as a flavor enhancer, often found in gelatin, desserts and candy. It is not known to be toxic, and does not contain gluten or dairy.

ADULTS/OLDER CHILDREN

While it is true that younger children generally respond better to dietary intervention, older children and even adults have made remarkable improvements. How much response you will see depends on many factors, including current level of functioning, condition of the gut, immune function, and of course, the subtype of their disorder.

"Many people believe that it is pointless to try dietary intervention once early childhood is past. I wondered what difference this could make for my autistic daughter, who is 16. After all, we cannot fix whatever neurological damage has been already been done. I'm gratified to say that Dina has recently entered high school, and the diet has made a real difference in her quality of life.

When she was only six or seven, we had a psychologist tell us that searching for the cause of her disability was akin to a fishing expedition that would net nothing. I certainly wish I could have a

conversation with that doctor today. I am the Chair-Elect of the State Council on Developmental Disabilities in California. After seeing how this intervention has helped my daughter, I am hoping to bring this issue to the state level and to bring this information to parents, schools, and doctors."

-Sherri L. Martin, reprinted from The ANDI News

Although it may take longer to notice significant results, the improvements over several months can be anywhere from mild to profound. Don't be afraid you missed the boat—it is never too late to get started. Anything that alleviates symptoms of illness should be welcome, at any age. Despite the fact that most older children and adults with developmental disabilities have not "recovered," many have achieved functioning far beyond their caregivers' expectations. Remember that foods may be causing discomfort and pain in addition to behavioral problems.

Keep in mind that even high-functioning people with autistic disorders may need a great deal of support as they make this transition:

"I am 32 years old and have autism. For the last four years I have attempted to maintain the GF/CF diet. The results were astounding with many symptoms disappearing and my getting full-time work for the first time. Someone wrote it is like 'a fog lifting,' and I think this is a good way to describe it.

After being on the diet for some time I was able to talk to people much more comfortably, deal with complex situations without fear, sleep better, maintain eye contact much more easily, not obsess about things and basically look after myself properly. I did have to be on the diet strictly, or else I regressed. My friends said they thought I was like a new person.

Due to the addictive nature of the peptides, I am having difficulty sticking to the diet and think that peer support would really help."

-Nick Douglas, Queensland, Australia, reprinted from The ANDI News

ALGINATES

Also known as algin, algin gum, calcium alginate, potassium alginate, algae and propylene glycol alginate. Derived from seaweed, alginates stabilize foods and are used to achieve desirable textures. Safety during pregnancy has been questioned. These are gluten and casein free, but are not allowed on monosaccharide diets such as the SCD™.

ALLERGENS

An allergen is any substance that specifically induces an *allergic* response - a specific type of immune reaction (see ALLERGIES & INTOLERANCES). Different people react to different allergens, and it is possible to be allergic to an extraordinary range of substances, including chlorine and perfume. Foods such as milk, wheat, peanuts (and other legumes), nuts, seafood and shellfish are the most common food allergens. Dust, grass, pollen, and pet dander are common environmental allergens. Other common causes of serious allergy are wasp, fire ant and bee stings, penicillin, and latex.

Some allergens, such as poison ivy, poison sumac, and poison oak, will cause an allergic reaction in everyone, given enough repeated contact.

One thing that most people don't realize about allergens is that the body doesn't usually react to them during the first exposure. Once the immune system has identified the allergen, its "memory" will trigger a reaction during a later encounter. These can grow increasingly severe with each exposure.

ALLERGIES & INTOLERANCES (See also MULTIPLE FOOD SENSITIVITIES)

An allergic reaction can be caused by any form of direct contact with an allergen: eating or drinking a food you are sensitive to (ingestion), breathing in pollen, perfume or pet dander (inhalation), or touching the allergen (direct contact). Classic allergy (also called "Type-I" or "IgE" allergy) refers to the type of allergy in which a reaction is almost always immediate.

Most Type-I allergic reactions are expressed as hay fever, sneezing, itching and redness of the eyes. There can be skin reactions such as swelling, itching or hives. Inhaled allergens can also lead to asthmatic symptoms, shortness of breath, coughing and wheezing. Sometimes, an allergic reaction to food is confined to the mucus membranes in and around the mouth (see ORAL ALLERGY SYNDROME). Food allergy can also cause stomach pain and/or vomiting. In its most serious presentation, food allergy can be fatal (see ANAPHYLAXIS).

According to the American Academy of Family Physicians, about 8 percent of children and 2 percent of adults have a Type-I food allergy. Milk allergy is much more common in children than in adults. Children usually outgrow allergies to milk, eggs, soybean products, and wheat by the time they are six years old, but people usually do not outgrow allergies to nuts, fish, and shellfish.

Many autistic children do have classic allergies, but are they more "allergic" than age-matched controls? A recent study found that 30% of the autistic subjects had a family history of classic allergy, compared to only 2.5% of the controls.[15] However, actual prevalence of classic allergy in both groups was not much different.

Not as well-understood are IgG allergies (also called "Type-II allergies," "intolerances," or "sensitivities"). These allergies are not life-threatening, and usually present with subtler symptoms, including red cheeks or ears, itchy skin, stomach aches, diarrhea, gas, headaches, joint pain, sleeplessness or hyperactivity. For some reason, children with autism and their typical siblings tend to have higher values on IgG tests than children in a normal population. Most allergists do not place much value on, or test for, IgG reactivity. They will usually acknowledge that foods can cause a reaction or intolerance in some people, even though the reaction is not strictly a "classic" allergy.

Meanwhile, researchers at the New Jersey Medical School found that there were "intrinsic defects of innate immune responses (to cow's milk protein) in ASD children with gastrointestinal symptoms."[16] Another study concluded that food allergies and severe constipation are an extremely common finding in autistic children.[17]

Based on the premise that autistic children have something awry in their immune systems, here are some possibilities as to why autistic children are more likely to be intolerant to food:

---

[15] Bakkaloglu B, Anlar B, Anlar FY, Oktem F, Pehlivantürk B, Unal F, Ozbesler C, Gökler B. "Atopic features in early childhood autism." *Eur J Paediatr Neurol.* 2008 Feb 11.

[16] Jyonouchi H, Geng L, Ruby A, Zimmerman-Bier B."Dysregulated innate immune responses in young children with autism spectrum disorders: their relationship to gastrointestinal symptoms and dietary intervention." *Neuropsychobiology.* 2005;51(2):77-85.

[17] MacDonald TT, Domizio P. "Autistic enterocolitis; is it a histopathological entity?" *Histopathology.* 2007 Feb; 50(3):371-9; discussion 380-4.

1. They have a genetic vulnerability to food allergies *and* to the environmental trigger(s) leading to autism.

2. They have a genetic vulnerability to the environmental trigger(s) leading to autism. The trigger sets off an immune problem that leads to allergy. For example: if the gut-immune system is damaged by a viral insult, the gut lining is weakened, foods leak into the bloodstream and trigger a sensitivity or an allergic response.

3. Early exposure to allergens (especially cow's milk) in an allergic infant creates a vulnerability to the environmental trigger(s) leading to autism.

Some speculate that infants with IgG milk intolerance may be more prone to ear infections, leading to antibiotic use, gut dysbiosis, leaky gut, and food allergy/peptiduria. It is also possible that an IgG gluten intolerance, either inborn or acquired, is responsible for the breakdown of the intestinal lining in some children (analogous to celiac disease). This may explain why some older children, after the gut has healed and the autistic behaviors have resolved, will regress several weeks after gluten is re-introduced. See also ALLERGY TESTING.

ALLERGY TESTING (See also TESTING)

Allergies - IgE ("Type I") allergies are most commonly tested for with skin tests and blood tests. In a skin test, a series of needle pricks are made on the patient's skin (usually the patient's back) to introduce small amounts of suspected allergens. If the patient is allergic to a given substance, a visible response (a small welt) will occur, usually within 30 minutes. Positive responses can range from a slight redness to full-blown hives. Any allergist can perform these tests in-office; it usually takes a couple of hours, so bring something to keep your child busy. Do not give your child Benedryl™ or any other antihistamine for 24 hours before the test: this will invalidate the results.

While skin tests are simple and cheap, they are not terribly accurate. Some people show delayed reactions as long as six hours after the tests. The introduction of potential allergens during the test may sensitize some individuals to the allergen, that is, they could cause a new allergy that won't show up until the next time the patient is exposed to the allergen.

In a blood test, the amount of serum IgE contained within the patient's serum is measured using different immunoassays.

Sensitivities - IgG ("Type-II") allergies can be measured in blood using an ELISA test. It is a simple blood draw, and some insurance companies will reimburse the cost. However, this type of testing is not 100% accurate, since the response will be higher to antigens currently in the diet.

For information on having your doctor or allergist order the test, contact the lab directly and request that a test kit be sent to your home or doctor's office. If the doctor is reluctant to order it, tell her that you are prepared to pay out of pocket if the insurance claim is rejected. Since most hospital labs are unfamiliar with the test, instructions are included for the lab technician. You may need to wait 30 minutes for the blood to be processed and have an express delivery company pick it up from your home (at no cost to you), but many hospital labs will send it directly. Some of the most commonly-used labs for IgG food allergy testing are listed in the APPENDIX.

Defeat Autism Now! Doctors report that there is a great deal of inconsistency in the test results from every type of food allergy testing. When a sample is split and sent to several labs, or even to one lab, the results can vary widely. False negatives are the most common problem reported, which is why many doctors recommend a program of eliminating and reintroducing foods, in addition to food allergy testing.

Even with these limitations, IgE allergy testing is reasonably inexpensive, and can prove to be useful. And an IgG food allergy panel can be a good guideline when getting started on an elimination diet. If a food tests very high (+3 or +4, for example), there's a good chance that your child will not tolerate it very well. Keep in mind that IgG intolerances tend to subside when the food has been avoided for a period of weeks or months - so if your child is sensitive to eggs and strictly avoids them for a few months, he may be able to better tolerate them in the future (at which time rotating the food into the diet every few days is a wise policy, since constant exposure is likely to increase sensitivity again).

A child with multiple intolerances is likely to have a significant problem with gut permeability, and when these values go down, it's a good sign that the gut may be beginning to heal. Re-testing every six months is the best way to get an overall sense of what's working. The tests usually cost between $150 and $400, and the techniques can vary, so do a little research to find out which labs you think are best.

ALLERGY TREATMENTS

There are limited mainstream medical treatments for allergies. Probably the most effective is the removal of sources of allergens from the home environment, and the general avoidance of exposure to allergens.

"Hyposensitization" is a form of immunotherapy where the patient is gradually vaccinated against progressively larger doses of the allergen in question. Delivery can occur via allergy injection, or sublingual immunotherapy (these are allergy drops taken under the tongue - though not commonly offered in the U.S., sublingual immunotherapy is gaining attention internationally). This can either reduce the severity or eliminate hypersensitivity altogether.

A second form of immunotherapy involves the intravenous injection of monoclonal anti-IgE antibodies. This kind of treatment uses a drug called Xolair (omalizumab). It should only be given in a doctor's office, and is typically used only when allergy triggers asthma.

ALMONDS (See also NUTS)

Almonds are the fruits of the almond tree. Although considered a nut, botanically, the almond is a fruit, which may explain why it is generally better tolerated than some other nuts. One ounce of whole almonds contains 164 calories, 6 grams of protein, and they are a good source of Vitamin E.

Almonds are an important component of restricted carbohydrate diets, since they can be ground into flour and used in baking and cooking. Almonds, like other nuts, can go rancid, so store them in an airtight container in the refrigerator or freezer. Soaking them in water (preferably filtered or spring water) for six or more hours makes them more digestible (see PHYTIC ACID). For baking, snacking, or grinding into nut flour, you can re-crisp almonds for 7-10 minutes in a 300° oven.

Almonds are high in oxalates, so if your child has not done well on almonds, the LOW OXALATE DIET might be helpful.

AMINO ACIDS

Amino acids are known as the basic structural building blocks of proteins. They bind together to form short polymer chains called peptides. Longer chains formed by several peptides are called polypeptides, which in turn form very long molecular chains called proteins.

If this sounds complicated, picture a bowl of colored beads (amino acids). Each bead color represents a different molecule, such as nitrogen, hydrogen, oxygen or sulphur. A bracelet made from these beads represents a short chain of molecules called a peptide. Link a few of these bracelets together into a necklace, and you've got a polypeptide. Link a few of those into a belt, and you've got a protein.

There are 22 amino acids, of which 10 are "essential." All are necessary for optimal health, but ten are considered essential because the body cannot manufacture them; they must come from the food proteins we eat. See also OPIOID EXCESS.

AMINO ACID DEFICIENCIES

In 2002, Defeat Autism Now! Doctor Sidney Baker analyzed 61 urine amino acid tests done on autistic children, and found a significant number suffered from amino acid deficiencies. In fact, deficiencies in taurine, lysine, phenylalanine or methionine occurred in over 50% of the subjects. He strongly recommends that autistic children be evaluated for amino acid deficiency with a 24-hour urine test (tell your doctor that the test should not be scaled to creatinine, since that will give a false normal result for those deficient in creatine and creatinine).

Carnitine, a naturally occurring amino acid derivative, is produced in the kidneys and liver and derived from meat and dairy products in the diet. Carnitine deficiency should be of special concern to those whose children are eating very few animal products.

Most amino acid supplements can be purchased online, or wherever supplements are sold. Be sure to check ingredients for potential allergens. Keep in mind that amino acid supplementation could be harmful for those with certain rare metabolic disorders. Further, supplementing with amino acids that you child does not need diverts money better spent on treatments that will help. For these reasons, test for amino acid deficiencies and work with your doctor to determine which, if any, supplements are needed.

ANAEROBIC BACTERIA (See also GUT FLORA)

Anaerobic bacteria are organisms that thrive in environments with little or no oxygen.

Clostridium difficile is a well-known variety of anaerobic bacteria that causes severe diarrhea and has recently created special concern. According to a new study, "C-diff" has been growing by more than 10,000 cases a year, especially in hospitals and nursing homes.[18] The germ has grown resistant to antibiotics that work against other types of colon bacteria. When patients take those antibiotics, competing bacteria die off and C-diff rapidly reproduces.

Clostridium infection has been a concern for several children on the autism spectrum, many of

---

[18] Zilberberg M, "Increase in Adult Clostridium difficile–related Hospitalizations and Case-Fatality Rate, United States, 2000–2005" *EIF,* Volume 14, Number 6–June 2008.

whom have displayed an improvement in autistic behaviors when given Flagyl, or a combination of Flagyl and Vancomycin (antibiotics specifically aimed at anaerobic bacteria). The improvement sometimes requires repeated treatment. Probiotics, especially *Saccromyces boulardii,* can be extremely helpful. While more research is needed, the impact of *Clostridium* on autistic symptoms supports the theory that abnormal microbiology plays a role in autism disorders.

ANAPHYLAXIS (See also ALLERGIES & INTOLERANCES)

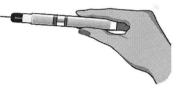

Anaphylaxis is a severe and rapid multi-system allergic reaction affecting the digestive system, respiratory system, and circulatory system. Anaphylaxis may occur after ingestion, inhalation, skin contact or injection of an allergen to which a person has been previously sensitized. Even tiny amounts of allergens may cause a life-threatening anaphylactic reaction in a sensitive person.

The most severe type of anaphylaxis—anaphylactic shock—can lead to death in minutes if untreated. Common foods that cause anaphylaxis in allergic people include peanuts and shellfish, among others. Early signs include vomiting, weakness, and/or difficulty breathing. If such a reaction is suspected, seek immediate medical help.

Those known at risk for anaphylaxis are usually advised by their doctors to keep an "EpiPen®" (an epinephrine shot) with them at all times. An antihistamine drug such as Benedryl™ can be helpful if no other treatment is readily available. Even after treatment, a person having an allergic reaction should be taken to the hospital, because the symptoms can start again hours after the epinephrine is taken.

ANDI (AUTISM NETWORK FOR DIETARY INTERVENTION)

ANDI was founded in 1997 by Lisa Lewis and Karyn Seroussi, to provide support and information to other parents interested in pursuing dietary interventions. Lewis and Seroussi became regular speakers on dietary interventions at Defeat Autism Now! and other conferences worldwide. They developed and maintained the listing of an international network of support volunteers, and published a newsletter, *The ANDI News,* for seven years, from 1999-2005. At the request of their readers, and to support their efforts, they helped develop a protein bar suitable for children with multiple food sensitivities ("ANDI Bars").

You can write to ANDI, the Autism Network for Dietary Intervention, at PO Box 335, Pennington, NJ 08534-0335, or visit *www.autismndi.com.*

ANNATTO

Annatto is a yellow vegetable dye derived from Asian and South American trees. It is often used to color cheese, sausage casings, margarine and baked goods, and is not usually problematic for people on special diets.

ANTIBIOTICS

Antibiotics include any medication that treats bacterial infections. Developed in the 1940's, these "miracle" drugs have saved millions of lives from previously untreatable diseases. Unfortunately, they kill not only harmful bacteria, but many of our beneficial bacteria as well (see DYSBIOSIS). Overuse has led to many bacterial strains that are drug-resistant, and the use of antibiotics in rats has been shown to hinder the detoxification of mercury by the body,[19] which some claim to be a trigger or side effect of autistic disorders (see MERCURY).

Higher usage of oral antibiotics in infancy may also partially explain the high incidence of chronic gastrointestinal problems in individuals with autism. One study found that children with autism had significantly higher usage of oral antibiotics during their first 12 months of life, and possibly higher usage of oral antibiotics during their first 36 months of life.[20]

If your doctor determines that you need antibiotics, you can ask for an additional prescription for Nystatin, a mild anti-fungal medication, for the duration of the treatment plus one or two weeks (see YEAST & FUNGUS).

Many drugs (including the pink Amoxicillin™ liquid) contain sugar, gluten, and/or dairy. Ask your pharmacist to check all ingredients before giving any drug, or have your prescriptions filled at a COMPOUNDING PHARMACY.

ANTIFUNGAL TREATMENTS (See DYSBIOSIS; YEAST & FUNGUS)

ANTIGEN (See also ALLERGIES & INTOLERANCES)

Any substance that induces an immune response. This is different from an *allergen*, which is any substance that specifically induces an *allergic* response. All allergens are antigens, but not all antigens are allergens.

ANTIOXIDANTS (See also OXIDATIVE STRESS; SUPPLEMENTS)

Antioxidants are substances that protect cells in the body from being damaged by oxidation. They combat the destructive effects of "free radicals," which are highly reactive molecules that can harm healthy cells. Many people are becoming more conscious of eating foods that are high in antioxidants, in hopes of slowing the processes of aging and disease. Antioxidants are also used by food manufacturers as a preservative. Some are natural, such as vitamins A, C and E, whereas others are synthetic (see BHA & BHT).

Natural antioxidants include:

- Vitamin C (also called ascorbic acid): This powerful antioxidant is not stored by the body, so it's important to maintain a regular intake. Important sources include citrus fruits, green peppers, broccoli, green leafy vegetables, berries, raw cabbage and potatoes. Blueberries are especially known for their antioxidant properties. Excessive vitamin C is not recommended on a Low Oxalate Diet.

- Vitamin E: Important sources include nuts, seeds, whole grains, green leafy vegetables, vegetable oil and fish-liver oil.

- Beta-carotene: The most studied of more than 600 different carotenoids that have been discovered, beta-carotene protects dark green, yellow and orange vegetables and fruits from solar radiation damage, and it is thought to play a similar role in the body. Carrots, squash,

---

[19] Rowland, IR, Robinson, RD, Doherty, RA "Effects of Diet on Mercury Metabolism and Excretion in Mice Given Methylmercury: Role of Gut Flora." *Archives of Environmental Health* V39, 401-408, 1984.

[20] Adams JB, Romdalvik J, Ramanujam VM, Legator MS. "Mercury, lead, and zinc in baby teeth of children with autism versus controls." *J Toxicol Environ Health A.* 2007 Jun;70(12):1046-51.

broccoli, sweet potatoes, tomatoes, kale, collards, cantaloupe, peaches and apricots are rich sources of beta-carotene.

- Selenium: Good food sources include fish, shellfish, red meat, grains, eggs, chicken and garlic. The selenium content in many foods has been reduced due to soil depletion, so there is some concern that selenium deficiency is becoming a common problem. This is another good reason to eat organic foods - vegetables can be a great source of selenium if grown in nutrient-rich soil.

There is emerging evidence that oxidative stress is a factor in autism and related disorders (see METHYLATION), so antioxidants are recommended by most autism physicians and nutritionists. Melatonin is known to be an extremely powerful antioxidant, which may be part of the reason why it ranks high among successful autism therapies in parent ratings.

APPLIANCES

Appliances we use for regular cooking are not always ideal for gluten-free or starch free cooking and baking. For example, the point of the modern bread machine is to do the labor-intensive part of regular bread making—i.e. kneading dough. However, bread dough is kneaded to enhance the *gluten*. Since this is not necessary for gluten free breads, you may prefer to invest your appliance money and kitchen counter real estate in a heavy "stand" mixer, such as the KitchenAid™, or another good brand. Keep it accessible, because you'll be using it a lot. Gone are the days of sifting flour and combining the wet and dry ingredients separately. Powerful stand mixers have gyrating paddles that thoroughly blend every part of the dough or batter, and are easy to rinse clean.

A high-quality blender can be used for making soups, shakes and smoothies, grinding nuts or grains, and even making your own "ice cream." If you decide that you do want a bread machine, make sure to buy one that has a gluten-free setting.

Any appliance that can be run through a dishwasher (e.g. blenders, food processors, kitchen utensils, etc.) can be used for all your cooking. Toasters and other hard-to-clean items would be most likely to result in contamination. But rather than having two toasters, you may want to purchase a toaster oven with two trays, reserving one just for your child's special foods. Some people use "Toast-It Bags™," reusable heat resistant bags that keep bread from coming in contact with the toaster. These are available at kitchen stores and online.

Potholders are very likely to touch your food as it is removed from the oven. Consider using a second set, in another color or clearly labeled, for use when handling gluten or dairy free meals. You can also look for silicone oven mitts, which can be easily wiped clean.

Waffles are a gluten-free favorite, since the taste and texture of gluten free or nut flour based waffles are very similar to those made from wheat. This is a case when it makes sense to invest in a second waffle iron, or make gluten free waffles for everyone in the family. See also CROSS-CONTAMINATION.

ARROWROOT (See THICKENERS)

ARTIFICIAL COLORS & FLAVORS (See FOOD ADDITIVES)

ARTIFICIAL SWEETENERS (See SUGAR SUBSTITUTES)

ASCORBIC ACID

Ascorbic acid is another name for vitamin C. It is used in packaged foods to preserve color, and is safe for use in special diets. For more about vitamin C, see SUPPLEMENTS.

ASPARTAME (See also SUGAR SUBSTITUTES)

Of the many sugar substitutes on the market today, aspartame (Equal®, NutraSweet™), has evoked the greatest concern among consumer groups. Aspartame breaks down into aspartate, a known neurotoxin (see EXCITOTOXICITY), and numerous scientific studies have connected it with headaches, brain tumors, epilepsy, movement disorders, depression and mood disorders, and the production of toxic formaldehyde adducts.[21] [22] [23] [24] [25]

Other studies have shown aspartame to be safe, leading to accusations of poor study designs and conflicts of interest. In 1992, a survey of 166 studies of aspartame in peer reviewed medical literature found that 74 studies had Nutrasweet™ industry-related funding and 92 were independently funded. Not surprisingly, 100% of the industry funded research attested to aspartame's safety, whereas 92% of the independently funded research identified a problem.[26]

Here is the conclusion drawn by a 2002 study funded by the NutraSweet™ company itself:

> *"The safety testing of aspartame has gone well beyond that required to evaluate the safety of a food additive. When all the research on aspartame, including evaluations in both the pre-marketing and post-marketing periods, is examined as a whole, it is clear that aspartame is safe, and there are no unresolved questions regarding its safety under conditions of intended use."*[27]

From the FDA website (www.fda.gov):

> *In 2005, the European Ramazzini Foundation (ERF) published new findings of a long-term feeding study on aspartame in rats. ERF scientists concluded that aspartame causes leukemia and lymphoma and that current uses of aspartame should be reevaluated. After reviewing the study data, however, the European Food Safety Authority (EFSA) released a statement in May 2006 that said the ERF's conclusion was not supported by the data. After learning of the ERF study results, the FDA requested*

---

[21] Van den Eeden SK, Koepsell TD, Longstreth WT Jr, van Belle G, Daling JR, McKnight B, "Aspartame ingestion and headaches: a randomized crossover trial." *Neurology* 1994 Oct;44(10):1787-93.

[22] Olney JW, Farber NB, Spitznagel E, Robins LN. "Increasing brain tumor rates: is there a link to aspartame?" *J Neuropathol Exp Neurol* 1996 Nov;55(11):1115-23.

[23] Camfield PR, Camfield CS, Dooley JM, Gordon K, Jollymore S, Weaver DF. "Aspartame exacerbates EEG spike-wave discharge in children with generalized absence epilepsy: a double-blind controlled study." *Neurology* 1992 May;42(5):1000-3.

[24] Walton RG, Hudak R, Green-Waite RJ, "Adverse reactions to aspartame: double-blind challenge in patients from a vulnerable population." *Biological Psychiatry* 1993 Jul 1-15;34(1-2):13-7.

[25] Trocho C, et al., "Formaldehyde derived from dietary aspartame binds to tissue components in vivo." *Life Sci* 1998;63(5):337-49.

[26] For details about this survey, see www.dorway.com/peerrev.html.

[27] Butchko HH et. al. "Aspartame: review of safety." *Regul Toxicol Pharmacol.* 2002 Apr;35(2 Pt 2):S1-93.

the study data and received a portion of the data in February 2006. The FDA will announce its conclusions after completing its review.

"At this time, our position that aspartame is safe is based on the large body of information previously reviewed… Our conclusions are based on a detailed review of more than 100 toxicological and clinical studies on safety."

Due to the controversy around the safety of aspartame, as well as anecdotal reports of adverse reactions from members of the autism community (especially in those with seizure disorders), its use is not generally recommended for those with autism or related disorders.

Note: *Aspartame contains phenylalanine, which is unsafe for those born with phenylketonuria, a rare genetic condition that is sometimes associated with autism.*

ASPERGERS (See RELATED AND/OR CO-EXISTING DISORDERS)

ASTHMA (See RELATED AND/OR CO-EXISTING DISORDERS)

ATTENTION DEFICIT HYPERACTIVITY DISORDER (AD(H)D) (See RELATED AND/OR CO-EXISTING DISORDERS)

AUTISTIC ENTEROCOLITIS (See BOWEL DISEASE & AUTISM)

AUTOIMMUNITY

Autoimmunity describes a condition in which the body mounts an immune response against its own cells and tissues.

Is autism an autoimmune disease? Several studies have found marked immune abnormalities in autism. Researchers at Immunosciences Laboratory in California measured auto-antibodies against antigens and peptides in blood from autistic patients, and their results suggest a mechanism by which bacterial infections and milk antigens may modulate autoimmune responses in autism.[28] A Dutch study found that autism is characterized by increased serum concentrations of IgGs, which may point towards an underlying autoimmune disorder and/or an enhanced susceptibility to infections resulting in chronic viral infections.[29] However, it is also possible that the altered immune system in autism is the result of a different type of dysregulation, and could be reversed when the underlying causes are addressed.

AVOCADO

Avocados have proven to be a very good addition to the diet for children with multiple allergies and low nutritional status. They are low in carbohydrates, high in "healthy" fats, folic acid, pantothenic acid, potassium, B6, Vitamin C, and Vitamin E. They can be a good choice for underweight children, since the average avocado contains about 320 calories. Many children will eat avocado if it is salted and spread on rice cakes or toast, or mashed and mixed with salt

---

[28] Vojdani A, Campbell AW, Anyanwu E, Kashanian A, Bock K, Vojdani E: "Antibodies to neuron-specific antigens in children with autism: possible cross-reaction with encephalitogenic proteins from milk, Chlamydia pneumoniae and Streptococcus group A." *J Neuroimmunol* 2002 Aug;129(1-2):168-77.

[29] Croonenberghs J, et al. "Increased serum albumin, gamma globulin, immunoglobulin IgG, and IgG2 and IgG4 in autism." *Psychol Med.* 2002 Nov;32(8):1457-63.

and leftover rice. Avocados turn brown when exposed to air – if you don't like the way that looks, try adding a little lemon juice. Avocados shouldn't be heated – they will become bitter and unappetizing.

BACTERIA (See ANAEROBIC BACTERIA, GUT FLORA)

BAKING (See COOKING & BAKING)

BANANAS

Bananas are rich in Vitamin B6, Manganese, Potassium, and Vitamin C. Unfortunately, many autism spectrum children react badly to them. Some question whether this is due to a high phenol content, but in any case, bananas are high in sugar, and seem to worsen a yeast problem more quickly and noticeably than almost any other fruit. Some children would happily eat several bananas a day to feed their sugar cravings, while others do not tolerate them, and feel sick after eating just a few bites. However, using half of a ripe banana to sweeten a zucchini bread or some pancakes may work for your child.

BARLEY

Barley is a gluten grain, and must be avoided by those on a gluten-free diet. Barley is found primarily in soup, cereal, beer and animal feed, but it is also added to some breads due to its high fiber count. Malt, barley malt and some miso pastes are derived from barley and should be avoided. Barley is a component of most beer, though there are now some specialized gluten-free types on the market.

BEANS

Beans are an excellent source of protein and fiber. They contain the B-vitamins that may be deficient in those avoiding wheat, and they can be added to soups, stews, dips, and tacos. There are many creative ways to use beans on a special diet: if you are avoiding potatoes, you could soak some white beans overnight, cook them until very soft, and mash them with salt and oil for a side dish resembling mashed potatoes. You can also use puréed white beans as a thickener for stews.

In recent years, many gluten free recipes have called for the addition of bean flours. Bette Hagman introduced two new bean flour mixes in her book, *The Gluten Free Gourmet Bakes Bread*. Adding bean flour to breads and cakes give a terrific texture and a lighter final product. Some brands carry "garfava" flour, which is a combined garbanzo and fava bean flour. Note that bean flours usually have an unpleasant taste before baking, which does not indicate how the final product will taste. For best flavor, use bean flours for no more than one third of your recipe's total flour content.

Cautions: Some people find beans difficult to digest, especially those with impaired digestion or enzyme deficiencies. To be on the safe side, beans should be added to the diet gradually. It is a good rule of thumb to soak beans overnight before cooking, which breaks down some of the gas-causing compounds (some say that adding lemon juice to the water increases this effect). Be sure to use fresh water for cooking the soaked beans. Enzyme supplements can be a good addition to bean-containing meals, but remember to check the ingredients: Beano® lists wheat as an ingredient. A similar product called Bean-Zyme® appears to contain no grain products, and is available online.

Those avoiding polysaccharides are advised to introduce certain low-starch varieties of beans only after they are symptom-free, some time after starting the diet, and to follow special recommendations for preparing them.[30]

BED (See BODY ECOLOGY DIET)

BEHAVIORAL THERAPIES

Very few people would rely upon diet alone to treat symptoms of autism. In addition to removing the underlying causes of autistic behaviors, most of these children need systematic re-training of the social, adaptive, language, and behavioral skills they have lost or never acquired.

There are several books about various therapies for autism, including Applied Behavior Analysis (also called ABA or the Lovaas method), the Greenspan approach, the Son-Rise program at the Option Institute, occupational therapy, speech therapy, play therapies, etc. Although this book deals exclusively with dietary and biomedical interventions, it is extremely important to discuss these therapies with your child's school and developmental pediatrician.

A child cannot recover lost skills on the diet alone. While dietary and biomedical treatments may be necessary precursors to make improvements possible, other therapies are usually needed to bring a child up to speed, socially and academically. All of the documented cases of recovery include other biomedical treatments as well as educational and therapeutic interventions.

BENZOIC ACID (See SODIUM BENZOATE)

BETA-CAROTENE

Beta-carotene is the organic compound in carrots that makes them orange. It is sometimes used as a natural coloring agent in food, and should be safe on most diets. Excessive amounts in foods or supplements can temporarily turn the skin orange; the dose should then be reduced.

BETTE HAGMAN'S BASIC FLOUR MIX (See COOKING & BAKING)

BHA & BHT

BHA (Butylated hydroxyanisole) is an artificial preservative used in chocolate, popcorn, sodas, candies, cereal, frozen foods and many other foods. BHA is known to cause allergic reactions and must be avoided by those following the Feingold Diet.

BHT (Butylated Hydroxytoluene) is also a commonly used artificial preservative that may be added to packing materials as well as to food. BHT residues have been found in human fat. It is banned in some countries due to its questionable safety, although it is in use in the USA. A related preservative called TBHQ (tertiary butylhydroquinone), is found in many fast food items.

Autism families appear to be more sensitive to food additives than the general population; many decide to avoid foods containing artificial preservatives whenever possible (see FOOD ADDITIVES).

BIFIDUS

A probiotic strain used to enhance intestinal health (see PROBIOTICS).

---

[30] *Breaking the Vicious Cycle*, by Elaine Gottschall, 1994, Kirkton Press.

BISPHENOL (BPA)

Bisphenol or Bisphenol-A is a substance found in certain plastics (including many water and baby bottles), the linings of cans, and dental sealants. It can mimic estrogen, which may cause hormone disruption. There have been no studies proving that this ingredient is non-toxic and new studies are raising serious concerns about its safety, especially for pregnant women and children. Since products intended for children (including baby bottles and sippy cups) may contain bisphenol, it is especially important for parents to be aware of its risks. Until more is known about this substance, look for products labeled BPA free, and consider limiting the use of canned foods. Details can be found at the website www.bisphenolafree.org.

B-12 SHOTS/NASAL SPRAY (See SUPPLEMENTS)

BIRTHDAYS (See HOLIDAYS)

BLOATING (See DIGESTION)

BLOOD-BRAIN BARRIER (BBB)

The blood-brain barrier is a semi-permeable structure that protects the brain. The cells lining the BBB are packed together so tightly that large molecules do not easily pass through. The purpose of the BBB is to protect the brain from foreign substances in the blood, hormones and neurotransmitters in the rest of the body, and to maintain a stable chemical environment. Because the BBB is known to allow the passage of opioid peptides from the blood into the brain, it is theorized that these compounds from food or other sources will affect brain function (see OPIOID EXCESS).

BLOOD SUGAR (See also DIABETES, GLYCEMIC INDEX)

Blood sugar is simply the amount of glucose in the blood. Glucose, transported via the bloodstream, is the primary source of energy for the body's cells. Glucose levels are usually lowest in the morning before breakfast, and rise after meals. When the blood sugar level is too high it is called hyperglycemia. Low blood sugar is called hypoglycemia.

Concern about blood sugar levels is another reason to avoid sugary snacks between meals. When eaten without other foods like proteins and fats, sweets can raise blood sugar levels significantly. The body responds by releasing insulin, to send blood sugar levels down into the safety zone. However, the body doesn't always know exactly how much insulin to release, and it tends to err on the side of caution, sending blood sugar levels *below* the safety zone. This drop can make one reach for a sweet snack that will cause the fastest rise in blood sugar. The result is a rapidly fluctuating levels of blood sugar and insulin release. This is part of where the "addictiveness" of sugar comes in. The cycle begins again, creating energy highs and lows, and adding unnecessary, non-nutritive calories into the diet.

Some nutritionists suggest that protein (such as nuts or a hard boiled egg) should be included with snacks of fruit or other sweets, to prevent these highs and lows. Sensible advice to is to consume low-sugar fruits (such as apples and berries) together with a meal that includes vegetables and some protein and fat. In other words, if you snack on an apple between meals, a handful of almonds will slow down the rate at which the sugar is metabolized. The food-combining principles from the BODY ECOLOGY DIET may be helpful for your family.

BLOOD TYPE DIET (*"Eat Right For Your Type"*)

This diet was created by Dr. Peter D'Adamo, who proposes that blood type is an evolutionary marker that tells which foods a person can best utilize and tolerate.[31] There are two schools of thought on the Blood-Type Diet: some avow that it has tuned them in to foods that were negatively affecting their health, while others argue that since several of the foods to be eliminated are common allergens, improvements will be noticed for that reason alone.

In the autism population, multiple allergies, enzyme deficiencies, gut flora and maldigested proteins play a large role in food restrictions, so this diet may not be an extremely useful tool. However, you may decide that it can provide additional information for your family.

BODY ECOLOGY DIET (BED)

The Body Ecology Diet[32] is a dietary program targeting fungal infections (see CANDIDIASIS), viruses, and parasites, and promoting health and healing using high quality, easily-digested foods plentiful in healthy fats and minerals. The diet draws from the principles of several other types of diets, including macrobiotics, raw foods, blood type, Weston A. Price, and the Yeast Connection.

The BED has been used to address symptoms of fungal overgrowth associated with ulcerative colitis, Crohn's disease, and various autoimmune diseases, including AIDS. In 2003, The diet began to receive interest from the autism community, since unhealthy flora is linked with food allergies and GI dysfunction (see DYSBIOSIS, GUT FLORA, YEAST & FUNGUS).

The premise of the diet is that many cases of chronic illness begin with a fungal infection in the gut. The gut becomes unable to perform its job as the first line of defense for the immune system, which leads to various secondary illnesses. Incompletely digested nutrients inside the gut wall lead to allergic reactions, and nutrients are improperly absorbed, leading to nutritional deficiency. If these pathogenic organisms escape the intestines (see LEAKY GUT), they can provoke symptoms affecting the rest of the body.

The solution, then, is to first heal the gut by reestablishing the correct gut flora, and then nourish and rebuild the body. The BED is designed to do those two things, based on the following principles:

1. **The Expansion/Contraction Principle:** This is a principle from macrobiotics, which looks at the "energetic" properties of food. Certain foods are seen as "contracting," such as meat, eggs and salt. Other foods are seen as "expanding," such as sugars. The BED encourages primary food selection from the middle of this continuum, emphasizing lots of vegetables.

2. **The Acid/Alkaline Principle:** This is a commonly-used principle in alternative medicine/ nutrition. It is based on the idea that the blood should be kept slightly alkaline, which is thought to discourage candidiasis and discourage the growth and spread of cancer. It is

---

[31] *Eat Right for Your Type*, Peter D'Adamo, 1996

[32] *The Body Ecology Diet*, Donna Gates, 2002

suggested that every meal contain 20% "acid-forming" foods and 80% "alkaline-forming" foods.

3. **The Uniqueness Principle:** This principle acknowledges that one size does not fit all in diets. For example, some people may do better with a slightly higher percentage of protein in their diet, and some people may tolerate animal protein better than others. Each person is encouraged to respect the signals that their body sends, and to avoid foods that do not work for them.

4. **The Cleansing Principle:** This principle states that we must be continually cleansing to attain and maintain good health. Modern-day living is full of exposures to toxins and these toxins must be continuously removed. Regular bowel cleansing is recommended to assist with this process.

5. **The Food Combining Principle:** The basic premise is that different macronutrients need different conditions in the stomach to be properly digested. For example, protein requires a high-acid environment. Starch, on the other hand, requires a more alkaline environment to digest properly. If you mix starch and protein in a single meal, the stomach cannot properly set the conditions to digest, so it cannot do a good job with either component. By eating fruit separately, and separating starch and protein into separate meals, you increase the efficiency of digestion and reduce unwanted fermentation. (It has been suggested that this is a good way to start the diet for sensitive children, and then move onto the other principles.)

6. **The 80/20 Principle:** This principle is taken from Oriental medicine, which states that you should never eat more than 80% of your stomach capacity in one meal. This leaves you with 20% of your stomach empty, giving it room to properly mix the meal with enzymes and acid.

7. **The Step by Step Principle:** This principle states that healing comes in steps which happen in their own time and their own order. When people are really sick, they may not have the capacity to handle a full-blown "healing crisis." So the body will go through cycles of progress followed by a rest period. Each step reaches deeper into the body to pull out toxins and heal the affected organs.

By healing the gut, reestablishing the healthy microflora, providing the body with nutritious foods, the body is then able to build itself up to the point that it can then begin to detoxify. The liver is able to do its job of removing the toxins from the body. The gut will allow the nutrients through to feed the brain, thyroid and adrenals to begin detoxifying and healing. The BED has also been suggested for the mothers of the children with autism, as they may also suffer from fungal infections and complaints of fibromyalgia, chronic fatigue, and eczema.

Specifics of the diet: The BED is a gluten-free diet focusing on the use of minimally processed, healthy foods. It consists of large amounts of vegetables (including sea vegetables), meats, eggs, good fats, Celtic sea salt, and herbs for seasoning. The grains recommended in the BED are quinoa, amaranth, buckwheat and millet. All of these grains are gluten-free, and said to "alkalinize" the body. The BED also recommends certain therapeutic foods, which are specifically aimed at reestablishing the intestinal flora and healing the body. Those on the diet must eat and drink foods that are fermented or cultured every day (see CULTURED VEGETABLES, YOUNG COCONUT KEFIR).

Overview of the Body Ecology Diet

Gluten-containing grains (wheat, barley, rye, spelt, kamut, and possibly oats)	Not Recommended
Rice	Not Recommended
Corn	Some OK if tolerated
Soy	Not allowed unless fermented (miso, tempeh)
Millet, Quinoa, Amaranth, Buckwheat	Unlimited (80/20 rule), pre-soaked
Eggs and Meat (incl. beef, lamb, fish, chicken, turkey)	Recommended; organic free range/wild caught preferred; use 80/20 rule
Vegetables	Unlimited and recommended to be 80% of the diet. Fermented vegetables are highly recommended and should be consumed regularly
Fruit	Not recommended except lemon, lime, cranberry or black currant. Tomatoes not recommended.
Dairy Products	Raw butter *("ghee" may be used for people with casein sensitivities)*
Sweeteners	Stevia or Lakanto only
Vinegar	Raw apple cider only- foods pickled in vinegar not recommended
Juice	None except pure cranberry, black currant, lemon or lime
Oils	Olive, coconut and pumpkin seed recommended
Condiments	Limited to wheat-free tamari, herbs and spices, Celtic sea salt
Nuts, Seeds	Prefer raw and soaked for 12 hours. Pumpkin seeds recommended
Seaweed	Highly recommended
Beans	Not recommended- soak 12 hours if used. Adzuki beans preferred
Alcoholic Beverages	Not recommended
Coconut Products	Young Coconut Kefir, coconut oil, and raw coconut meat recommended (cultured preferred), unsweetened flake coconut for occasional use
Gelatin	Not recommended, substitute agar agar
Coffee and Tea	Not recommended, herb/green tea OK

Note: This is not an exclusionary diet, so nothing is "illegal" with the exception of sugary foods and hydrogenated oils; certain foods are recommended as particularly healing and followers of the BED are advised to eat them preferentially over other foods. Grains or meat should be only 20% of a meal that is 80% vegetable.

If you decide to try the BED, do so with the support of experienced people who have been using the diet for several months or years, and under the supervision of a qualified medical professional. Details can be found in the book *The Body Ecology Diet* by Donna Gates, and additional information, including products helpful in implementing the diet, can be found at www.bodyecologydiet.com. For online info about the BED and children with autism, and to join a support group/message board, go to www.bedrokcommunity.org. For BED support for adults and teens, try www.yahoogroups.com/group/BodyEcology_Antiviral-Raw_Diet.

BOWEL DISEASE AND AUTISM (See also COLONOSCOPY, LEAKY GUT)

Parents have been reporting signs of chronic gastrointestinal (GI) distress in their autistic children for many years. As awareness of dietary interventions among parents increased sharply between 1997 and 2001, as the autism population grew, and as Internet use became widespread, these parents began to compare notes. It became quite clear that for many, something was going wrong in the gut, not just the brain.

In February, 1998, Dr. Andrew Wakefield and his colleagues at the Royal Free Hospital in London published a research paper reporting an unusual type of enterocolitis (inflammation of the small and large intestine) in a small group of autistic children.[33] This study was considered controversial because the authors raised the question of whether the inflammation could be related to the MMR (measles-mumps-rubella) vaccine.

A well-publicized British study, while concluding that there was insufficient evidence for MMR-related autism, reported that there were abnormal GI symptoms in 18.8% of the children.[34] No immediate steps were taken to investigate this finding. Sick children, many of whom couldn't verbally express their suffering, continued to go untreated. But in the past decade, several researchers have found a higher incidence of gastrointestinal illness in autism. One study reported an abnormal stool pattern in 18% of autistic children, versus 4% of typical controls.[35] In another, 24% were found to have a history of at least one chronic gastrointestinal symptom (the most common symptom was diarrhea, which occurred in 17%).[36]

Dr. Wakefield and a small team of physicians and medical researchers, using private funding, continued to conduct studies and publish papers in scientific journals regarding bowel disease and autism.[37] They reported that their subjects frequently suffered from chronic diarrhea or constipation, fecal impaction, colitis, moderate to severe lymphoid nodular hyperplasia, bacterial infection, pancreatic insufficiency, and other GI disorders. They began to recognize a specific pattern of disease in these children not seen in normal patients, and dubbed the condition "autistic enterocolitis." They reported that in most cases, after treatment, these patients were relieved of extreme pain or discomfort, and had significantly reduced autistic symptoms or self-injurious behaviors (see COLONOSCOPY).

Dr. Timothy Buie, a gastroenterologist at Harvard-Mass General, performed more than 500 colonoscopies on autistic children who had GI symptoms, and concluded that more than half had treatable gastrointestinal disorders, including abdominal pain, gas, bloating, and chronic diarrhea or loose stools, food allergies, and maldigestion or malabsorption issues. In a study of his first four hundred patients, 20% had esophagitis, 12% had gastritis, and 10% had duodentitis. Lymphoid nodular hyperplasia was found in 16%. Tests of pancreatic function performed on ninety patients were also illuminating. Very low enzyme activity was found in 11%, and multiple enzyme defects were found in 6%. Several had markedly impaired starch

[33] Wakefield AJ, Thomson MA, Harvey P, Valentine A, Davies SE, Walker-Smith JA. "Ileal-lymphoid-nodular hyperplasia, non-specific colitis, and pervasive developmental disorder in children." *Lancet*. 1998 Feb 28;351(9103):637-41.

[34] Richler J et al. "Is There a 'Regressive Phenotype' of Autism Spectrum Disorder Associated with the Measles-Mumps-Rubella Vaccine? A CPEA Study." *Journal of Autism and Developmental Disorders*. 2006; April 28.

[35] Valicenti-McDermott M, McVicar K, Rapin I, Wershil BK, Cohen H, Shinnar S. "Frequency of gastrointestinal symptoms in children with autism spectrum disorders and association with family history of autoimmune disease." *J Dev Behav Pediatr*. 2006 Apr;27(2 Suppl):S128-36.

[36] Molloy CA, Manning-Courtney P. "Prevalence of chronic gastrointestinal symptoms in children with autism and autistic spectrum disorders." *Autism*. 2003 Jun;7(2):165-71.

[37] Wakefield AJ, Anthony A, Murch SH, Thomson M, Montgomery SM, Davies S, O'Leary JJ, Berelowitz M, Walker-Smith JA. "Enterocolitis in children with developmental disorders." *Am J Gastroenterol*. 2000 Sep;95(9): 2285-95.

digestion: two hundred and six autistic individuals with diarrhea demonstrated significantly lower maltase activity than non-autistic individuals with diarrhea. Frequency of lactase deficiency in autistic individuals with failure to thrive was significantly higher (80% vs. 25%) than in non-autistic failure-to-thrive subjects, and frequency of palatinase deficiency in autistic individuals with diarrhea was significantly higher than in non-autistic individuals with diarrhea.[38] [39] [40] (These findings support the use of digestive enzyme tablets with meals.)

There is no doubt that autism can be the result of a variety of different causes and triggers. It remains to be seen whether a chronic viral infection is one of the triggers of autism in a subset of these children, the result of an immune system weakened by a high mercury load, or simply an artifact of an abnormally functioning immune system. In other words, it remains to be seen which is cause, and which is effect. But it is clear that children with regressive autism have a higher incidence of food allergies and severe constipation, and a dysregulated gut-immune system.

According to pediatric gastroenterologist Arthur Krigsman, a New York physician who has performed colonoscopies on hundreds of autistic children, evidence of chronic bowel problems in an autistic child should be taken seriously. "The similarities of these children from a GI perspective is very clear to me now," he explains. "They frequently have the same issues: multiple food allergies and intolerances, diarrhea, constipation, fecal loading of the colon, abdominal pain and distention, reflux, vomiting, and/or growth failure. Some of them make great improvements after dietary changes, removing foods that might cause an immune reaction, but it isn't enough. Even after they improve on a special diet, their stools may be soupy or pudding-like, or gritty, or yellow, or mucousy or malodorous.

"You don't always know for sure the extent of the symptoms in a child with autism," explains Dr. Krigsman. "Abdominal pain will lead to irritability and crying in a child who can't communicate. They often demonstrate such pain with odd posturing, such as bending over tables, putting pressure on their lower abdomen, etc. In many cases, we have demonstrated that aggression, violence, and self-injurious behavior disappear after appropriate identification and treatment of the bowel disease. It is conventional practice that any child with chronic, unexplained abdominal pain, particularly in the presence of abnormal stool patterns such as diarrhea, should undergo a diagnostic endoscopy. You would need to investigate these symptoms, whether a child has autism or not."

Whether the pattern of pathology described as "autistic enterocolitis" is a diagnosis exclusive to autism is still under investigation. One researcher concluded that "ileal lymphoid hyperplasia may be more prevalent in children with regressive autism, but is also seen in

---

[38] Buie T, Winter H, Kushak, R. "Preliminary findings in gastrointestinal investigation of autistic patients." Harvard University and Mass General Hospital, 2002.

[39] Kushak, R. Winter H, Buie T, Farber N, Rafail Kushak. "Gastrointestinal symptoms and intestinal disaccharidase activities in children with autism," Abstract of presentation to the North American Society of Pediatric Gastroenterology, Hepatology, and Nutrition, Annual Meeting, October 20-22, 2005, Salt Lake City, Utah.

[40] Kushak R, Winter H, Farber N, Buie T, "Gastrointestinal symptoms and intestinal disaccharidase activities in children with autism," *Journal of Pediatric Gastroenterology and Nutrition*, Vol. 41, No.4, October 2005.

children with food allergies and severe constipation, the latter being an extremely common finding in autistic children. The histopathological diagnosis of autistic enterocolitis should be treated with caution until a proper study with appropriate methodology and controls is undertaken." [41] [42]

Dr. Buie sums up the opinion of a growing number of clinical researchers and practitioners treating autistic patients: "These children are ill, and they are sometimes in distress and pain. They are not just mentally, neurologically dysfunctional."

Parents of children with evidence of GI problems can educate their physicians about this problem, and ask to have their children referred to a knowledgeable gastroenterologist.

BREAD

You will probably find several different gluten free breads and bread mixes at your natural foods store. Breads made from mixes are generally cheaper and better tasting than frozen breads (see APPENDIX for suppliers), and once you get the hang of it, baking gluten free bread at home can become an inexpensive and easy part of your routine (see BREAD BAKING).

Keep in mind that "Wheat-Free" doesn't necessarily mean gluten free, and some food chains (e.g. Whole Foods) carry gluten free breads with and without dairy. Read labels carefully.

BREAD BAKING

If you bake gluten-free bread, you probably know that a thick batter or sticky wet dough makes a better loaf than a firm, kneadable dough. The problem is that the batter often rises too much in the center, which creates an odd shape, or worse, a giant air pocket. An air pocket means bread that looks gorgeous coming out of the oven but collapses within minutes. This happens when the outside crust browns too quickly; the bread looks done, but the inside is wet and the weight of it pulls down the crust.

The first thing to try is covering the bread with oiled foil after 20-30 minutes in the oven. This will allow you to bake the bread longer without over-browning the crust. You can also try covering with foil from the beginning, and raising the oven temperature.

If this doesn't help, the best solution is to use a smaller loaf pan, or to make rolls. The smaller the bread the less likely you are to have problems. For sandwich rolls, keep the dough a little sticky, put a glob on a baking tray lined with baking paper, and use a pastry brush dipped in water or milk substitute to shape and flatten the rolls. Mix in a little honey with the liquid to give the rolls a golden brown color, and sprinkle with sesame or other seeds. Let them rise before baking. If your result is too flat and dense, try fresh yeast for a fast, fluffy rise.

The grind of the flour can make a big difference, since finely ground flours will absorb more liquid. Humidity and altitude may also affect your results. After some trial and error, you will

[41] Turunen S, Karttunen TJ, Kokkonen J. "Lymphoid nodular hyperplasia and cow's milk hypersensitivity in children with chronic constipation." J Pediatr. 2004 Nov;145(5):606-11.

[42] MacDonald TT, Domizio P. "Autistic enterocolitis; is it a histopathological entity?" *Histopathology*. 2007 Feb; 50(3):371-9; discussion 380-4.

be able to recognize the right dough consistency, and adjust the amount of liquid or flour as needed.

If your bread rises to a sharp, high crust in the middle and you'd like a flatter top, use the back of a spatula or large mixing spoon to make a long, wide, deep slash down the center of the batter just before baking. Don't be afraid to make it too deep—it will level out in the end, and your bread will bake far more evenly.

Home-baked breads are best when eaten fresh; leftovers should be sliced and frozen as soon as possible. Gluten free bread is one of the few foods that actually improves with a brief reheating in the microwave (do not overheat - remove as soon as the bread is soft).

Red Star Yeast has tips and recipes for gluten free breads on their website at www.redstaryeast.com/collection.html. The King Arthur Flour Company sells a hamburger bun pan and some other home baking gadgets that you may find useful, at www.kingarthurflour.com.

BREASTFEEDING (See also PREGNANCY & INFANCY)

In addition to providing nourishment, breastfeeding plays a critical role in preventing infections in infants. Fever or illness in very young infants can be serious because of the ease with which pathogens, viruses, and bacteria can gain access to the baby's brain and nervous system, carrying with them the risk of meningitis. Breastfed babies are protected from a vast range of pathogens and have a lesser risk of developing fevers in the first six weeks of life, before the blood-brain barrier is fully intact. This is referred to as "passive immunity."

The pediatric community recommends that all infants be breastfed for as long as possible and practical. However, based on the OPIOID EXCESS theory, there are some concerns raised by parents of autistic children who are on a dairy-free diet and still crave breastmilk, at age two, three or older. Could this be due to the casein in breastmilk?

Biochemists tell us that the breastmilk of all mammals (including humans) does contain casein and casomorphin of different types (human casein has a slightly different amino acid sequence than cow casein). Sensitivity to this peptide probably explains why some babies are more likely to fall asleep while nursing. Human milk has a higher whey-to-casein ratio, which means less casein per ounce. Certainly, with most of our children, human breastmilk is tolerated far better than cow's or goat's milk. But there is some concern that it still may interfere with the benefits of this diet.

Another significant consideration is the mother's diet. Mothers nursing GF/CF children should also be gluten and casein free, as both molecules do cross into breastmilk. Women who are nursing younger siblings of spectrum children often choose to keep their babies gluten and casein free for the first couple of years, and in this case they must be on the diet themselves.

"The milk protein in cow's milk does cross into the breastmilk. My oldest, who is now informally considered Asperger's, was quite ill, and finally had an anaphylactic reaction at 8 weeks old due to cow's milk in my breastmilk. This was documented and tested at the time by our pediatrician and

then trial-tested in the allergist's office [with a dairy challenge] when he didn't believe us. I had to avoid cow's milk in any form until he was weaned at 2 ½." -Pamela Jann

Some nursing mothers who were gluten and casein free saw significant developmental improvements in their children when they were weaned from the breast:

"I have a three year old son with autism. I mentioned in a previous email that Daniel was still breast-feeding and had not responded as well as hoped to a GF/CF, corn & soy free diet. I've just weaned Daniel this week and after four days have definitely noticed an improvement in his behavior, including happier moods, fewer tantrums, more eye contact, more verbal and more physical.

I would also like to note that I was on the GF/CF, corn & soy free diet while nursing, my husband went on it, and that we allowed nothing in our home that would contaminate with those items. Prior to starting the diet we had the house professionally cleaned, including steam cleaning on the furniture and carpets, the cars professionally detailed and we purchased new strollers and car seats so our environment was truly GF/CF, corn & soy free.

I sadly must conclude that the casein in the breastmilk must have been toxic to him as well. I chose to nurse this long because Daniel was so nutritionally deplete, and I don't regret the decision because it truly kept him bonded to me in a way that his autism otherwise would not allow. I thought you might be interested in this fact and perhaps publish some any research you are familiar with regarding breastfeeding and the GF/CF diet." -Joyce DeMio

It appears to be common for some autism children on the diet to want to continue nursing until a time long past their siblings lost interest. This is especially nice for the mother, since it is a way of staying close to a child who may otherwise be emotionally remote. This can make it especially difficult to consider giving up that special time together. And for some less-sensitive children, a small amount of breastmilk may not make a difference:

"I thought I should give an update about what happened when my son (age 3) had no breastmilk for four days while I was away at a Defeat Autism Now! Conference. On the fifth day breastmilk was reintroduced with no noticeable differences. I did work, for the two weeks preceding my four-day absence, to get the nursing down to a couple of times a day, in order to make my absence less difficult for him. Since returning, he still nurses 1-2 times most days, though some days not at all.

Anyway, that's what happened! My plan is to keep nursing up to two times per day until he weans himself." -Amy

For a child over 12 months old, you may want to do at trial to determine if your breastmilk is a problem. Pump and store breastmilk for a few days while giving the child a milk substitute in a sippy cup during normal nursing times. This should allow you to see there is a difference in his health or behavior. (Don't use a baby bottle, since some children may refuse the breast after using a bottle for a few days.) If there is an addiction issue, he or she may react very poorly in the beginning, and then improve. There may be no change in the child after a week or two, for better or worse. With this information, you can make an informed decision about how to proceed (see also INFANT FORMULA).

Recently, there have arisen some concerns about the presence of metals, pesticides, and other toxins in breastmilk, which should be of particular concern to mothers of children with immune problems or impaired methylation and detoxification issues. Some labs, such as Doctor's Data (see APPENDIX), will measure levels of heavy metals in any substance, including breastmilk. For those using baby bottles in addition to nursing, look for products labeled "BPA-free" (see BISPHENOL).

BROTH

Broth made with chicken, beef or fish bones contains vitamins and minerals in an easily digestible form. When making a meat-based broth, first brown the meat in a pan to give added flavor, then place it (and the bones) in a large pot of cold water, adding any vegetables you have on hand. A bit of vinegar added to the broth helps extract calcium from the bones. Broth should be boiled for at least two hours. Carefully remove any "scum" forming on top with a spoon. After cooking, strain the broth and refrigerate or freeze. Use for soup or in cooking to add flavor, vitamins and minerals. Canned or powdered broth provides very few of the benefits of homemade, and may contain starch, gluten, and/or MSG.

BUCKWHEAT

Despite its suspicious-sounding name, buckwheat is a gluten-free grain. In fact, it is more closely related to rhubarb than to wheat. While cross-contamination between buckwheat and other grains has been reported, many brands state specifically that they are gluten free (such as Wolff's Kasha®).

Buckwheat is also a common allergen,* and is exceptionally high in oxalates. But when tolerated, it adds a nutty flavor and excellent texture to baked goods. Buckwheat contains protein and B vitamins, phosphorus, potassium, iron, and calcium. It is an excellent source of magnesium. In the United States, most buckwheat is marketed in the form of flour, and it is an ingredient in many pancake mixes. The flour is dark, almost blue in color, because hull fragments are not usually removed during the milling process. In addition to flour, buckwheat is available in the form of groats (the part of the grain left after the hulls are removed from the kernels) and grits. Groats are commonly called Kasha and are available in most grocery stores. They are delicious in soups, stews or pilafs. Buckwheat noodles (sometimes called soba) are delicious and widely available (read the labels carefully, however, as some buckwheat noodles are made with a combination of buckwheat and wheat). Buckwheat is higher in oil than many grains and may go rancid in hot weather. Store in a glass jar and refrigerate after opening.

Note: For those who have a buckwheat allergy, bed pillows made from buckwheat may also cause a reaction.

BUTTER

If you have ever over-beaten whipping cream, you've seen butter begin to form - butter is cream that has been churned into a solid state. To be called butter in the United States, it must contain at least 80% milkfat. The other 20% is made up of water, lactose (milk sugar), and proteins. Despite claims that butter is casein free, most commercial butter contains 3-5% casein, and should be avoided on a casein free diet. Clarified butter is a safer choice for those avoiding milk proteins (see GHEE).

BUTTER, RAW (see also BODY ECOLOGY DIET)

The Body Ecology Diet recommends the use of raw butter (butter made from unpasteurized milk). Butter is made almost entirely of milkfat, with vitamins A, D, E and a short-chain fat called butyric acid, which is said to be healing to the gut. In addition, raw g~ contains large amounts of conjugated linoleic acid (CLA) and an additional called "factor x" by Weston A. Price, which is particularly high in butter from sprin~

One reason milkfat promotes healing of the gut is that it may help beneficial bacteria adhere ~ the gut lining. Since butter contains a small amount of casein, it's something that most children with autism will need to avoid until they have achieved some gut healing. Knowledgeable BED-ers attest that the Body Ecology Diet can be done completely casein free for sensitive children.

Ginger Houston-Ludlam, a BED advocate, points out that there are *reactions* to raw butter, and then there are *cleansings*. "It is not unusual to have mild behavioral regressions when you add these foods. If your child starts passing bile (loose, green or yellow stools), the liver may be detoxifying. If he starts acting like a drug addict with contracted pupils,[43] that is probably a casein reaction, and the butter should be removed until further healing has taken place."

She adds, "According to the BED approach, you don't introduce any dairy, raw or otherwise, cow or goat, until the gut has been "preloaded" with appropriate gut bacteria. This may be why people who start using young coconut kefir, a rich probiotic drink, have an easier time proceeding with goat yogurt and other dairy. I'm not sure you can entirely separate the raw dairy/casein issue from the gut bug issue, and I think you need to understand the child's flora status before you declare the issue settled. If you dump a high casein food into a dysbiotic child, then I would imagine you would see bad results. If you give raw butter to a child who has been preloaded with dairy-loving organisms for a week or so, I'd expect a better result."

> *Raw milk and butter are not available in every state. To find a source near you, visit www.realmilk.com.*

If you have concerns about trying raw butter, or if you have a child with a dairy allergy, consider using organic GHEE.

CALCIUM (See also SUPPLEMENTS)

Calcium is a mineral that works with phosphorus to create healthy bones and teeth. The body must have sufficient vitamin D in order for calcium to be properly absorbed. Calcium also helps the body use iron and helps nutrients pass through cell walls. Proper absorption can also be inhibited by large amounts of fat, oxalic acid (from plants) and phytic acid (from grains). To prevent deficiencies, babies up to six months should have at least 400 mg/day. Toddlers need 600 mg, four to ten year olds need 800 mg/day and from age 11 to 18 children need 1200 mg.[44] Children on the autism spectrum should have calcium levels checked, especially if there is any sign of eye poking or gouging, which has been associated with low levels of calcium.[45]

Many people worry that they will be deficient in calcium if they do not drink milk or eat dairy

---

[43] One of the symptoms of opiate use is contracted (small) pupils while under the influence of opiates, and dilated (large) pupils during the withdrawal period.

[44] Mindell, Earl (1992) *Parents' Nutrition Bible: A Guide to Raising Healthy Children.* Hay House: Carson, CA.

[45] Coleman, M. (1994). "Clinical presentations of patients with autism and hypocalcinuria." *Brain Dysfunction,* 7, 63-70.

products. However, the calcium in many other foods can be easy to digest and absorb, particularly where the food also contains magnesium, necessary for using calcium in the body. Countries where little dairy produce is eaten, such as China, have very small percentages of osteoporosis, showing that it is possible to eat a balanced diet without dairy sources (see below).

Kirkman Labs (see APPENDIX) makes flavored and flavorless calcium supplements in various forms. Custom-made calcium liquids can also be mixed up by compounding pharmacies using a maple, sucrose syrup, stevia or water base.

Some Non-Dairy Sources of Calcium:

Almonds	Cauliflower	Melon
Apples	Dates and raisins	Nut milks
Baked beans	Green beans	Pears
Blackberries	Green Leafy Vegetables	Pumpkin seeds
Broccoli	Hazelnuts	Seaweeds
Cabbage	Kidney beans	Spinach & Kale*
Canned pink salmon	Kiwi fruit	Sunflower seeds
Canned sardines	Leeks	Tofu
Carrots	Lentils	Watercress

To boost calcium in a dairy-free diet, try these pointers:

Substitute Almond Butter for peanut butter on toast and in sandwiches. Almond butter has 76 mg. more calcium than peanut butter.

Dried figs (one half cup) 286 mg

Collard greens (one cup) 226 mg

Great northern beans (one cup cooked) 120 mg

Spinach and kale do contain calcium, but because of their significant oxalate content the calcium is not well absorbed.

CAMP, SLEEP-AWAY

Having special dietary needs should not prevent a child from attending summer camp. The key is good communication and planning. When her son Matt went away to camp for five days (a camp for typical and special-needs children), ADI member Peg Tipton put together a booklet for the camp staff, to make sure that her son Matt had a great time without getting the wrong foods. Here's what the booklet included:

Page 1: A photograph of Matthew, and the following letter:

"Thank you so much for helping Matt stay on his diet for Autism. We are grateful that he has the opportunity to experience Sargent Camp. We know he will have a wonderful time here.

Matthew is intolerant to the following foods:

Gluten (including all products made with wheat, rye, barley or oats), Casein (including all dairy products), Soy, Eggs, Peanuts & Tree Nuts, Corn, Legumes, Strawberries (hives), Raspberries (hives), Chocolate, Xanthan Gum.

Matt has been on a special diet to avoid these offending foods for 8 years now (since age 5). He requires supplements, and must stay completely off those foods. Even the slightest bit of contamination is a problem for him. At home we don't use wheat flour for other family members, because of airborne contamination. Using utensils and cutting boards that have been used for foods would be a problem. Therefore, we have provided everything that you will need for his stay, including dishwashing liquid, and towels to hand wash his utensils.

Thank you so much for keeping Matt 'clean.' If you have any questions please call us at [phone number].

Sincerely, Peg & Jim Tipton"

Page 2: A list of Matthew's supplements, and a schedule for giving them to him.

Page 3: Matthew's menu for the week, based on the menu for the other children (Peg had previously requested this). Also, instructions for making breakfast, lunch, and dinner.

Page 4: An "inventory" of each item she had provided, which were divided into refrigerated, frozen and room temperature boxes. She also included a list of which box contained each item. Here is what Peg sent for Matthew that week:

Refrigerated Items (in plastic food-storage containers)

Cooked bacon

6 apples, 2 pkgs. cauliflower, 2 pkgs. broccoli, 2 pkgs. spinach leaves, 2 cucumbers

3 pkgs. celery sticks (1 extra for picnic lunch)

Muir Glen ketchup

1 small water bottle for picnic lunch

Frozen Items (in individual plastic bags, inside one bigger plastic bag)

5 bags of chicken for sandwiches, bread for sandwiches

3 hamburgers (1 extra, in case one falls on the floor!)

French fries

2 pkgs. chicken wings

8 muffins (apple & pumpkin)

5 pkgs. cookies (nutmeg/flax or ginger flavor)

Room Temperature Items

> *5 bags potato chips, 4 bags rice cereal, 2 bags rice pasta*
> *5 bottles apple juice, 1 bag prunes*
> *Cutting board, knife, vegetable peeler, tongs, salt shaker, serving spoon*
> *Pot holders, dish cloths, dish towels, paper towels*
> *2 round cake pans for heating food in convection oven, pasta pan w/cover*
> *Scouring pad for cleaning utensils & pans, dishwashing liquid, moist towelettes*
> *Matt's lunch box for picnic day (freezer packs are in box w/frozen food)*

Page 5: A section that told about Autism, a copy of Karyn Seroussi's *Parents Magazine* article, Matt's success story, and a page called "Autism is Treatable," with links for further information.

The booklet worked out well because there were three different staff members who worked on Matt's food throughout the week. They had a lot of experience with food allergies; there was no peanut butter served at the camp. And Peg was not the first parent to bring 100% of her child's food.

A week before camp, Peg drove up with Matt's provisions. The kitchen staff was happy to find a place for it in the storage room and walk-in refrigerator and freezer. Matt took the bus with his classmates. On the day he came home, Peg went back to pick everything up. Matt had a wonderful time, which made the planning and effort worthwhile.

CANDIDA & CANDIDIASIS (See YEAST & FUNGUS)

CAROB

The carob tree is an evergreen native to the Middle East, where it has been cultivated for thousands of years. It is sometimes called St. John's bread or locust bean, because the pods were thought to have been the "locusts" that were eaten by John the Baptist in the wilderness. The beans are dried and ground into a powder used for cooking or baking. Carob is relatively high in oxalates, but it is popular with those who avoid chocolate because it can be substituted ounce for ounce with cocoa powder in cooking and baking, with similar results. It is caffeine-free, and does not have addictive or mood-altering properties. It contains no fat, has only a third of the calories of cocoa powder, is low-allergenic, gluten and casein free, and contains protein. Though the flavor is unusual, those who must avoid chocolate usually come to enjoy it very much. Like chocolate, flavor can vary, so if you are unsure about whether you like carob, try more than one brand.

CARRAGEENAN

Carrageenan is a thickener made from red seaweed. A fat-soluble polymer (also known as a gum), carrageenan adds a pleasant 'mouth-feel' to non- and low-fat foods, and serves as a stabilizer. It has been used in cosmetics, toothpaste and even air fresheners. Carrageenan continues to enjoy its FDA status of GRAS (generally regarded as safe), although consumers have raised some concerns, and a recent study at the University of Iowa shows that in animal models carrageenan causes ulcerations or malignancies in the GI tract.

As with so many food additives, it's hard to know whether reports of ill-effects are legitimate or whether they are unnecessarily alarmist. But since many of our children have compromised intestinal health, when choosing packaged foods, you may want to add carrageenan to the list of foods to avoid or to use in moderation. Like all gums, carrageenan is not allowed on the SCD.™

CASEIN (see also CASOMORPHIN, MILK)

Casein is one of the main proteins found in milk and other dairy products, and used as a filler or binding agent in many non-dairy foods and some medications. Casein is a common allergen, as well as being one of the primary proteins restricted by those using special diets for autism spectrum disorders.

CASOMORPHIN

A peptide resulting from the incomplete breakdown product of casein, casomorphin is a known opioid, and abnormally high amounts have been reported in the urine of some individuals with autistic or behavioral disorders (see OPIOID EXCESS).

CELIAC DISEASE & GLUTEN SENSITIVITY

Celiac disease (also referred to as *celiac sprue* and *gluten enteropathy*) is a digestive disorder that prevents absorption of nutrients from food due to damage to the small intestine. It is caused by a reaction to *gliadin*, a protein found in gluten-containing grains. Because the body's own immune system causes the damage, celiac disease is considered an autoimmune disorder. When people with celiac disease eat foods containing gluten, their immune system response damages the intestinal villi: tiny, finger-like protrusions lining the wall of the small intestine. Normal villi allow nutrients from food to be absorbed into the bloodstream. When villi are damaged, a person becomes malnourished, regardless of the quantity of food eaten.

Celiac can result in a variety of symptoms such as diarrhea, constipation, fatty, floating stools, abdominal pain, excessive gas, health problems associated with vitamin deficiencies, iron deficiency (anemia), chronic fatigue, weakness, weight loss, joint pain, easily fractured bones, abnormal or impaired skin sensation. They may report feelings of burning, prickling, itching or tingling, water retention, cdcma, headaches, white flecks on the fingernails, fuzzy-mindedness after gluten ingestion, or burning sensations in the throat.

Those who do experience GI symptoms may be misdiagnosed with IRRITABLE BOWEL SYNDROME. But with such a wide range of symptoms, it's not all that surprising that most doctors will only think to screen for CD due to unexplained weight loss or chronic diarrhea.

The treatment for celiac disease is, quite simply, a strict gluten free diet. In many cases, patients are instructed to avoid dairy products as well, at least until some healing has taken place.

If a person has been on a gluten-free diet for more than a few weeks, lab tests for celiac will be negative even if a person does have celiac disease. Doctors often suggest going back on gluten for testing, but many do not believe this is a wise choice if gluten removal has been effective.

Dr. Arthur Krigsman, pediatric gastroenterologist, warns, "I wouldn't suggest re-introducing

48

gluten to an autistic child responding positively to the diet. This is why it's crucial for all physicians caring for these patients to do some baseline blood testing *before* gluten is removed. Ask your physician to have them tested for total IgA, gliadin IgA and IgG, and tissue transglutaminase IgA."

Celiac disease is genetic. The prevalence of CD is 1 in 22 in first-degree relatives, and 1 in 39 in second-degree relatives.[46] This indicates a strong need for people with a family history of CD to get tested as soon as possible. Understandably, those without symptoms may not want to undertake a gluten-free diet, and thus avoid being tested. However, the consequences of going untreated are weight loss, anemia, and vitamin deficiencies that may result in fatigue, stunted growth, and neurological problems such as depression, anxiety, neuropathy, balance disorders, seizures, and severe headaches. There are also increased risks of gastrointestinal cancer (such as lymphoma), kidney stones, and osteoporosis due to decreased calcium levels and bone density.[47]

Celiac Disease: Another 'Epidemic'?

In recent years, researchers have come to realize that CD is much more common than previously thought. In all likelihood, its incidence has not changed, but testing and diagnosis have improved greatly. Celiac disease is now known to be one of the most common genetic diseases, affecting more than two million people in the United States. According to gastroenterologist Dr. Allessio Fasano, the prevalence may be as high as 1% of all Americans.

In a 2004 study, Dr. Fasano and his colleagues found that about 40 percent of those testing positive reported no symptoms, while many suffered from a variety of health problems without realizing that celiac disease was to blame.

It is common to hear that autism spectrum children or their relatives have celiac disease, but it's unclear whether celiac disease is actually more common in this group than in the general population. Statistically, those with autism *may* have the same chance of having celiac as typical children, but due to other GI problems, are more likely to be tested and diagnosed.

There is an excellent summary of diagnostic criteria for celiac disease at the American Academy of Family Physicians at www.aafp.org. In the search box, type "detecting celiac disease."

CHAPSTICK® (See LIP BALM)

CHELATION THERAPY

Chelation is included here because it has relevance to dietary intervention and anti-fungal treatments. Some children have had increased yeast problems while on a chelation regimen, so doctors report that it's important to "clean up the gut" before starting the process. Some children have been reported to transition to a less restricted diet after chelation, adding to the question of whether toxic metals are causing the gut-immune issues that may lead to problems with dietary or bacterial peptides.

[46] Fasano A, Berti I, Gerarduzzi T, Not T, Colletti RB, Drago S, Elitsur Y, Green PH, Guandalini S, Hill ID, Pietzak M, Ventura A, Thorpe M, Kryszak D, Fornaroli F, Wasserman SS, Murray JA, Horvath K. "Prevalence of celiac disease in at-risk and not-at-risk groups in the United States: a large multicenter study." *Arch Intern Med.* 2003 Feb 10;163(3):286-92.

[47] National Institutes of Health Consensus Development Conference on Celiac Disease, Consensus Development Conference Statement: June 28–30, 2004.

Chelation therapy, also called *heavy metal detoxification* or *toxic metal elimination*, is defined as the administration of chelating agents to remove heavy metals (usually lead, arsenic or mercury) from the body. These agents bind to the metals, allowing them to be freed up from the tissues and flushed out. Some physicians prescribe chelating drugs (such as DMPS, DMSA and Calcium EDTA), while recommending natural substances with purported chelating effects, such as alpha lipoic acid (ALA), cilantro, chlorella, glutathione, vitamin C, and certain antioxidants from fruits and plants.

Drug-based chelation therapy has been somewhat controversial in the treatment of autistic children, possibly due to the implication that an excess of toxic metals would have to be the direct result of mercury-containing vaccines or dental amalgams. However, chelation therapy is not intended to treat autism, it is intended to treat heavy metal toxicity. Members of industrial societies are exposed to varying levels of toxic metal exposure from many sources, including water and air pollution. All children (and adults) who have been found to have increased levels of aluminum, cadmium, lead, mercury, and/or nickel are candidates for chelation therapy.

Metal toxicity is usually tested using oral and IV challenges, followed by a 24-hour urine collection. Depending on the type of chelating agent, the treatment can be oral (pills to swallow), intravenous (a release of the drug from an IV tube into the bloodstream), transdermal (skin patches or creams) or suppository (rectal).

> *Chelation therapy is not intended to treat autism, it is intended to treat any child or adult suffering from heavy metal toxicity.*

Concerns about oral chelation have arisen from trouble with yeast overgrowth during treatment, so many doctors opt for the IV or transdermal method. They usually instruct patients to supplement heavily with minerals during the process, even though some of these may be also removed by the chelating agents.

Some parents report that their children have an immediate and dramatic positive response to intravenous treatments with chelating drugs. One explanation could be that the drugs are acting as antioxidants, relieving oxidative stress and temporarily restoring healthy immune and detoxification function.

Although thousands of autistic children have been treated for heavy metal toxicity, only two chelation-related deaths in children took place in the past few years. Both were due to a drug error, when Disodium EDTA was accidentally substituted for the intended drug, Calcium Disodium EDTA.

CHEWING GUM

Chewing gum can be an important tool for overcoming sensory issues. For some, it can help with concentration: people with ADHD may find that they can sit longer and concentrate better if allowed to chew gum. Not all gum is gluten-free, however. Even those without gluten on the label may have been dusted with starch or flour to keep them from sticking to the wrapper. Ingredients often change, so call the manufacturer or do an Internet search for "gluten free chewing gum." Celiac groups are diligent about keeping up with ingredient changes and are a good source of information.

CHICKEN STOCK

Chicken stock is the broth made by boiling chicken until the meat is fully cooked, and the bones have released proteins and other nutrients into the liquid (see BROTH). Long believed to help alleviate the symptoms of a cold, stock is the basis for many dinner entrées. Many commercially prepared chicken stocks contain gluten or MSG, so read labels carefully or make your own in large batches, and freeze it in small containers.

CHOCOLATE

Chocolate comes from the seeds (often called beans) of the cacao tree. It is a common allergen, and is high in fat, oxalates and phenols. Due to its natural bitterness, it is usually prepared with large quantities of sugar. Chocolate has mildly addictive properties and can affect mood for brief periods after eating it.[48] It contains caffeine and should be avoided, especially later in the day, by those who have trouble sleeping. CAROB is frequently used as a substitute for chocolate in recipes.

CHRISTMAS (See HOLIDAYS)

CHRONIC FATIGUE (See RELATED AND/OR CO-EXISTING DISORDERS)

CITRUS

Citrus fruits include many varieties of oranges, grapefruits, limes and lemons. They are known for being particularly rich in vitamin C, and when eaten whole are a good source of fiber. Most are peeled before eating, but some, like the kumquat, are eaten peel and all. The peels contain fragrant oils, and their zest is often used to flavor foods. Allergies to citrus fruit are common.

CLOSTRIDIUM (See ANAEROBIC BACTERIA)

COD LIVER OIL (CLO) (See also OMEGA-3 and OMEGA-6 FATTY ACIDS)

Cod liver oil is a nutritional supplement derived from codfish liver. It is rich in omega-3 fatty acids, EPA and DHA, vitamin A, and vitamin D. It can be purchased at most pharmacies, health food stores and supermarkets, and comes in capsules and a liquid form. When fresh, it has a mild, fishy flavor. As it oxidizes, the flavor becomes rancid, so it should be kept refrigerated and used as quickly as possible after opening.

Defeat Autism Now! Doctor Ken Bock, MD of the Rhinebeck Health Center suggests 2500-5000iu of cod liver oil per day for an autistic child. This should not be exceeded, since CLO is very rich in vitamin A, and an excess of vitamin A could lead to toxicity. Take into account all other supplements in the diet (see VITAMINS). Vitamin E should also be taken, to prevent oxidation of the fish oils.

Look for suppliers who guarantee that their products are are free of PCBs and mercury, and who regularly test them for purity.

---

[48] Bruinsma K, Taren DL. "Chocolate: food or drug?" *J Am Diet Assoc.* 1999 Oct;99(10):1249-56. Review.

COLON

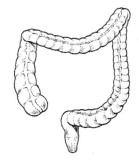

The colon is the arch-shaped length of bowel that runs from the beginning of the large intestine to the rectum. The first part runs vertically up the right side of the body from the small intestine and is called the ascending colon. The horizontal section at the top is referred to as the transverse colon. The downward vertical section is the descending colon, and the loop at the bottom, just before the rectum, is the sigmoid colon.

COLONOSCOPY

If typical children present with abdominal pain, gas, bloating, chronic loose stools and maldigestion issues, doctors thoroughly investigate the source of the problems and determine appropriate treatment. As recently as a few years ago, doctors overlooked these symptoms in their autistic patients, regarding them as "just part of the autism picture." Fortunately, doctors and parents now know that serious investigation is warranted in *any* child who is suffering from serious or chronic bowel symptoms (see BOWEL DISEASE & AUTISM).

Before scheduling a child for a colonoscopy, there are several things your gastroenterologist may suggest. A fairly non-invasive test is an abdominal x-ray (also called a KUB), which will reveal problems such as blockages from tumors, or impacted stools. Fecal impaction is a common finding in these children, even in those who appear to have normal stools or diarrhea (see ABNORMAL STOOLS).

Your child may also undergo an "Upper GI," in which he is asked to drink a chalky liquid that will show up on an x-ray, and give clues about the health and condition of the pharynx, esophagus, stomach and first part of the small intestine (the duodenum). *Note: this liquid may not be gluten-free. Before the procedure, ask your doctor to check and order the powdered form from a compounding pharmacy if necessary.*

Based on these findings, and on reports from the parents regarding abnormal stools or pain, a colonoscopy may be scheduled. This involves inserting a tube with a tiny camera into the colon from the rectum, and examining the walls of the colon. Pictures or even videos of the colonoscopy will be taken, and tissue samples will be taken from any inflamed area or lesions. The tissue samples will later be biopsied. For children, this procedure is done under sedation or light anaesthesia.

A colonoscopy may be scheduled if your child presents with one of the following symptoms:

- Chronic loose stools, diarrhea, constipation, or alternating constipation and diarrhea
- Excessive gas; floating or fatty stools.
- Multiple food intolerances
- Abdominal pain (sometimes characterized by nighttime awakening, odd posturing, screaming or self-injurious behavior)

If your child is a candidate for colonoscopy, it is imperative that you find an experienced pediatric gastroenterologist, preferably one who has researched the abnormal GI findings that have been recently associated with autism. If a child is not already on a gluten-free diet, request that a small-bowel biopsy be taken during the procedure - in a small number of autistic patients, this has led to a diagnosis of celiac disease. Since biopsy is the only definitive test for celiac disease, it may determine the presence of celiac in children who tested negative with a blood test. In addition, you can request a secretin infusion during the procedure to test pancreatic function. There is some preparatory work that must take place before the procedure. Your doctor should give you detailed guidelines, but here is some general information.

In order for the doctor to get a clear picture of what's going on, all stool must be cleaned out of the area. There is a two-prong approach to this goal:

First, the diet must consist of only clear liquid the day before the procedure. Water, plain broth, clear juice, Jell-O®, and Popsicles® are allowed, but no red fluids or gelatins since they could be mistaken for blood in the colon. Milk substitutes and other opaque liquids are not allowed.

Then, the afternoon before the colonoscopy, the child will need to start drinking a laxative formula recommended by your doctor.

Within a few hours, the child will experience diarrhea. This will continue until it runs clear and the bowel is empty. This diarrhea should not be painful. If the child will not drink the laxative (some will, surprisingly, even though it tastes quite odd), you can try squirting it into his or her mouth with a dropper or syringe. If this fails you have no alternative but to give an enema. It is wise to have an enema on hand as a last resort, but an enema will not clear the bowel as effectively as the oral preparation. Look for a Fleet Pediatric Enema — they are available at most large pharmacies.

On the morning of the procedure, your child will probably feel weak and listless, but young children are usually scheduled very early in the day to minimize their discomfort.

The procedure is completely painless, except for the minor discomfort of the insertion of the IV (intravenous line). If you feel this will be scary or painful to your child, ask your doctor for a prescription for EMLA cream, which is a topical anesthetic (a cream that has a numbing effect when applied to the skin). Make sure you have the cream beforehand, so it can be used on the morning of the test, before you leave the house. At least an hour before the test, spread a thick layer on the inside of both arms (to be safe, ask the doctor where the IV will be inserted - it may be in the back of the arm or hand), and gently wrap the area with plastic kitchen wrap.

The anesthesiologist will carefully review your child's medical history. Make sure that he/she is aware of all allergies and sensitivities. The actual procedure takes about an hour, and it may take another hour before the child wakes up. Shortly afterward, he will be able to start eating again (small amounts at first). By the end of the day, he should be feeling just fine. In fact, having had his bowels cleaned out, he may feel better than usual.

So why should you put your child, and yourself through this ordeal? The answer is simple. If your autistic child has any signs or symptoms of chronic gastric distress (abnormal stools, food allergies, gas, bloating, constipation, etc.) the odds are fairly high that the colonoscopy will reveal some important results that can provide relief. In some cases, the damage may be severe enough to warrant immediate treatment.

For those with intestinal inflammation or pathology, various treatments have proven to be useful. According to Dr. Krigsman, a pediatric gastroenterologist specializing in autistic patients with bowel disease, the best form of treatment is based on many factors. If inflammation is found, 5-aminosalicylates medications are often very helpful, as are related salicylate-based anti-inflammatory drugs. These medications were developed to treat Crohn's disease and mild to moderate ulcerative colitis. If these treatments are not effective, the intermittent use of immunosupressive drugs can be tried. A cytokine called TNF- (tumor necrosis factor alpha) is sometimes used, because it triggers and sustains the inflammation response that has been found to be markedly elevated in autistic colitis.[49] A low dose of immunomodulators may be used to control a hyper-alert immune system. Some doctors are also trying montelukast taken orally, since the allergic response is in many ways similar to that in asthma.

COLOSTRUM

In the earliest stage of breastfeeding just after giving birth, female mammals produce a thin yellow liquid called colostrum. A bovine (cow) version of this substance is available as a supplement, and is said to have some benefit for those with autism and gut-immune disorders. If you decide to try colostrum, be sure to find a brand that is obtained from hormone, pesticide and antibiotic free cows, during the first 24 hours after they give birth. Colostrum is derived from milk, so be sure to use a product that is casein free at detectable laboratory levels.* Do not give colostrum or any milk product to a child with a severe milk allergy.

*Note: Kirkman Laboratories reports that their Colostrum Gold® is casein free, and comes in a hypoallergenic formula. (The flavored version contains sucralose, which may cause bowel problems in sensitive individuals.) See www.kirkmanlabs.com.

COMPLIANCE

Even children who are home-schooled spend some time outside of the house, and are at risk for getting hold of food that is not allowed on their special diet. Here are some tips for minimizing those risks, with family and friends, at school, and in the world at large.

Compliance from Family and Friends: If your family members are not supportive about your efforts with the diet, there are several things you can try. First, print a list of studies about the diet (see STUDIES). Second, see if you can get a letter from your child's physician about any medical test results that support the dietary restrictions (see DOCTORS). Your doctor should be able to write a note saying that the restricted diet should be carefully followed for some period of time, while being evaluated as a helpful option for your child. Show the letter to your family members, and explain that you and your doctor are engaged in some careful record-keeping which will be fouled up by any dietary infractions. It may be helpful to say something like, "this is something we are trying for three months, and it's important that we are extremely strict about it so we can evaluate the results." At a family party, try taking a couple of guests aside, and quietly ask them to help you keep an eye on your child, so that he isn't accidentally or deliberately fed a forbidden treat. Choosing potential diet saboteurs as your "co-conspirators" may prove effective.

> Before a party, ask your hosts to make sure that all sources of gluten, including bowls of dog or cat food, are out of reach. This is usually less awkward than making the request when you arrive.

When asking friends or family to babysit, keep in mind that they may feel intimidated by the idea of caring for your child, and be reluctant to

---

[49] Ashwood P, Wakefield AJ. "Immune activation of peripheral blood and mucosal CD3+ lymphocyte cytokine profiles in children with autism and gastrointestinal symptoms." *J Neuroimmunol.* 2006 Apr;173(1-2):126-34.

take that responsibility. Unless they are experienced with food allergy issues, they are very likely to feel insecure about understanding the rules. You should not expect them to remember to stick only a clean knife into the jelly jar, or wash the cutting board before using it for GF bread. Let them know that you are aware that this diet can be an inconvenience, and that you are going to keep it as simple as possible. *Do not expect others to cook for the child, even if your rules are fairly specific, unless you are certain they can do so without making mistakes.*

As with school compliance, the key is preparation. Prepare and provide all of the food in advance. If you are leaving your child at the sitter's house, bring a cooler bag with meals, snacks, and drinks, and a small bottle of digestive enzyme tablets. Pack extra food in case you are delayed. If it is a place where your child will visit frequently, ask if you can keep a few emergency items in the cupboard. Be very clear that nothing must go into your child's mouth unless it was provided by you. Emphasize that they shouldn't hesitate to phone you with any questions.

Compliance from Spouses and Ex-spouses: One of the most stressful situations is when one parent has trouble getting their child's other parent to cooperate with dietary changes, especially in the case of a difficult or contentious divorce. Sadly, there are parents whose ex-spouses refuse to comply. This is a situation where testing and a doctor's note will be necessary. Although digestive enzymes should not be a substitute for the diet, if a spouse simply will not cooperate, then enzymes are the best approach. Even the most difficult "ex" may be willing to give enzymes with meals, especially if the child has had bowel problems in the past. If there are tests to show that the child needs to be on a special diet and your doctor is supportive, you may be able to have a lawyer get an injunction requiring compliance.

Compliance from School: Some parents are extremely careful with their children's diets at home, but unsure about what they may be getting at school. How can you be certain that the school staff is cooperating with your child's dietary restrictions? To be certain that there is no room for misunderstandings, the child should never, ever be allowed to put anything in his mouth that was not provided by you. This means sending in all lunches, snacks, food-based art supplies, and reinforcers, and having a serious conversation with every teacher, therapist, and bus driver who will supervise your child throughout the day (see INFRACTIONS).

Despite your best efforts, you might find that your child's diet is being sabotaged by teachers or therapists who are ignorant of the importance of strict dietary compliance. Luckily, some determined parents have developed excellent strategies for making sure that their children get the dietary support they need in the classroom.

Here are some tips from ANDI member Lynne Arnold:

"Although it may be hard to get grandparents, babysitters, therapists and respite workers on board with dietary restrictions, these difficulties often pale in comparison to getting compliance from school personnel. Fortunately, the law is on your side. If any child has a medical prescription from a doctor for a special diet, the school *must* put it into the IEP. Jaquelyn McCandless, MD, author of *Children with Starving Brains*, recommends that the prescription state that the child can *only* eat food provided from home. A prescription for the diet is the best way to inform staff and get compliance.

General guidelines are most easily met if they are also written into the IEP. Your child's IEP could include the following, or similar language:

> *The school will keep a supply of treats (which his mother will provide) in the freezer to be used when a parent unexpectedly brings in a non-GF/CF treat that "Johnny" cannot eat. All food and drink for "Johnny" will be clearly labeled.*

> *The school must give the parents at least 3 days notice of any food-related classroom event so they may provide an alternative.*

> *Safe substitutes will be used for any school supplies containing gluten or casein, such as Play-doh®, macaroni, painting with yogurt, etc.* If white school glue is used, "Johnny" must be carefully supervised and his hands washed afterward.*

> *All children in the classroom will be instructed to not share or trade food or drink with other children unless permission is given by the teacher.*

> *A staff member will be in attendance for every snack, drink, or meal activity to prevent trading or sharing of foods with other children.*

> *If, despite these precautions, "Johnny" accidentally ingests a forbidden food, enzyme tablets will be immediately administered and his parents will be immediately notified.*

These guidelines can be printed, signed by all teachers and staff members, and filed in the nurse's office. I also go over the diet with the teacher, telling her that I would rather provide food for everyone than for him to have something different/special. I point out that there is no appropriate substitute for cheese, but there is one for practically everything else. I also strongly encourage everyone on staff to feel free to call me anytime if they have questions."

* See PLAYDOUGH for a gluten free recipe.

Support for the diet can be worked into the IEP as goals and objectives. The following examples were provided by Moira Giammatteo:

GOAL 1: Johnny will deny offers of foods that are not brought from home.

Incremental objective #1 related to the goal: When adult asks Johnny if he can eat food not brought from home, he will answer "No" 70% of the time.

Incremental objective #2 related to the goal: When adult asks Johnny if he can eat food not brought from home, he will answer "No" 80% of the time.

GOAL 2: Johnny will self monitor the consumption of safe foods and non-edible items.

Incremental objective #1 related to the goal: Will be able to decline offers of unsafe foods that look similar to his by asking "Am I allergic to this?" 2 out of 5 opportunities.

Incremental objective #2 related to the goal: Will refrain from eating non edible items (such as rocks, plastic and wood) at all times independently or by asking an adult 4 out of 5 opportunities.

GOAL 3: Will self-monitor safe food consumption (gluten and casein free diet).

Incremental objective #1 related to the goal: Will be able to consume only foods from home.

Incremental objective #2 related to the goal: Will be able to decline offers of unsafe foods.

If you are new to the world of developmental disabilities, don't be intimidated – there are many sources of support that can help you to be the advocate your child needs you to be. *The Complete IEP Guide: How to Advocate for Your Special Ed Child*, by Lawrence M. Siegal, is an easy-to-understand resource for learning about the IEP process. For accurate, reliable information about special education law, education law, and advocacy for children with disabilities, visit www.wrightslaw.com.

Compliance from Strangers: Sometimes, in the course of a day, it becomes necessary to explain your child's food sensitivities to total strangers: when speaking to a waiter at a restaurant, when talking to another parent at a school meeting, or when bringing a cooler bag full of special food through customs at the airport. Most of us would prefer not to take the explanation too far, but we need to tell them something. Most people are not familiar with gluten or casein and even fewer have heard of monosaccharides!

Technically, it is correct to say that your child has a food intolerance. But that can sound trivial to some people, who then might underestimate the risk of exposure. Some of the parents on the ANDI-ADI support group have chosen other ways of handling this problem:

> *"We tell people the kids have a gluten allergy, which means they get very sick from regular bread or most kinds of flour, including wheat flour."*

> *"Most often I just say he's allergic to wheat and everybody gets it."*

> *"Not so long ago, before the tests were available, if a person reacted favorably to the diet, he was given a celiac diagnosis. That's good enough for me."*

> *"At the airport, I had to explain why there were six loaves of gluten free bread in my carry-on to Switzerland. My son was five, and overheard my explanation. Next time somebody asked him why he couldn't eat bread, I heard him tell them, 'I have celiac.' After that, he decided it just made his life a lot easier, and he's said so ever since. Nobody has ever asked to see a copy of his diagnosis. No doctor, no teacher, nobody. I'm not saying that everyone should do the same thing, but it worked for us. His dietary restrictions make things tough enough for him without a big blah blah blah every time he has to go to a birthday party. He's almost 13 now, and thinks of himself as a kid with celiac disease."*

In some cases, especially when it comes to medical care or school compliance, a celiac diagnosis will pull a lot more weight than a gluten allergy or a parental report of gluten sensitivity. Unfortunately, celiac tests will only be positive after the patient has been eating gluten for several weeks, and few parents run the tests before starting the diet (see CELIAC DISEASE).

Some doctors will suggest a trial of gluten for several weeks, since the long-term risks of temporary gluten ingestion for a person with celiac disease are probably not very serious. However, for our population, it usually presents a real problem:

"We agreed to a trial of gluten to see if my little guy could get a celiac diagnosis. I can't tell you how sorry I am about that. It took weeks to get him back to where he was beforehand."

"My non-autistic daughter has been gluten-free for several years because of severe eczema. The doctor suggested a month of gluten, so they could do a celiac test. After two days we stopped the experiment because she started projectile vomiting after every meal. And still, the doctor thought we should keep giving her gluten for the next few weeks so we could get a 'proper diagnosis.'"

"What I realized is that the only person who stands to benefit from a gluten challenge at this point is me! I want the credibility of a celiac diagnosis so badly, but I can let it go when I see that my son will not gain anything from it."

"Calling it celiac started as a matter of expediency, but taught me to act like the parent of a child with a 'legitimate' disorder: non-apologetic and with certain rights and privileges."

COMPLIANCE FROM MEDICAL PROFESSIONALS (See DOCTORS)

COMPLIANCE FROM YOUR CHILD (See PICKINESS & FOOD ADDICTION, SOCIAL ASPECTS OF THE DIET)

COMPOUNDING PHARMACIES

Many medications include gluten, starch, lactose and food dyes. People with allergies and intolerances might need a pharmacy that can prepare medications without these problematic ingredients. A compounding pharmacy mixes prescription medications on-site, rather than buying them ready-made. To find a compounding pharmacy in your area, visit the International Academy of Compounding Pharmacists online at www.iacprx.org.

CONSTIPATION (See STOOLS, ABNORMAL)

COOKING & BAKING

Whatever diet you are using for your child, the easiest way to cook is to keep it simple, serving a meat or protein, fresh fruit and vegetables, and rice or potatoes (if tolerated). This type of cooking is the most healthful and economical, and saves the time of having to make more than one family meal at a time. There are times, however, when you will want to adapt fancier recipes to work for special diets.

Many of the suggestions below will be more useful for those who are using grains and starches, but several can also be made using nut flour. There are detailed guidelines for cooking and baking on the Specific Carbohydrate Diet™ in the book *Breaking The Vicious Cycle,* and on www.pecanbread.com.

For those following the LOD, there is no better source of recipes than the *Low Oxalate Cookbook* (see LOW OXALATE DIET). You can create your own recipes based on food lists. Baking may still be a challenge, since nut flours shouldn't be used, and many other types of flour are high in oxalate. But baked goods in small amounts usually fall within the LOD guidelines.

To adapt a recipe for baked goods, you generally just replace regular flour with a gluten free flour mix. Different types of flour have different qualities, so for most recipes, a combination will work best. The following are some excellent cooking and baking tips, adapted from an article by Jay Berger, of Allergy Grocer (www.allergygrocer.com). Again, many of these will not work for some of the special diets.

The Bette Hagman original flour mix (see below) is an excellent basic mix, but better texture can be achieved by modifying the recipe to meet your specific application. Knowing how many changes might be needed for a particular use requires some testing, and changing flours may necessitate a change in the amount of liquid needed. Use your raw dough texture as your guide.

Sandwich and other loaf breads call for heavier, denser, "grittier" flour mixtures, with a higher ratio of heavy to starchy flours. Gluten-free breads require binding agents or gums. In general, you will need two teaspoons of xanthan or guar gum for every cup of flour used.

Cakes, cookies, quick breads, and more delicate baked goods turn out better using a higher ratio of starchy to heavy/gritty flours. Less binder is needed: for cakes, use a teaspoon of xanthan or guar gum per cup of flour. No binder is needed for cookie recipes.

Heavy flours include:

- White rice flour
- Brown rice flour
- Sorghum flour
- Buckwheat flour
- Millet flour
- Quinoa flour
- Potato flour (not potato starch)

Starchy flours include:

- Tapioca starch
- Potato starch (not potato flour)
- Arrowroot powder
- Cornstarch

Some popular flour blends:

(For each, combine and store in an airtight container. Use cup for cup as an equal substitution for wheat flour.)

Bette Hagman Original Flour Blend:

- Two parts white rice flour
- Two thirds part potato starch flour
- One third part tapioca starch

Variations:

Substitute brown rice or sorghum for white rice

Substitute starches for other starchy flours.

Bette Hagman Featherlite Flour Mix

3 cups rice flour

3 cups tapioca starch

3 cups cornstarch

3 tablespoons potato flour (not potato starch)

Bette Hagman Light Bean Flour Mix

- 3 cups garfava bean flour
- 3 cups tapioca starch
- 3 cups cornstarch

Wendy Wark's Gluten-Free Flour Mix

This Multi Blend Gluten-Free Flour mix is used cup for cup in recipes such as tortillas, pancakes/ waffles, and cookies. If you plan to use this flour mix for cakes, sweet breads or brownies, add an additional ½ teaspoon of xanthan gum per cup flour mix.

- 1 cup brown rice flour
- 1¼ cup white rice flour
- ¼ cup potato starch flour
- ⅔ cup tapioca starch flour
- ¾ cup sweet rice flour
- ⅓ cup cornstarch
- 2 teaspoons xanthan or guar gum

Substitution Ideas for Recipes

Instead of evaporated milk:

- DariFree®, soy, rice, or other non-dairy powder, mixed double-strength
- Rice or soy concentrate, undiluted
- Light cream alternative (dairy free)
- Dairy free coffee creamer (carefully check ingredients, many do contain milk proteins)

Instead of regular condensed milk

- Coconut cream in a can (drain liquid)

- Combine 1 cup powdered dairy alternative (such as DariFree®), 3 Tbsp melted margarine, ⅔ cup sugar, and ½ cup boiling water in a blender. Process until smooth and creamy. Use to replace standard condensed milk in recipes.

Instead of sweetened condensed milk (14-oz. can)

- Combine ½ cup powdered dairy alternative (such as DariFree®), 2 Tbsp melted margarine, ¾ cup sugar, ½ tsp xanthan or guar gum, and ½ cup boiling water in a blender. Combine all ingredients, mix well. Bring to slow boil over medium heat until thick and bubbly, stirring constantly. Chill before adding to recipe. (Recipe courtesy of Allergy Grocer and Diane Hartman.)

Instead of cream

- Coconut cream in a can
- Rich's Richwhip® Non Dairy Topping (in many stores - see www.richs.com).
- Hip Whip: chocolate and plain versions can be found at health food stores.
- Some non-dairy coffee creamers (check ingredients carefully).
- Soyatoo® vegan whipped topping (at groceries, health food stores or online at www.cosmosveganshoppe.com)
- Mix ⅔ cup dairy alternative and ⅓ cup melted margarine or canola oil (this will not whip).
- Chill a large bowl and a whisk in the refrigerator for 10 min. Open 3 cans of coconut cream and carefully remove the liquid. Whisk the cream together with 2 Tbsp confectioner's sugar until thick and stiff. Store covered in the refrigerator.

Instead of sour cream or yogurt:

- Tofutti® Sour Supreme
- Soy or Nut Yogurt (see YOGURT)
- Blend ¾ cup buttermilk substitute (see below) + ⅓ cup margarine
- Combine 1 package soft Silken tofu, drained, with a few Tbsp lemon juice to form a smooth texture when puréed in a blender.

Instead of buttermilk:

For each cup of dairy alternative, replace 1 Tbsp liquid with 1 Tbsp apple cider vinegar or lemon juice. Stir & allow to stand for 4-6 minutes before adding to a recipe.

Instead of corn syrup

(To make any of these "dark," just add 1 Tbsp molasses per cup syrup)

- Combine equal amounts of Lundberg Farms Brown Rice Syrup, cane Syrup, and vegetable glycerin (made from coconut)
- Combine 2 cups sugar and 1 cup water in a saucepan over medium heat. Bring to a full boil.

Boil for 1 min or until all sugar particles are dissolved. Transfer mixture into airtight container and store in refrigerator until use.

Instead of solid shortening:

- Spectrum shortening

- Coconut Butter (do not confuse with cocoa butter).

Cake decorating tip: Sprinkle shredded coconut over frosting before it hardens to create a realistic looking Santa's beard, lamb or other animal fur, etc.

Allergy Grocer is an online store that produces and distributes a wide range of gluten free goods and baking mixes, including those for people with multiple food sensitivities. There is an excellent collection of recipes for making special holiday foods at the Allergy Grocer website (www.allergygrocer.com).

COOKWARE

Those with increased sensitivity to environmental toxins have begun to re-think their choices in cookware. There are concerns that aluminum could leach into the food and contribute to Alzheimer's or Parkinson's disease. Stainless steel is a composite of several metals, any of which could possibly leach into food if the pots and pans become dinged or badly scratched. Cookware containing copper, pewter or lead should never be used for preparing or storing food.

Although the EPA scientific advisory board determined that one of the chemicals used to make Teflon® is a "likely carcinogen" (cancer-causing agent), such non-stick products are said to be safe until there are visible scratches in the cooking surface. Use only flexible plastic utensils to prevent scratching, and watch the pan carefully for signs of wear. Some experts contend that Teflon® is never safe and should not be used at all.

Brands such as Calphalon® and All-Clad® are examples of "anodized" aluminum, which has undergone a process that locks in the metals. Cast-iron cookware provides even cooking due to excellent heat distribution, and has a surprisingly non-stick surface after a process called "seasoning.*" Some brands of cast-iron have enamel cooking surfaces, which are also excellent for cooking. The main drawback for cast-iron is that the cookware is very heavy, and therefore cumbersome to clean and store. It might leach small amounts of iron into the food, which is usually considered a benefit, but food stored in the pot after cooking can take on a "rusty" flavor.

Whichever choice you make, it is always a good idea to transfer leftovers into a clean covered glass container for storage (see FOOD STORAGE).

* To season a cast-iron pan or pot, coat the pan lightly with olive oil, place it upside-down on a baking tray lined with foil or baking paper, and heat in a 300°F oven for one hour. Wash with hot water (no soap) and wipe lightly with oil after each cleaning.

CORN

Agricultural sources say corn has gluten, but celiac sources say it doesn't. Although corn gluten may not be affecting autistic spectrum children for the same reason that wheat gluten does, it often turns out to be a big problem. In a poll of members of the ADI discussion list, comprised mostly of parents who have been using dietary intervention for at least several months, over 50% of the respondents reported that they had eliminated corn, usually based on allergy tests or observation. Hyperactivity, eczema and feces smearing are on the list of things reported by parents as reactions in the corn-sensitive, and it may not show up on food sensitivity panels because there are so many genetically modified species of corn. See also GENETICALLY MODIFIED ORGANISMS (GMO FOODS).

If your child cannot eat corn, he or she will have to avoid many pre-packaged baked goods, beverages, candy, canned fruits, cereals, cookies, jams, jellies, lunch meats, snack foods, and syrups. Corn is an inexpensive food to produce, and a great deal of it can be hidden in food labels. Many processed foods, such as catsup, and even instant coffee, contain hidden corn flour. Again, be sure to read labels carefully.

Corn is also known as maize, hominy, and grits. The following ingredients *may* contain corn protein:

May Contain Corn:		
baking powder	fructose	monosodium glutamate
calcium powder	glucose	powdered sugar
caramel	golden syrup	sorbitol
cellulose	invert sugar or invert syrup	starch/food starch/
confectioner's sugar	lecithin	modified food starch
dextrin, maltodextrin	linoleic acid	sugar/sweeteners
dextrose	malt, malt syrup/extract	treacle
excipients	maltidextrin	vanilla extract
flavorings	maltitol	xanthan gum
	maltose	zein
	mono- and di-glycerides	

Any food ingredient with the word "vegetable" in it is also highly suspect, such as vegetable oil, vegetable broth, vegetable protein, vegetable shortening, hydrolyzed vegetable protein, and vegetable mono- and diglycerides.

If your child is sensitive, and you are uncertain, call the manufacturer and check. Many can ensure that their products are safe. For example, several types of syrup, starch, vanilla extract, and baking powder are corn free.

If your child can't have corn, you can use the following items as sweeteners, thickeners, and leavening agents:

Sweeteners:	Thickeners:	Leavening Agents:
cane sugar	arrowroot	baking soda
fruit juices	kuzu	
honey	potato starch	
maple syrup	rice starch	*Note: these products are usually*
molasses	tapioca	*corn-free, but it's always a good*
rice syrup (GF)		*idea to read labels and check with*
stevia		*the manufacturer.*
vegetable glycerin		

Like other grain oils, corn *oil* is generally considered safe for a person with an allergy. You can find more information from "The Food Allergy Network," a national nonprofit organization, at www.foodallergy.org.

CORN SYRUP

Since food "allergies" are a reaction to proteins, corn sensitive children should not, theoretically, react to corn syrup. Corn syrup is derived from corn starch, which is diluted with water before being washed, filtered, and centrifuged to remove the protein. The resulting starch is more than 99.5% pure (usually less than .5% protein).

However, a great number of sensitive children do react to it. The Feingold Program suspects that the problem with corn syrup is usually not caused by an allergy to corn, but is a reaction to the chemicals used in processing the corn, especially sulfur (sulfites). Corn starch may contain up to 50 parts per million of sulfur dioxide.

Other concerns about corn syrup, especially high-fructose corn syrup, are that it is metabolized differently than other sugars, which could stimulate appetite and affect weight control. Studies on this have been inconclusive. However, high-fructose corn syrup is so inexpensive to manufacture that it has found its way into many of our packaged foods, enhancing the flavor just enough to make us want to eat more than we probably should.

Most people think that soft drinks, candy, gum, jams, and jellies are the main sources of this ingredient. But if you start checking labels, you'll find it in products such as bread, oatmeal, peanut butter, and more.

COSMETICS, CREAMS & LOTIONS (See SKIN CARE PRODUCTS)

CROHN'S DISEASE (CROHN'S COLITIS/REGIONAL ENTERITIS)

Crohn's Disease is a chronic, progressive autoimmune inflammatory bowel disease (IBD). It usually occurs in the lower part of the small intestine, called the terminal ileum, but it can affect any part of the digestive tract, from the mouth to the anus. The inflammation extends deep into the lining of the affected organ, and can also involve nearby lymph nodes. It is a serious disease, which can cause pain and frequent bowel movements and diarrhea, as well as severe abdominal pain, nausea, fever and weight loss.

For children with chronic GI symptoms, doctors may want to rule out Crohns's disease. In addition to blood tests for anemia and white blood cell counts, a stool analysis will be performed. The doctor may perform an upper GI series and/or a COLONOSCOPY. If Crohn's disease is indicated, more detailed x-rays of the entire digestive track will be required to see how much of the system is affected by the disease. In serious cases, surgery may be necessary.

CROSS-CONTAMINATION

Some foods that should be appropriate for a special diet are off limits due to cross-contamination. Foods can be corrupted during production, storage, grinding processing, handling or even shopping (think of a salad bar, with croutons sitting beside the lettuce). With grains, the contamination can take place in the field (seeds may have been left behind from the harvesting of last year's crop). Though oats do not contain gluten, they are usually milled and packaged in the vicinity of other grains (see OATS). Individual tolerance to cross-contamination is variable, but for most people avoiding gluten and casein, it seems to be necessary to avoid even the tiniest amounts (milligrams) of offending protein.

Another common source of cross-contamination comes from health food stores that sell in bulk, especially when they encourage self-service. Each food is supposed to have its own scoop, but people often put them in multiple bins. Although bulk buying can be economical, it is probably best to avoid it.

You can order rolls of customized return-address labels that read, "WARNING - NOT SAFE FOR SPECIAL DIET." Another set, in a different color, can say "SAFE FOR SPECIAL DIET." Keep them in the kitchen to label foods quickly and easily.

There may be unexpected sources of contamination in your own kitchen. Double-dipping of spoons or other serving utensils can transfer food between "safe" and "unsafe" containers. See also APPLIANCES.

CULTURED FOODS AND CULTURE STARTERS

Cultured (fermented) foods have been used for thousands of years in many countries. The cultured food most familiar to Americans is yogurt, but there are others, such as kefir and cultured vegetables. Fermentation can refer to the use of yeast to change sugar into alcohol, or the use of bacteria to create lactic acid in certain foods, such as vegetables or yogurt. Fermenting food has many benefits: it can enhance the flavors of certain foods and make them last longer. Some fermentation processes increase the amount of protein, essential amino acids, essential fatty acids, and vitamins. Eating cultured foods is a natural way to replenish our beneficial gut flora (see PROBIOTICS).

The first time food is cultured, commercial starter mixes are usually preferred (after that, a small amount of an existing batch of a cultured food may be used as a base to start a fresh batch). Several different varieties are available. The culture starter sold at www.bodyecologydiet.com contains a robust bacterium called *Lactobacillus plantarum*, a species of lactobacillus which is commonly found in fermented and pickled foods. *L. Plantarum* has been shown to be resistant to several strains of antibiotics, and has proven to be beneficial for those with Irritable Bowel Syndrome.[50] [51]   Other starters typically contain *Saccaromyces unisporus, Bifidobacterium longum* and several varieties of *Lactobacillus,* including *L. acidophilus.* Defeat Autism Now! Doctor Elizabeth Mumper, MD suggests using several different species of probiotics to ensure diverse colonization of the gut with friendly bacteria (see DYSBIOSIS). For more information on fermentation of foods, see www.healingcrow.com. Look for culture starters online, or at your local natural foods store.

CULTURED VEGETABLES (See also PROBIOTICS)

For people who do not tolerate dairy products, cultured vegetables offer another good source of natural probiotics. Donna Gates describes how to make cultured vegetables in her book, *Body Ecology Diet, 9th edition*:

> "Cultured vegetables are made by shredding cabbage or a combination of cabbage and other vegetables, combining them with water, and then packing them tightly into an airtight container. They are left to ferment at room temperature for several days or longer. Friendly bacteria naturally present in the vegetables quickly lower the pH, so the bacteria can reproduce. The vegetables become soft, delicious, and somewhat sour.

> The airtight container can be glass or stainless steel. Use an appropriate size container that will hold all the ingredients. The container must be airtight and seal with a rubber or plastic ring or a clamp down lid.

> Room temperature means 72 degrees Fahrenheit, for at least 3 days. You can taste them at different stages and decide for yourself. In the winter months, you can wrap the container in a towel and place it inside an insulated or thermal chest. In the summer months the vegetables will culture faster. They may be ready in just three or four days.

"I have had my son on fermented vegetables for a month and for the first time that I remember, he has formed stools. Some healing is going on!"

-Maryjo Sliwinski

> During this fermentation period, the friendly bacteria are having a heyday, reproducing and converting sugars and starches to lactic acid. Once the initial process is over, slow down the bacterial activity by putting the cultured vegetables in the refrigerator. This greatly slows the fermentation, but does not stop it completely.

> Even if the vegetables sit in your refrigerator for months, they will not spoil; they do, however, become more sour. Also, over time, the beneficial microflora will slowly consume all of the sugars in the vegetables. The vegetables will still be fermented and safe to eat, but they will not be as rich in friendly microflora."

While it is not necessary to add a culture starter to your vegetables, doing so will ensure that your vegetables begin fermenting with a hardy strain of beneficial bacteria (see CULTURE STARTERS). Adding a spoonful of honey before fermenting will add a pleasant flavor without adding sugar to the final product (the bacteria will digest the sugars during fermentation). If

---

[50] Mathara JM, Schillinger U, Kutima PM, Mbugua SK, Guigas C, Franz C, Holzapfel WH. "Functional properties of Lactobacillus plantarum strains isolated from Maasai traditional fermented milk products in Kenya." *Curr Microbiol.* 2008 Apr;56(4):315-21.

[51] Niedzielin K, Kordecki H, Birkenfeld B. "A controlled, double-blind, randomized study on the efficacy of Lactobacillus plantarum 299V in patients with irritable bowel syndrome." *Eur J Gastroenterol Hepatol.* 2001 Oct; 13(10):1143-7.

your child doesn't like the texture of cultured vegetables, you can start by giving him small amounts of the juice, which is also rich in probiotics. Adding salt may help.

"DAN!"

"DAN!" is the former nickname for an organization called DEFEAT AUTISM NOW!

DARIFREE™ (See MILK ALTERNATIVES)

DEFEAT AUTISM NOW!

Defeat Autism Now! began in 1995, when Dr. Bernard Rimland of the Autism Research Institute brought together thirty of the field's most innovative autism researchers for a brainstorming session. Since then, Defeat Autism Now! has developed into a large movement of parents, researchers and practitioners working together to unravel the biochemical, genetic and nutritional puzzle responsible for autism spectrum disorders. Defeat Autism Now! holds major conferences for parents and professionals twice a year, in large cities on the East and West Coasts. Additionally, smaller conferences ("Mini-Defeat Autism Now Conferences") take place throughout the year in various locations, some international.

On the Defeat Autism Now! website (www.autism.com/dan), you can view scientific talks, presentations and panels featuring researchers, physicians, and parents. You will also find information about conference dates, locations, speakers, and registration details, and a list of participating doctors (see below).

DEFEAT AUTISM NOW! DOCTORS

Defeat Autism Now! Doctors (formerly called "DAN! Doctors") are physicians interested in autism who have attended at least one Defeat Autism Now! Conference. They are required attend a special clinician seminar at least once every two years, and to sign a statement that they subscribe to and conduct their practice in accordance with the Defeat Autism Now! philosophy. They will know what sorts of tests to order, and how to interpret the results. They usually network with other Defeat Autism Now! doctors to discuss difficult cases.

The Autism Research Institute keeps a geographical list on their website of these doctors, naturopaths, homeopaths, and nutritionists, with the disclaimer that "it does not endorse or support any individual or entity listed, makes no representations, warranties, guarantees or promises on behalf of or for those listed, and assumes no liability nor responsibility for any service or product provided. ARI does not 'certify' practitioners or guarantee competence, skill, knowledge or experience."

Within the United States, see: www.autism.com/dan/danusdis.htm. Outside of the United States: www.autism.com/dan/danforeigndis.htm

If you think your doctor might be interested in acquiring new patients who are looking for knowledgeable autism practitioners, suggest that they attend a Defeat Autism Now! conference, and refer them to www.autism.com/medical for more information. For more on finding a good physician, see DOCTORS.

DERMATITIS HERPETIFORMIS (DH)

Dermatitis herpetiformis is a chronic inflammatory disease, characterized by red, slightly-raised lesions that itch and burn intensely. DH is linked to intestinal sensitivity to gluten in the diet, and is more common in individuals with celiac disease.

The bumps or blisters usually appear on the elbows, knees, back, and buttocks. In most cases, the rash is roughly the same size and shape on both sides of the body. DH can be diagnosed with a blood test, a skin biopsy or an intestinal biopsy, and is treated with strict adherence to a gluten-free diet. You can find photos of patients with this rash online, by searching *dermatitis herpetiformis pictures.*

DETOXIFICATION

There is increasing concern over the apparent difficulty autistic children have with excreting toxins from the body (see METHYLATION, SULFATION). Aside from concerns about exposure to mercury and toxic metals, children are bombarded with viruses, pesticides, flame-retardant chemicals such as organophosphates, and other chemicals and environmental toxins. These can all disrupt or block the body's detoxification pathways.

There are several supplements that may be helpful in addressing this problem, including glutathione (GSH) and the amino acid N-acetylcysteine. GSH works to detoxify many environmental toxicants in pesticides, herbicides, fungicides, solvents and petrochemicals. Antioxidants are also highly recommended: Taurine is both an antioxidant and a detoxifying agent, protecting cells from exposure to toxins like household detergents, and chlorine from bleach or swimming pools.

DIABETES (See also BLOOD SUGAR)

Diabetes is a metabolic disorder that is characterized by persistently high blood sugar levels. After eating, the pancreas (a gland in the digestive system) releases a hormone called insulin. Insulin allows glucose, the sugar that is the body's main source of energy, to move from the blood into our cells. If the pancreas either produces too little insulin, or the cells do not respond to the insulin that is produced, glucose will build up in the blood and pass into the urine. If this imbalance isn't corrected, blood sugar will remain high but the body won't be able to use it.

Some symptoms include increased thirst, frequent urination, increased appetite or weight loss, fatigue, irritability, and/or blurry vision. Type I diabetes, most often seen in children, can have a fairly sudden onset, and lead to serious complications including permanent nerve damage, so if you see any of these symptoms, ask your doctor to do some testing without delay.

Dietary recommendations include planning meals that are approximately the same size and combination of carbohydrates and fats at the same time every day, to help to keep blood sugar regular and predictable. Complex carbohydrates such as whole grains, fruits and vegetables are preferable over simple carbohydrates like soft drinks and candy (see GLYCEMIC INDEX).

DIAPER RASH

Diaper rash can be caused by several different things. The skin can become irritated by prolonged contact with urine and feces, especially diarrhea, due to increased pH. In some cases, especially after antibiotic treatment, yeast and fungus such as *Candida Albicans* can get trapped in the folds of the skin - this is usually characterized by redness and/or a yeasty smell, and can be treated with over-the-counter anti-fungal cream.

Diaper rash can also be caused by food allergies and sensitivities. Because of this, breastfed babies are less likely to have diaper rash than those who are bottle-fed. In fact, diaper rash often begins with a change in diet, probably as a result of sudden direct skin contact with food allergens in the urine and feces. This can also lead to eczema, which is an extremely itchy and persistent rash in other parts of the body.

Obviously, identifying and removing food allergens is a primary concern - it is pointless to keep putting cortisone cream on a rash caused by something in the diet. Other treatments includesavoiding or using only hypoallergenic baby wipes, removing the diapers for a period to let the skin dry out, or coating the skin with petroleum jelly or cod liver oil while it heals.

Occasionally, diaper rash can be caused by bacterial infections such as *Staphylococcus,* so if a diaper rash persists, talk to your pediatrician.

DIARRHEA (See STOOLS, ABNORMAL)

"DIE-OFF" REACTIONS (See also DYSBIOSIS, YEAST & FUNGUS)

"Die-off" refers to a medical term called the *Herxheimer reaction*, named for an observation made by German dermatologist Karl Herxheimer. Dorlands Medical Dictionary defines the Herxheimer reaction as a *"transient, short-term, immunological reaction commonly seen following antibiotic treatment...which is manifested by fever, chills, headache, myalgias (muscle pain), and exacerbations of cutaneous lesions. The reaction has been attributed to liberation of endotoxic substances or antigens (a substance which causes an immune reaction) from the killed or dying microorganisms."*

In other words, when we take antibiotics, toxins are released by the dying bacteria as they are killed by the medication, causing symptoms of illness such as pain, headache and muscle aches. The same thing can happen when we treat yeast infections, and can explain why children often get worse when they first start anti-fungal medication, special diets, or probiotic foods and supplements.

A "healing crisis" occurs when the body is detoxifying too rapidly and toxins are released faster than the body can eliminate them. This may occur when the body is in the process of elimination, and the symptoms can be mild or severe. When treating yeast and bacteria in the GI tract, one can recognize this as a temporary condition that occurs before healing begins.

Recommendations for reducing the symptoms of die-off include adding fermented foods to the diet, taking epsom salt baths, increasing fluid intake, rest, and taking digestive enzymes or activated charcoal. If these reactions are severe, talk to your doctor about backing off on the treatment a bit, and proceeding more slowly.

DIFLUCAN (See ANTIFUNGAL MEDICATIONS)

DIGESTION

Many people are vaguely aware of what goes into the process of digestion, but since it's not very complicated, it's worth grasping. This way, if GI problems are diagnosed in your child, you will have some basic knowledge of where the problem is occurring.

The digestive process consists of four stages: Ingestion (eating the food), Digestion (breaking down the food), Absorption (using the food), and Elimination (getting rid of the waste products from the food that the body can't use).

Ingestion: Some foods are simply easier to digest than others. A basic rule is that the more the food is broken down *before* it enters the body, the easier it will be to break down once it is inside the body. For example, flax seeds and corn kernels may pass into the stools virtually undigested, whereas ground seeds and corn can be utilized more efficiently. Complex carbohydrates require more digestion than simple sugars. So for those with impaired digestion, it's important to choose foods that your body can use. If a single food causes diarrhea, then many of the nutrients taken in with the rest of the meal will be lost. (The Specific Carbohydrate Diet™ and The Body Ecology Diet, among others, focus on foods that will give the best nutrition without causing digestive problems.)

Digestion: Digestion begins in the mouth, with the secretion of an enzyme called *ptyalin*. Saliva containing ptyalin mixes with the food during chewing, and begins to break down certain carbohydrates before they even reach the stomach. (This is one of the many reasons why autistic children, who are notoriously bad at chewing their food, can benefit by taking digestive enzyme tablets along with their meals.)

> *"You are not what you eat. You are what you digest."*
> -Patrick Holford, *Improve Your Digestion*

The food then travels down the throat, along the esophagus, and into the stomach. The stomach lining produces highly acidic digestive juices - about half a gallon a day. These are so strong that they can break down proteins and kill most types of dangerous bacteria. At this point, the content of the stomach is unrecognizable as food, so it is given a new name: *chyme*.

After a few hours, the chyme is released into the twists and turns of the small intestine, where it goes on a roller-coaster ride thanks to peristaltic motion (a muscular wave that moves the chyme along). At the top of the small intestine, called the *duodenum*, it is bombarded with another flood of digestive juices, this time from the liver and pancreas.

Absorption: As the chyme moves along, digestion continues, and by the time it reaches the middle of the small intestine (the *jejunum*), the nutrients are ready to be absorbed by the body through the intestinal walls. This digestion and absorption continues until the end of the small intestine, called the *ileum*.

Elimination: Digestion and absorption slow down as the chyme starts a new journey around the bends of the large intestine, or *colon*. What's left of it now is mostly waste. Fiber, bacteria, dead cells from the digestive tract, and all things that haven't been digested are passed along. The colon re-absorbs most of the liquid back into the body, and the rest makes its final journey into the last part of the colon, called the *rectum*. When the rectum is full, it triggers *defecation*, and the process is complete.

It's an efficient and essential system. But as you can imagine, there are a lot of things that can go wrong. Food may not be properly chewed. Caffeine, alcohol, carbonated beverages, and other foods can affect the speed of the peristaltic motion in certain individuals (see IRRITABLE BOWEL SYNDROME). Allergens can trigger problems. Lactose intolerance is common in some societies that have embraced milk-based diets, resulting in gas and diarrhea. Excessive amounts of unhealthy gut flora combined with sugars can lead to fermentation, and viral infection or gluten intolerance could possibly damage the intestinal walls, affecting the production of other digestive enzymes. If the gut walls are damaged and "leaky" for any number of reasons, particles of food can escape into the bloodstream before they are fully broken down.

But luckily, most of these problems can now be identified, and treated. It is generally acknowledged that digestive health is closely related to overall health, which is why it is so important to investigate these issues.

See BOWEL DISEASE AND AUTISM, DIGESTIVE ENZYME TABLETS, DYSBIOSIS, ENZYMES & ENZYME DEFICIENCY, GUT FLORA.

DIGESTIVE ENZYME TABLETS (See also BOWEL DISEASE AND AUTISM)

Various glands in the body secrete digestive enzymes, and some of them are produced on the walls of the intestinal tract. Their job is to break down the foods we eat, starting in the mouth, and continuing throughout the digestive system (see DIGESTION). Different types of enzymes handle the digestion of different food components: fats, starches, proteins, sugars, and so on. When there is a deficiency in certain digestive enzymes, the result can be bloating, cramping, diarrhea or pieces of undigested food in one's stools. Growth of undesirable intestinal flora is a frequent result of carbohydrate and sugar maldigestion.

Sometimes enzyme deficiency is due to a genetic disorder. In those with a "leaky gut," viruses, infections or allergies can cause inflammation, which gets in the way of adequate enzyme production. And, even when enough enzymes *are* being manufactured by the body, some children with autism gulp down their food without chewing it properly, which makes it harder for the enzymes to do their job.

Some digestive enzyme tablets have been specially formulated to aid the breakdown of many types of food, including gluten and dairy proteins, dietary fats, and disaccharidases for digestion of complex sugars. These have proven to be very useful in addressing digestive problems and peptidurea, and are now highly recommended. Parental reports to the Autism Research Institute (San Diego, CA) indicate that digestive enzyme use has had beneficial results in about 60% of the 1500 reported cases.

"Enzymes are not a substitute for an exclusionary diet," explains biochemist Dr. Jon Pangborn, co-founder of Defeat Autism Now! and consultant for Kirkman Labs. "But they assist digestion and may help reduce intestinal inflammation. They may be especially helpful as a safeguard when eating away from home, or when you cannot be positive that the food is actually safe. Without certain enzymes, such as DPP-4, we end up with harmful exorphins, especially from gluten and casein, but also from other foods like zein, from corn. That's one of the reasons why I believe that we need digestive enzyme tablets *plus* a GF/CF diet."

Here are some other key points from Dr. Pangborn:

• Digestive enzyme tablets can facilitate the process of changing a diet. When changing a child's diet to avoid some types of food (casein, gluten, soy, etc.), it becomes necessary to rely upon different types of foods. Good quality, broad-spectrum enzymes will help the body cope with changes in the types of dietary proteins, carbohydrates and fats.

- Investigators including Horvath,[52] Winter, Kushak[53] and Buie[54] have found that carbohydrate-digesting enzymes can be subnormal in autistics, especially disaccharidases such as maltase, isomaltase and palatinase. That means that some have problems digesting even potatoes and seemingly innocuous starchy foods. Digestive enzyme tablets should help correct or alleviate that problem.

- Dr. Jeffrey Bradstreet found that over fifty percent of autistic children in his practice, after stool analyses, had fat malabsorption. Since fats cannot (and should not) be avoided, good quality digestive enzyme tablets that include lipase can help correct or alleviate a fat malabsorption problem.

- If present, mercury may be released by heavy metal detoxification. This can inhibit the production of the digestive enzymes documented to be inadequate in autism, such as DPP-4, lactase, and maltase. Some children's dietary intolerances worsened during the detoxification process. Enzymes might be especially helpful during this period.

- For parents who simply will not or cannot implement the diet, enzyme use may be better than nothing.

The digestive enzymes designed for autism should be taken at the beginning of each meal. The dose depends on the amount of food that's eaten, not the age or weight of the individual. You may notice a period of worsened behavior and autistic traits when enzymes are started, similar to what you might see when gluten and casein are removed. According to the opioid excess theory, this could be due to the body's withdrawal from opioid peptides, which are now being properly broken down instead of leaking into the bloodstream undigested. There may also be some discomfort due to "die off" of dysbiotic flora. These effects should be temporary, and can be seen as a sign that improvements are likely to occur within a few days or weeks.

> *If food isn't being properly broken down, a person can become malnourished even while eating an adequate diet.*

A great deal of information on enzymes and autism has been compiled online at www.enzymestuff.com. To join an online support group for those using digestive enzymes, visit www.yahoogroups.com/group/enzymesandautism. For a list of manufacturers who produce digestive enzymes specific to the needs of those with autism spectrum disorders, see APPENDIX.

In short, enzyme supplements are recommended with every meal. If a child is accidentally contaminated with dairy or gluten, swift administration of the enzymes may alleviate the reaction, or at least reduce its severity. Enzymes can also be useful as a clean-up for stray peptides which may be getting through unbeknownst to the parents, and for the other reasons stated above.

My high-functioning son is twelve years old and has been strictly GF/CF since he was five. He's

---

[52] Horvath, K et. al., *J. Pediatrics*, 135 (199)

[53] Kushak, R. et al. *N. Am Soc Ped Gastroenterol, Hepatol and Nutr.* October 2005 (poster) Salt Lake City

[54] Buie, T. Winter H. Kushak, R. 2002. "Preliminary findings in gastrointestinal investigation of autistic patients."

been taking enzymes for three months, and we have started letting him have small gluten and dairy treats. We really don't notice any negative effects. The diet made a huge difference for him, but he wants to eat the same foods as his friends. Has anyone successfully stopped this diet with enzymes?

After some gut healing takes place, small or occasional amounts of these foods will often be tolerated. It is possible, however, that the damage from repeated infractions could add up and prove ultimately damaging (see INFRACTIONS).

Enzymes instead of Diet?

Parents of autistic children usually observe and report that enzymes improve digestion of many foods, reduce the severity of a withdrawal when the diet is first started, and reduce the duration of infraction-related adverse reactions. However, many parents who tried to take their children off the diet by using digestive enzyme tablets at each meal have been disappointed with the long term effect, and have returned to strict monitoring of food in addition to digestive enzyme tablets.

Dietary intervention should be strictly maintained, but what about those children or teenagers who are sneaking forbidden foods, or getting them from adults who don't understand the importance of their special diet? Unfortunately, these events are the *least* likely times that the child will be offered such a pill. To be effective, enzymes need to be given with the food; they will not be effective if you find out that your child ate a forbidden food while at school or at his grandparents' house earlier in the day.

Dietary intervention is most successful when everyone understands that it is a necessary part of life, and not something to be discarded frivolously (see COMPLIANCE). Allowing slip-ups for "special occasions" because you think the enzymes will handle them will undermine this understanding.

Defeat Autism Now! Doctors recommend giving enzyme supplements during all meals and snacks, in addition to keeping a bottle handy in case of accidents. Those following the Specific Carbohydrate Diet™ can find a list of approved enzymes at www.pecanbread.com.

Until the mechanism for restoring a normal diet in these children can be determined, consider enzyme tablets to be one of the important weapons in our arsenal against autism and related disorders.

DI-METHYL GLYCINE (DMG)

Di-methyl glycine is an amino acid found in both plant and animal cells, which serves as a metabolic enhancer and improves the ability of cells to use oxygen. It is also involved in detoxification, cell protection and immune system regulation. DMG supplements have been said to benefit children even when there is no deficiency, and are considered to be safe. Dr. Bernard Rimland was a strong advocate of giving DMG to children on the autism spectrum, based on the Autism Research Institute's "Parent Ratings of Behavioral Effects of Biomedical

Interventions:" 42% of the nearly 6000 parents who responded said that their children improved on DMG.

> *"Ten minutes after taking DMG, he was sitting at a desk, drawing an original picture and coloring it (something he had never done before). The next day he attended a religious meeting at which he walked around, shaking people's hands and engaging them in conversation. We were astounded! He asked to be tickled. I said, "Did you not know how it felt to be ticklish?" He had never experienced it in his seven years!*
>
> *One morning I was cooking his breakfast and inadvertently touched him with a hot spatula and he flinched. He had never flinched before! I asked him, "What happened when you took the 'stomach pill?'" He said, "Mommy, a noise turned off in my head." -Barbara Broome, reprinted from The ANDI News*

DOCTORS

If you are lucky, or live in a large town or city, finding a knowledgeable autism specialist may be easy. However, many parents decide to travel with their children, sometimes for hours, to get the appropriate testing and treatment they need. Audun and Kathrine Rør, a couple from Tønsberg, Norway, have flown their son Kristoffer to the U.S. three times, to attend Defeat Autism Now! conferences and to see physicians specializing in biomedical interventions (see "DEFEAT AUTISM NOW! DOCTORS").

> *"Some medical professionals may not understand the full impact of having a child with these issues - nor do they realize that there's more that we can do than just sit, wait and watch. These are our children, and there's plenty that we can do to help ... and why that's called unconventional is beyond me!" -Liz Gribbon*

For Americans, the journey should be considerably easier. Many specialists are now treating patients who come from distant locations. After taking an initial in-depth examination, a detailed history, and urine and blood samples, many of these doctors will follow up with the test results by telephone, make recommendations, prescribe supplements or medications if needed, and then see the child again when necessary.

A doctor who doesn't know the difference between wheat and gluten will not be worth your time and money, so find out what they know before committing yourself. Don't be afraid to ask the receptionist the following questions before booking an appointment:

- How has this doctor been trained to specialize in the biomedical treatment of autism spectrum disorders? Has he/she attended a Defeat Autism Now! Practitioner Training?
- Is there a waiting list to see this doctor? How long is it?
- Is the doctor willing to follow up by telephone and maintain communication with the child's regular pediatrician?
- What is the exact cost of the initial consultation, follow-up visits and phone calls? What can I expect to spend on testing or additional fees?

For a comprehensive list of questions to ask the doctor before and during the first consultation, see www.autism.com/dan/ques2ask.htm.

Although some people are easily disgruntled and will give a bad review to a good doctor, there are some doctors out there who have "earned" their bad reputation due to poor follow-up or by charging excessive fees. It's a good idea to get onto a busy Yahoo list or two and ask flat out – "I am considering taking my child to see Dr. Whatsit. Does anyone have any experience with her? Can anyone recommend another doctor in the Southern California area?" Write privately to anyone who replies and get details. If they liked the doctor but felt that she wasn't good at returning phone calls, you can discuss this during the consultation.

Of course, there are no guarantees. In difficult cases, it could take a lot of time and tinkering to find the right treatments for your child, and even the best doctor might not be able to help. Audun and Kathrine, however, report that Kristoffer has surpassed everyone's expectations, and in two years has gone from a severely handicapped, hypotonic four-year-old to a bright, talkative little boy who is catching up with his peers. For them, the travel and expense has been worthwhile.

No matter who you choose to address your child's special medical needs, remember that your child's regular pediatrician needs to be your ally. You must have a doctor who will cooperate with you to make sound decisions for your child's health. If your local doctor intimidates or patronizes you, or ridicules your efforts to explore biomedical treatments, get another doctor. It could be the single most important choice you make for your child's health and well being.

DOWN'S SYNDROME (See RELATED AND/OR CO-EXISTING DISORDERS)

DPP-4 (Dipeptidyl peptidase-4) (See OPIOID EXCESS)

DYSBIOSIS (See also LEAKY GUT, YEAST & FUNGUS)

Dysbiosis is a state of microbial imbalance anywhere on or inside of the body. Much of the time, you will hear the term used to describe an imbalance in gastrointestinal microflora (e.g., "good bacteria," "bad bacteria," yeast, parasites, etc.), living in the gut.

In a healthy person, colonies of beneficial microbes carry out a series of helpful and necessary functions, and protect the body by battling pathogenic (harmful) microbes. They also compete with each other, so the body has a variety of different species, each with their own purposes. In this way, no specific microbial colony becomes overpopulated. When this balance is disturbed, by such things as repeated and inappropriate antibiotic use, these colonies exhibit a decreased ability to check each other's growth. This can lead to an overgrowth of one or more of the disturbed colonies which then may damage some of the other smaller beneficial ones.

This type of situation can create a cascade of problems. The microbes are opportunistic; when given the chance, they will take over and diminish other species, creating problems with digestion and immune function. They excrete different types of waste, which in large quantities can affect overall health in various ways. Harmful bacteria may secrete enzymes which attack the gut lining, causing damage to the intestines and triggering an immune response.

The solution to this problem is to rebuild the immune system and heal the gut by reestablishing a healthy complement of gut flora (see PROBIOTICS). Several types of diet, including the Specific Carbohydrate Diet™, the Body Ecology Diet, and the Yeast Connection Diet, target this concern by limiting the amounts and types of sugars in the diet, and by repopulating the gut with fermented foods such as yogurts and cultured vegetables. If care is taken to encourage the re-growth of healthy flora, the balance can be restored.

Understanding Gut Dysbiosis *by Elizabeth Mumper, MD, reprinted from The ANDI News*

Working with developmentally disabled children has given me a renewed appreciation for the multiple roles of the gut. In addition to its obvious role in digestion, it functions as a vital barrier that protects our bodies from the harmful effects of what we ingest.

You may know that our intestines form an integral part of our immune systems, but did you also know that the gut, just like the brain, has receptors for many neurotransmitters? These are the chemicals that transmit nerve signals between synapses in the nervous system. Further, our guts support a thriving environment (or flora) of bacteria and yeast. This flora consists of about a quadrillion individual germs, which also live on the skin, eyes, digestive tract and vagina.

The guts of breast-fed infants are initially colonized with beneficial bacteria, including lactobacillus and bifidobacteria. In exchange for a place to live, our gut flora perform many important tasks, such as fighting off harmful microbes, manufacturing certain vitamins, and converting food into fuel for the body and brain.

When the delicate balance of the ecosystem in our intestines is disrupted, however, the good bacteria may be depleted. Even a single course of antibiotics can wreak havoc on normal intestinal flora. Harmful flora can produce substances which are biochemically similar to normal neurotransmitters, which is called "molecular mimicry." As these messages are processed, we may suffer from clouded thinking, feel drunk or achy, or develop symptoms that are hard to diagnose. The release of these toxins (often considered microbial "waste products") can also interfere with the body's detoxification mechanisms. Our bodies now find it more difficult than ever to handle pollutants, at a time when toxins are being added to our environment at warp speed.

Judicious use of probiotics and intermittent use of *Saccromyces boulardii*, a good yeast that fights bad yeast, can promote the normal balance of the many bacterial and yeast inhabitants of our guts. Probiotic supplements or cultured foods with active cultures can help reestablish beneficial flora in the intestines (see PROBIOTICS).

Children on the autism spectrum seem to be at particular risk for pathogenic bacteria, especially *Clostridium*. Stool analyses can be used to identify and quantify bacteria so that pathogenic species can be identified and treated. For example, *Clostridia* is treated with oral Vancomycin, sometimes in combination with Flagyl or oral gentamicin. Certain children with autism respond positively to treatment with anti-fungal agents like Diflucan, Sporinox, Lamisil or Ketoconazole. The reasons for this are still unclear, since studies to date do not demonstrate increased colonies of yeast in autistic children, compared to controls. Some symptoms to look out for are red rings around the anus, chronic constipation or diarrhea, or a history of multiple courses of antibiotics.

People know that they need to exercise to build muscles, take calcium to maintain their bones, and eat a "heart healthy" diet to prolong their lifespan. How many of those same people understand how crucial it is to take care of their guts, and the flora that live there symbiotically? Far from being a lowly corridor that simply turns food into waste, our gut performs many vital functions, and needs to be kept healthy in order for us to stay healthy.

Dr. Elizabeth Mumper is a general pediatrician treating a large number of children with autism and attention problems. She is Medical Director of the Autism Research Institute, CEO of Advocates for Children and the founder of the RIMLAND Center in Lynchburg, Virginia.

EAR INFECTIONS (OTITIS MEDIA)

Ear infections are the second most common childhood illness, after colds. More than 75% of all children have had at least one ear infection by the age of three. Normally, the eustachian tube allows drainage of mucus from the middle ear into the throat. When a cold or allergy (commonly a milk or wheat allergy) causes the nasal passages to block, the tube may also be blocked by mucus within the tube. The blockage allows the build-up of fluid within the middle ear, which is normally filled with air. Bacteria or viruses that have entered the middle ear through the eustachian tube can get trapped there, breeding and eventually leading to an ear infection (acute otitis media). Simply put, acute otitis media is the presence of fluid (usually pus) in the middle ear which becomes infected.

Children's immune systems are not fully developed at this young age and they can be prone to infection. Because their eustachian tubes are shorter and more horizontal than those of adults, bacteria and viruses find their way into the middle ear more easily. This is accompanied by pain, redness of the eardrum and sometimes, fever. Some cases of *otitis media* are chronic, with fluid in the middle ear for six weeks or more. When there is fluid present which is not infected it is called *"otitis media* with effusion."

For years, any redness or fluid in the ear triggered antibiotic treatment, leading to antibiotic-resistant bacterial strains, and the potential for an imbalance in gut flora. Doctors now know that the presence of fluid alone should not necessitate antibiotics, because many infections are viral in nature, and antibiotic treatment will not help. There are some naturopathic recommendations for preventing ear infections, including a low-sugar diet, and herbs such as echinacea to boost the immune system. In fact, naturopathic ear drops have been shown to be just as effective as anesthetic ear drops.[55] These usually contain some combination of St. John's Wort (*Hypericum*), Mullein (*Verbascum*), Garlic (*Allium*), and Calendula, and should be warmed before using.

Although they can be unpleasant and uncomfortable, most cases of otitis media resolve themselves. But while rare, there can be complications. If a child develops a high fever, redness on the ear or extreme pain you should seek medical care.

ECZEMA

Eczema is a type of chronic rash, consisting of itchy, dry, red skin and small bumps. The most common type is sometimes referred to as *atopic dermatitis* or *infantile eczema*, though it may occur in older children.

The word "atopic" describes a sensitivity to allergens in the environment such as pollens, molds, dust, animal dander, and certain foods. "Dermatitis" means that the skin is inflamed or sore.

Scratching tends to make the problem worse, so it can be difficult to treat. Doctors typically advise avoiding hot baths, using hypoallergenic soaps and detergents, steroid creams and moisturizing lotions, waiting for it to be outgrown. But eczema does not just happen, and it should not be ignored. It is an allergic reaction, which can usually be identified and treated. Eczema itches fiercely and constantly, and can cause an otherwise healthy child to become anxious and stressed. Stress makes eczema worse, thus creating a vicious cycle.

---

[55] Sarrell EM. "Efficacy of naturopathic extracts in the management of ear pain associated with acute otitis media." *Arch Pediatr Adolesc Med* - 01-Jul-2001; 155(7): 796-9

The allergic triggers can be caused by molds, pollen, dust, dander or foods. They may be hard to pinpoint, since these allergies may not show up on skin tests. However, IgG testing or an elimination diet can also prove useful. One child had an IgE allergy to cats, and an IgG sensitivity to oranges, tomatoes, dairy, and gluten. Removing one or two of these allergens alone did not solve the problem. But removing all five resulted in smooth, creamy skin after only two weeks.

If your child has a rash, show it to your doctor for a diagnosis. You can also find photographs on the Web, with examples of eczema and atopic dermatitis.

EGGS

If tolerated, eggs are an excellent source of protein, containing all of the essential amino acids. Eggs also provide B Vitamins, Vitamin D and Vitamin A. They make baking and cooking much easier, especially when grains and starches have been removed from the diet.

Unfortunately, some children are allergic to eggs. Others do not have a confirmed allergy, but do not tolerate them well. Some children are able to tolerate eggs after they have been off gluten, casein and other problem proteins for a period of time. In the absence of a confirmed allergy, let your food diary be your guide if you suspect eggs are a problem.

Some chicken feed contains trace amounts of arsenic, and since Defeat Autism Now! doctors report that impaired detoxification is often a problem for our children, this is of special concern. Whenever possible, buy organic eggs from free-range chickens (chickens who get to walk around and peck at grass).

Do eggs contain dairy? Most children can tell the difference between a milk producing mammal such as a cow or goat, and an egg-laying bird. So why do so many people believe that eggs are dairy products? It seems to be due to their close proximity in the refrigerated section of the grocery store.

EGG SUBSTITUTES

If you have tried baking cookies, cakes or breads without eggs, you know how hard it can be. Here are some ideas from the Vegan website, *The Post Punk Kitchen* (www.theppk.com). Each recipe substitutes for one egg, so double or triple them as needed. Some contain soy and should not be used if you are avoiding it.

Flax Seeds: Mix 1 tablespoon of finely-ground flax seeds with 3 tablespoons of water, and beat using a whisk or fork. Let stand for five minutes before using. The mixture will become gooey and gelatinous, much like an egg white. This works well in pancakes, muffins, and cookies.

Silken Tofu: For those who tolerate soy, whip ¼ cup blended silken tofu (with some of the liquid from the recipe) in a blender until completely smooth and creamy, not grainy or lumpy. Beaten tofu leaves virtually no taste, and works well in dense cakes and brownies. Use in smaller quantities for lighter cakes and fluffy baked goods (if the recipe calls for 3 eggs, use only 2 "tofu eggs"). In cookie recipes, it may make the cookie more cake-like and fluffy, but adding 1 teaspoon of starch (such as arrowroot or potato starch) will compensate for that. It may make pancakes a little heavy.

Ener-G Egg Replacer™

Mix 1½ tablespoons egg replacer with 2 tablespoons water. It may add a slightly chalky taste to cakes and cookies, but adds good texture to cookies, and baked goods that are meant to be a little crispy.

Bananas: Mash ½ of a medium banana. Bananas keep cakes moist and fluffy and give a nicely browned result. This works well in quick breads, muffins, cakes, and pancakes. Note that many children with autism spectrum disorders have problems with bananas.

Soy yogurt: ¼ cup of soy yogurt makes a good egg substitute for quick breads, muffins, and cakes (again, if soy is tolerated).

ELIMINATION DIETS (See also ROTATION DIETS)

Allergy testing can be a great way to determine which foods might be problematic for your child (see ALLERGY TESTING). However, because testing often fails to provide accurate data, many people believe that an elimination diet is the most accurate way to determine what foods, if any, cause a reaction. In some cases this may be a classic allergy, and in others it may be a food intolerance (see ALLERGIES & INTOLERANCES). It is especially hard to determine conclusively whether or not a food is causing physical or behavioral symptoms.

An elimination diet is simple, if not always easy: Foods suspected of causing symptoms are removed from the diet, and then added slowly back. For children the most common culprits are milk, wheat, eggs, peanuts, tree nuts and soy; grains, vegetables, fruits, spices, etc. may also cause problems. Often an elimination diet begins with just a few foods that are known not to provoke a reaction. Once you have taken the diet down to "bare bones," other foods are added back, one at a time, to see if they are a problem. It is important to add only one food at a time, and to keep a food diary. Keeping careful notes will help identify any delayed reactions. Usually, a food is added for one day, then removed for a few days. A second challenge with the same food should follow, or if you are unsure about whether a delayed reaction was caused by that food. When a food's safety has been determined, another can be added in the same manner.

Some people remove only one food at a time to see if symptoms disappear, then challenge with that food. However, this may not be useful if more than one food is problematic. A regular elimination diet is often the fastest and easiest way to determine food sensitivities. Since many children on the autism spectrum eat very few foods, this may be less difficult than it sounds.

Because the elimination diet is so spartan, it is often referred to as the "cave man" diet. In general, foods allowed include lamb (preferably organic and with no chemicals or antibiotics), wild game, deep water fish (halibut and wild caught salmon), turkey (if fresh, and contains no additives), vegetables (but no corn, white potato, tomato, peas or legumes), and very small fruit servings (no citrus or fruit juice). Only small servings of fresh, unprocessed fruit are allowed. Lemon and lime may be used to enhance flavor. Water and small servings of fruit juice are the only drinks given during an elimination diet. Oils used for cooking should be cold pressed (sunflower, sesame, safflower, sesame and extra virgin olive oil). Nuts may be eaten if they are not treated in any way. No peanuts (which are legumes).

If a food proves to be a problem, you may want to follow up with allergy testing. However it is important to remember that you are treating a child, not a test result. If a test is negative for eggs, but your child clearly reacts badly to them, avoid eggs. This common sense approach will generally lead to the best balance between sensitivities and nutrition. See also MULTIPLE FOOD SENSITIVITIES, ROTATION DIETS.

If your child has ever had an anaphylactic reaction to a food, that food should *never* be introduced.

ENDOSCOPY

An endoscopy is a diagnostic procedure used to examine the digestive tract and other internal organs. An endoscope, which is a flexible tube with a lighted camera attached, is inserted through the mouth, down the throat, or through the rectum (see also COLONOSCOPY).

Endoscopy is typically used to evaluate stomach pain, ulcers, gastritis, digestive tract bleeding or suspicious masses in the colon. Biopsies (tissue samples) can be taken during the procedure and analyzed for more information.

ENTEROCOLITIS

Enterocolitis is a severe form of infection that can affect the small or large intestine. The most common symptoms are fever, abdominal swelling and diarrhea (see BOWEL DISEASE AND AUTISM), but less acute forms of enterocolitis may go undiagnosed in a child who is not able to describe his symptoms.

ENVIRONMENTAL ILLNESS/ ENVIRONMENTAL TOXICITY

We know that illnesses such as cancer, emphysema and heart disease can be triggered by environmental factors, especially in people with a family history of these illnesses. We also know that toxins abound in modern society, such as those in industrial waste, chemicals, pesticides and solvents, and even in the water we drink and the food we eat.

And now, even breastmilk has been found to contain traces of heavy metals and a number of chemicals, such as tetrachloroethene, dioxins, and polychlorinated biphenyls (PCBs). It's impossible to know the long-term effects of this on our children's health and development.

The medical records from autism spectrum children commonly show a family history of cardiovascular disease, cancer, neuro-degenerative disease (such as Alzheimer and Parkinson's disease), allergies, thyroid disorders and other autoimmune diseases. Parents of these children also seem to have a high frequency of fibromyalgia, fatigue, joint and muscle pains, migraines, seizures, and related symptoms. It is logical therefore, that these families should minimize exposure to food additives, amalgam

"We have exposed our bodies and our children to a greater number of toxic substances than any prior generation. It's a tribute to the human immune system that it has stood up to this increasing burden of chemicals, pesticides, hormones, heavy metals, and other substances in our air, food, and water. But the reality is that not everyone is doing well. The dramatic increase in autism, ADD, ADHD, autoimmune diseases, neurodegenerative diseases, arthritis and cardiovascular disease may reflect this ever-increasing body burden of toxic chemicals in our environment."

-Defeat Autism Now! Doctor Stuart Freedenfeld, MD

fillings, smoke, cleaning fluids, pesticides, fungicides, and other chemicals. In addition, consider using filtered water, organic foods and environmentally friendly cleaning products and cosmetics.

ENZYMES AND ENZYME DEFICIENCY (See also DIGESTION, DIGESTIVE ENZYME TABLETS)

Digestive enzymes break down food so that the body can absorb it. Enzymes are produced in the mouth, the stomach, the duodenum and the jejunum. They are secreted by different glands: the salivary glands, the glands in the stomach, the pancreas, and the glands in the small intestines (see DIGESTION).

Dr. Timothy Buie, a pediatric gastroenterologist at Harvard/Mass General Hospital, found that 55% of the autistic children he examined showed below normal levels of disaccharide/glucoamylase, lactase, and sucrase enzymes.[56] (See also BOWEL DISEASE AND AUTISM.)

EPI-PEN® (See ANAPHYLAXIS)

EPILEPSY/SEIZURE DISORDERS

Epilepsy is a disorder in which recurring seizures are caused by abnormal electrical activity in the brain. The part of the brain that is affected determines the type of seizure that a person experiences. There are many types of epilepsy, and often the cause is unknown.

According to Dr. Stephen Edelson of the Autism Research Institute, about one in four individuals on the autism spectrum begins to have seizures during puberty. The exact reason for the onset of seizures is not known, but it is probably due to hormonal changes. Sometimes seizures are noticeable, (i.e., associated with convulsions), but for many, there are small, subclinical seizures typically not detectable by simple observation. Some parents have EEGs performed, but if the child does not have a seizure during testing, they may be missed. A 24-48 hour EEG increases the chances of detecting subclinical seizure activity.

Anticonvulsant medications are the usual means of treating seizures, but they have unpleasant or potentially severe side effects, and do not work for all individuals. Some dietary interventions have been used, including stabilizing blood glucose levels and the avoidance of allergenic foods, especially monosodium glutamate (MSG) and aspartame. Some have successfully used low carbohydrate diets like the Ketogenic Diet and The Atkins Diet.

In a double-blind, placebo controlled study of 63 children with epilepsy, identifying and avoiding food allergens was very successful in treating seizures.[57] Researchers used an elimination diet to determine foods to which the children were allergic and these were removed from the diet. The children who improved were those who also showed other signs of allergy, such as migraines, stomach symptoms or hyperactivity. Symptoms were caused by over 40 different foods, and most children reacted to more than one food.

---

[56] Buie T, Winter H, Kushak, R. "Preliminary findings in gastrointestinal investigation of autistic patients." 2002. Harvard University and Mass General Hospital.

[57] Egger, J, Carter CM, Soothill JF, Wilson J. "Oligoantigenic diet treatment of children with epilepsy and migraine." *J Pediatr* 1989; 114:51-58.

The incidence of celiac disease is higher in epileptics than in the general population.[58] Seizures have improved in those celiacs after starting a gluten free diet, but only when the diet was started very soon after seizure activity began. Most epileptic patients later found to have celiac disease showed no gastrointestinal symptoms, so it is reasonable to test for celiac disease when seizures begin.[59]

A rare form of epilepsy results from a deficiency of Vitamin B6, and is treated with supplementation. B6 may also be helpful for other types of epilepsy.[60]

Nutrients that may reduce seizures include magnesium, vitamin E, manganese, taurine, dmg and omega-3 fatty acids. Taurine, especially, has been documented to reduce seizures in some types of epilepsy.[61] [62] Thiamine may improve cognition in epileptic children. Folic acid, vitamin D, biotin and L-carnitine may be needed to treat deficiencies that result when anticonvulsant medication is used.[63]

ERYTHRITOL (See SUGAR SUBSTITUTES)

EPSOM SALTS

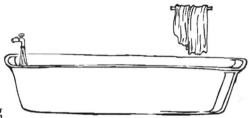

Epsom salts have been reported to have a calming effect when dissolved in warm bath water. It is suggested that this compound, when absorbed through the skin, helps correct imbalances in SULFATION, thus providing improved functioning in those with sulfation defects. They have also been reported to be useful for combating "die-off" reactions and for reducing the severity of sleep disorders.

If you notice a marked worsening of symptoms from an epsom salt bath, do not continue the treatment. It is theorized that in some, this effect may be caused by the production of too many sulfide groups.

You can read more about the use of epsom salt baths for detoxification at www.enzymestuff.com/epsomsalts.htm.

ESSENTIAL FATTY ACIDS (See OMEGA-3 and OMEGA-6 FATTY ACIDS)

EQUAL® (See ASPARTAME)

---

[58] Cronin, CC, Jacson LM, feighery C, et al. "Coeliac Disease and Epilepsy." *QJM* 1998;91:303-308.

[59] Pratesi R. Modelli IC, Martins RC et al. "Celiac disease and epilepsy: favorable outcome in a child with difficult to control seizures." *Acta neurol Scand* 2003;108:290-293.

[60] Hagberg, B, Hamfelt, Hansson O. "Tryptophan load tests and pyridoxal-5-phosphate levels in epileptic children. II. Cryptogenic epilepsy." *Acta Paedoatr Scand* 1966;55:381-384.

[61] Airakseinen EM, et al. "Effects of taurine treatment on epileptic patients." *Prog Clin Biol Res.* 1980;39:157-66.

[62] Fukuyama Y, Ochiai Y. "Therapeutic trial by taurine for intractable childhood epilepsies." *Brain Dev.* 1982;4(1): 63-9.

[63] Gaby, Alan R. "Natural Approaches to Epilepsy." *Alt Med Rev* Vol. 12 (1) 2007; 9-24.

EXCESSIVE THIRST

A number of children with autism are excessively thirsty. Some researchers have attributed this to a deficiency of essential fatty acids. Rosemary Waring of the University of Birmingham has suggested that excessive thirst is indicative of a problem with phenols, since many metabolic processes are disturbed by phenolic compounds and cause physical symptoms not usually associated with autism (including excessive thirst, night sweats, and facial flushing).

Excessive thirst is one of the first warning signs of Juvenile (Type I) diabetes, so have your child checked out by a doctor before looking into other causes.

EXCITOTOXICITY

Excitotoxicity is the process by which nerve cells are damaged and killed by an excess of certain neurotransmitters. The fact that MSG (see MONOSODIUM GLUTAMATE) and ASPARTAME are added to commercial foods as sweeteners and flavor enhancers has caused a considerable amount of concern among consumer advocacy groups, because these are broken down into excitotoxins called glutamate and aspartate.

Here's a very simplified way of understanding the communication of nerve cells in the brain: imagine giving a person some caffeine and a sedating medication. If you get the balance right, the person might function reasonably well. Now imagine that he suddenly gets too much caffeine and not enough of the sedative. The levels of each would have to be balanced in order for him to stay relaxed and alert.

Some neurotransmitters are *excitatory* (including glutamate and aspartate), and some are *inhibitory* (such as GABA). Excitatory neurotransmitters *increase* the electrical transmission between nerve cells. Inhibitory neurotransmitters *reduce* electrical activity. It is necessary for excitatory and inhibitory neurotransmitters to be in balance for proper brain function to occur.

The communication of the nerves is controlled by glutamate. If excessive glutamate is released or not properly recycled, it becomes neurotoxic. This "excitotoxicity" leads to death of the neurons. Excitotoxicity has been implicated in a number of acute and/or degenerative forms of neuropathology such as epilepsy, Alzheimer's, Parkinson's, stroke, hearing loss and tinnitus.

EZEKIAL BREAD

Ezekial bread is made from a blend of bean and grain flour. High in protein and fiber, it is a healthy product but contains wheat and other gluten flours.

FAILURE TO THRIVE (FTT)

Failure to thrive is a diagnostic label given to children who weigh consistently below the 3rd to the 5th percentile for age, or who have a sudden decrease in weight to below the 5th percentile. When FFT is caused by a medical condition, it is referred to as *organic failure to thrive*. FFT caused by environmental problems, like poverty or parental neglect, is referred to as *non-organic failure to thrive*.

There are several nutritional factors that can lead to organic FTT, such as celiac disease, parasitic infection, excessive fruit juice consumption, and food allergies (especially milk allergy). [64] [65] [66] Chronic diarrhea can result in malnutrition and FTT, since the food passes too quickly through the digestive tract for nutrients to be absorbed. [67]

According to Harvard researcher Timothy Buie, the frequency of lactase deficiency in autistic individuals with FTT was significantly higher than non-autistic individuals with FTT (80% vs. 25%). This puts these children into a predictably bad situation, since many of them are placed on a dairy-based liquid nutritional supplement, which may become the only food they will accept (see PICKINESS & FOOD ADDICTION). For more on Dr. Buie's findings, see BOWEL DISEASE AND AUTISM.

It has been theorized that autistic children with food allergies or bowel disease eat little because of the discomfort they feel after eating. For many of these children, the few foods they *will* eat are opioid-associated foods like gluten. It has been speculated that this is a way of "self medicating" their discomfort. It is also possible that these opioids mask the feeling of hunger.

Although parents often resist taking away an underweight child's favorite (or only) food, it is only after substituting foods *not containing gluten and dairy* that many of these children will begin to eat again. When the diet is being changed, it is extremely important that FTT children are monitored by qualified nutritionists working together with parents. These children should also be evaluated by a pediatric gastroenterologist for signs of bowel disease and/or malabsorption (see BOWEL DISEASE AND AUTISM, DIGESTION).

"My daughter refused all solids at 6 months old. By 12 months, we were very concerned as she stopped gaining weight, and wasn't developing in other ways. By 15 months she was diagnosed with Failure to Thrive. She entered Early Intervention and they tried all kinds of speech therapy, OT, developmental therapy, play therapy, ABA. you name it. Nothing. Not an ounce of progress. She scored at 4-5 months old in developmental testing.

At that point, my autistic son had been on the diet for about a year, and I was still concerned about his perpetual runny nose, so I scheduled skin scratch test with a local allergist, and decided to test her as well. She reacted to chicken, pork, shrimp, wheat, and dairy. I removed every trace of gluten, casein, chicken, pork, and seafood from her diet that day. She began putting on weight. Six weeks later she tested out at 18 months in developmental testing and was putting together 2-3 word sentences."

FATS & OILS (See also BUTTER, GHEE)

Though fat has become a dirty word in our diet-conscious world, fats constitute a critically important part of the diet. Fats provide a concentrated source of energy, and without them, fat-soluble vitamins A, D, E & K cannot be properly used by the body. Fats are also necessary for

---

[64] Tully MA. "Pediatric Celiac Disease," *Gastroenterol Nurs.* 2008 March/April;31(2):132-140.

[65] Ewing WM, Allen PJ. "The diagnosis and management of cow milk protein intolerance in the primary care setting." *Pediatr Nurs.* 2005 Nov-Dec;31(6):486-93.

[66] Smith MM, Lifshitz F. "Excess fruit juice consumption as a contributing factor in nonorganic failure to thrive," *Pediatrics.* 1994 Mar;93(3):438-43.

[67] Noimark L, Cox HE. "Nutritional problems related to food allergy in childhood." *Pediatr Allergy Immunol.* 2008 Mar;19(2):188-95.

proper brain development,[68] which is why a fat free regimen is never recommended for young children. In fact, since milk or formula provide fat in a typical child's diet, those using low fat or fat free milk substitutes must be sure to provide fat in other foods or via supplements. Over half the calories in human breastmilk are actually calories from fat. Here are some different types of fats and oils:

Polyunsaturated fat (PUFA): Omega-3 and Omega-6 fatty acids belong to this group. Although polyunsaturated fats are good for us, when they are heated or exposed to oxygen or moisture, they tend to turn rancid. Rancid oils contain free radicals (see OXIDATIVE STRESS), which attack cell membranes and can damage the skin and organs.

Monounsaturated fat (MUFA): Monounsaturated fats tend to be liquid at room temperature, but firm when cold. These fats are quite stable and do not easily go rancid. They can be heated for cooking. The most common monounsaturated fat is oleic acid, an omega-9 fatty acid found in olive oil, nut oils and avocado oil. It is one of the healthier forms of dietary fat, lowering the total cholesterol level. It also promotes the production of antioxidants.

Saturated fat: These are the fats that are solid at room temperature. Typically these are animal fats or tropical fats (coconut and palm); some are even made by the body. Saturated fats are very stable, which is why they are so commonly used in packaged foods. They do not go rancid easily and can be heated.

Trans fats: Hydrogenation is a process that turns PUFAs into saturated and over-saturated fats in products such as margarine. These "partially hydrogenated" fats are considered to be the most unhealthy of all fats, but because they have a very long shelf life they have been a mainstay of prepackaged foods. Fortunately, due to greater public awareness, food companies are beginning to remove them from their products.

Canola oil: Canola oil comes from a hybrid of leaf mustard and turnip rapeseed (hybridized using traditional propagation techniques, not genetic modification). While the original rapeseed plant was high in erucic acid, which is unpalatable and toxic in large concentrations, canola oil contains less than 1% erucic acid and is considered to be safe. Canola oil does have a high sulphur content and goes rancid easily; baked goods made with canola oil also tend to mold quickly.

Duck, goose & chicken fat: These animal fats are quite stable and are prized in some cultures for frying potatoes and other foods. The proportion of omega-3 to omega-6 fatty acids depends on the birds' diet.

Fish oil: See COD LIVER OIL, OMEGA-3 & OMEGA-6 FATTY ACIDS.

Lard or pork fat: Lard is also stable for frying. It is high in vitamin D, which may be important for some populations where meat is expensive.

Flax seed oil: Flax seed oil has an excellent omega-6 to omega-3 fatty acid ratio, so it is a very good excellent addition to the diet. It should never be heated, and should be taken in small

---

[68] Alfin-slater, R. B. and L. Aftergood,(1980) "Lipids," *Modern Nutrition in Health and Disease,*" 6th Ed. RS Goodhart and M.E. Shils, eds. Lea & febiger, Philadelphia.

amounts (one to two tablespoons per day). It can be used in salad dressings or dips. Flax seed oil tends to go rancid if not treated properly. It should come in a dark bottle, and be refrigerated after opening.

Olive oil: With a high percentage of oleic acid, olive oil is very good uncooked (e.g. in salad dressings or drizzled on vegetables). It can be used for cooking at low temperatures, but not for frying. Olive oil is believed to be the safest and healthiest oil when used in moderation.

Peanut oil: Peanut oil is relatively stable and can be heated. It is often used in stir-fried dishes. Its use should be limited because the proportion of Omega-6 fatty acids is high. Studies show that most allergic individuals can safely eat peanut oil, but *not* cold pressed, expelled, or extruded peanut oil - sometimes represented as "gourmet oils." Since it is impossible to verify the type of peanut oil used in restaurants, allergic individuals should make sure that their meal is being made without it. (See also PEANUTS.)

Sesame oil: Like peanut oil, sesame oil has a high percentage of Omega-6 fatty acids and should not be used regularly. It does impart a delicious, smoky flavor, and just a little bit will add a lot of flavor to a dish.

Safflower, sunflower, corn, soybean, cottonseed oils: These oils also have a high ratio of omega-6 to omega-3 fatty acids, so their use should be limited. Fallon and Enig (*Nourishing Traditions*) recommend against using these oils in cooking or baking.

Soybean oil: Soybean oil is generally considered to be safe for people who are soybean intolerant, because the processing removes the protein portion (and it is the protein that causes most allergic reactions). Therefore, a child with a soy allergy can still have soybean oil (and soy lecithin). It is not, however, considered a particularly healthy fat and is better avoided when possible.

Tropical oils: Tropical oils are more saturated than other vegetable oils, and for that reason they have gotten a bad reputation. Most people believe they should be avoided whenever possible. However, coconut oil and palm kernel oil are very high in lauric acid, as is human breastmilk. Lauric acid is known for its anti-fungal and anti-bacterial properties.

It is worth noting that in tropical populations that have introduced PUFAs, the incidence of intestinal problems is much higher than in populations that use only local tropical oils. These oils are very stable and can be heated to a high temperature. They are better for you than PUFAs and can be used successfully in cooking and baking.

Palm oil: Palm oil (not to be confused with palm kernel oil) is widely used in margarine, shortening, baked goods and candies. Though less harmful than partially hydrogenated oils (so-called "trans fats") it is high in saturated fat and low in polyunsaturated fat, and thus more likely to contribute to heart disease than are olive, canola and other oils.

On an environmental note, palm oil is grown largely in Malaysia and Indonesia on newly cleared rainforest or peat-swamp forests. In the last thirty years the area devoted to its production has grown 30-fold; it is forecast to be the world's most produced and traded fat by the year 2012. This translates to widespread destruction of tropical rainforest, endangering many species of animals and polluting the soil and water with pesticides and waste from processing plants. Palm oil production also causes soil erosion and increased sedimentation in rivers, and frequent forest fires increase air pollution.

"FEAST WITHOUT YEAST" DIET

This diet, meant to address problems with yeast overgrowth, was developed by Dr. Bruce Semon, MD, Ph.D. Semon is the father of an autistic child and co-author of *Feast Without Yeast: 4 Stages to Better Health: A Complete Guide to Implementing Yeast Free, Wheat (Gluten) Free and Milk (Casein) Free Living.* Dr. Semon is also the co-author, with his wife Lori Kornblum, of *An Extraordinary Power to Heal,* and a cookbook called *Extraordinary Foods for the Everyday Kitchen.*

The diet originally started as a way to find out what foods were causing severe headaches in a young child who was not developing well. Semon found that the foods that were eliminated from this child's diet all had something in common: they were either derived from yeast or were fermented. Upon further examination, Semon found that many of these foods actually contained or were contaminated with toxic chemicals. This diet is based on learning what chemicals in food are toxic, and also on knowing which foods encourage the growth of yeast. Semon found that some foods kill bacteria but do not harm yeast (vinegar, for example).

Some of the principles in *Feast Without Yeast* are quite different from those of other anti-*Candida* regimens discussed in this book. For example, Semon is less concerned about starches like rice and potatoes than he is about too much meat in the diet. He maintains that taking heavy probiotics can sometimes worsen *Candida*, because *Candida* and *Lactobacillus* grow well together. He also asserts that if you have *Candida*, you should avoid B vitamins, which could feed the yeast.

Here are some of the basic principles of the diet, according to Dr. Semon:

This is a four stage diet. Dr. Semon proposes first removing any foods promote the growth of *Candida*. He also removes all known neurotoxins from the diet, stating that they slow down brain as well as gut function. According to Semon, many people (especially those with depression or ADHD) can recover simply by removing malt and vinegar. In his experience, 80% of the people who try the diet need only do Stages I and II. Individuals on the autism spectrum usually need to go through Stage III, and possibly Stage IV.

Stage 1: Remove all malt and vinegar products. This includes anything with the word "malt" in it, including maltodextrin. Next, remove chocolate, pickled foods, aged cheese (but not fresh cheeses) and soy sauces. All fermented products must be removed from the diet. Rice syrup is considered a fermented food, so many traditional gluten free foods are off limits. Finally, apples and grapes are removed.

Aspergillus is a fungus that grows on cottonseed, and cottonseed is fed heavily to all livestock, chickens, turkeys, cows, pigs and farm fed fish. The aspergillus toxins end up in the fat of the meat. These toxins will be toxic to bacteria and could make room for the yeast. Aspergillus does not grow yeast directly, but if someone is having difficulty clearing yeast, eating meat could be one of the reasons.

Stage 2: Foods like corn, dried fruits, baked goods containing yeast, and sugar are removed.

Stage 3: Gluten and casein are removed next. Dr. Semon says that he sees much more improvement in his autistic patients when they remove neurotoxic foods in addition to gluten and casein, than with the GF/CF diet alone.

Stage 4: In this stage most processed and canned foods are removed, as well as bananas, grapes, apples, grapefruit and cantaloupe. Some fruit, such as oranges, can be eaten in season if they are not allowed to over-ripen. Tomatoes are also an acceptable food. Most of the meat is removed from the diet at this point - one relies more heavily on brown rice and potatoes for nutrition.

While Dr. Semon says that while patients generally improve significantly on this diet, the addition of the antifungal drug nystatin is necessary for most.

> *"When we discovered one of our children had Asperger's Syndrome, it answered many of our questions regarding her behavior. Her list of physical symptoms went on forever.*
>
> *We removed preservatives and hydrogenated oils from her diet. We replaced the ducts in our air conditioning and threw out all of our non-stick cookware. We avoided refined sugars and artificial coloring. I learned about gluten and casein. Then I found **Feast Without Yeast** at our local health food store and learned about Candida. We further restricted our daughter's diet: gluten free, casein free and yeast free, avoiding/limiting foods that may contain high levels of aspergillus. Within a few days we started to notice a difference. Within a few weeks it was incredible. Now the difference is profound.*
>
> *A year ago our daughter couldn't read two pages, and now she will read for hours. Her speech is improving rapidly, her vocabulary has quadrupled, and all physically painful symptoms are gone. Her hearing is perfect. People are able to engage her in conversations and she will initiate conversation as well. She is a bright, happy and focused child.*
>
> *Out of support for her diet, the whole family participates, and subsequently feels better. Our youngest daughter's asthma symptoms are much better and my own frequent headaches have disappeared. I understand not everyone will get these results, but I have to believe that if a drowning person is thrown a life preserver they would take it.*
>
> *My husband and I have created a website www.NourishToFlourish.net titled 'A Path to Recovery' along with information and support. We invite you to visit our website and appreciate any comments."* -Renee Osterhouse

FEINGOLD PROGRAM (FEINGOLD DIET) (See also FOOD ADDITIVES)

The Feingold Program is an elimination diet intended to eliminate common food additives that may cause hyperactivity or other behavioral and physical symptoms. The additives that are of greatest concern include:

- Artificial (synthetic) coloring
- Artificial (synthetic) flavoring
- Aspartame (the artificial sweetener in NutraSweet® and Equal®)
- Artificial (synthetic) preservatives such as BHA, BHT, and TBHQ
- Foods that contain natural salicylates, such as almonds and aspirin

In the first stage of the Feingold Program, aspirin and some foods containing salicylates are eliminated (see SALICYLATES).

Feingold is often referred to as a "program" rather than a "diet" because fragrances and non-food items containing certain chemicals are also excluded.

Feingold is run by volunteers who thoroughly investigate products and create a stage-by-stage food list. Prepared foods are included only when they have been investigated and determined to be free of additives and preservatives.

Largely due to years of public education and awareness by Feingold and the Center for Science in the Public Interest (CSPI), the need for proper research into food additives was finally filled by a well-designed study validating the connection between behavior problems and hyperactivity. The American Academy of Pediatrics now accepts this connection and has recommended that children with behavior problems avoid these food ingredients (see FOOD ADDITIVES for details).

For more information, visit www.feingold.org. You can find an online parent support group at www.yahoogroups.com/group/Feingold-Program4us.

FERMENTED FOODS (See CULTURED FOODS, CULTURED VEGETABLES, PROBIOTICS, YOGURT, YOUNG COCONUT KEFIR)

FIBER

Dietary fiber, sometimes called roughage, includes all parts of plant foods that your body cannot digest or absorb. Since fiber isn't digested by your body, it passes virtually unchanged through the stomach and small intestine and into the colon. Fiber prevents constipation because when the stool is softened and enlarged, it is easier to pass. A high fiber diet is believed to lower the risk of irritable bowel syndrome, control blood sugar and lower blood cholesterol.

There are two types of fiber: insoluble and soluble. Insoluble fiber (so named because it can't be dissolved in water) promotes the movement of food through your digestive system and increases stool bulk. It is particularly helpful to those with constipation or irregular bowel movements. Whole grains, nuts and many vegetables are good sources of insoluble fiber.

Soluble fiber does dissolve in water, taking on a gelatinous consistency. It can be found in acacia fiber, methylcellulose, guar gum, psyllium, cooked and peeled fruits, or starchy foods like white rice, oats, peas, beans, apples, citrus fruits, carrots, and barley. It is especially helpful for those who have alternating constipation and diarrhea, as it stabilizes the consistency of the stool (see also IRRITABLE BOWEL SYNDROME).

FIBROMYALGIA (See RELATED AND/OR CO-EXISTING DISORDERS)

FISH & SEAFOOD

Fish is an excellent source of protein and essential fatty acids, and fish oil is gaining attention for its many health benefits (see COD LIVER OIL). The primary concerns about fish and seafood have to do with increased levels of methylmercury that have been found in many varieties of fish. This could pose a problem for pregnant women, and for children or adults with poor detoxification. See MERCURY.

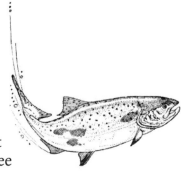

FISH OIL (See COD LIVER OIL, OMEGA-3 & OMEGA-6 FATTY ACIDS)

FLAGYL (See ANTI-FUNGAL TREATMENTS)

FLAX SEEDS (LINSEEDS) (See also FATS & OILS)

Flax seeds, found in most grocery stores and natural food stores, are an excellent source of fiber and omega-3 fatty acids, and lend a pleasant, nutty flavor and firm texture to gluten free baked goods. Grinding the seeds in a blender before use makes them easier to digest, but keep ground flax seeds in the freezer to prevent them from going rancid. Ground flax seeds can be used as an egg replacer (see EGG SUBSTITUTES).

FOLATES & FOLIC ACID (See SUPPLEMENTS, CEREBRAL FOLATE DEFICIENCY)

FOOD ADDITIVES

Preservatives, artificial colors and artificial flavors have long been blamed by consumers for side effects, long-term health concerns, and hyperactivity or learning disabilities. A handful of small scientific studies concluded that if there was an effect, it was not significant.

But in September 2007, new research, financed by Britain's Food Standards Agency and published online by the British medical journal *The Lancet*, presented evidence that "a mix of additives commonly found in children's foods increases the mean level of hyperactivity."[69] The team of researchers, led by Jim Stevenson, a professor of psychology at the University of Southampton, concluded that "the finding lends strong support for the case that food additives exacerbate hyperactive behaviors (inattention, impulsivity and overactivity) at least into middle childhood."

That study examined the effect of artificial colors and a sodium benzoate preservative, and found both to be problematic for some children. Further studies are needed to find out whether there are other additives that could have a similar effect, and it is unclear whether this is true of some adults, but it seems likely that some disturbances can occur in mood and concentration. In the February 2008 issue of its publication, *AAP Grand Rounds*, the American Academy of Pediatrics concludes that a low-additive diet is a valid intervention for children with ADHD:

> *"Although quite complicated, this was a carefully conducted study in which the investigators went to great lengths to eliminate bias and to rigorously measure outcomes. The results are hard to follow and somewhat inconsistent. For many of the assessments there were small but statistically significant differences of measured behaviors in children who consumed the food additives compared with those who did not. In each case increased hyperactive behaviors were associated with consuming the additives. For those comparisons in which no statistically significant differences were found, there was a trend for more hyperactive behaviors associated with the food additive drink in virtually every assessment. **Thus, the overall findings of the study are clear and require that even we skeptics, who have long doubted parental claims of the effects of various foods on the behavior of their children, admit we might have been wrong.**" (emphasis added)*

[69] McCann D, Barrett A, Cooper A, Crumpler D, Dalen L, Grimshaw K, Kitchin E, Lok K, Porteous L, Prince E, Sonuga Barke E, Warner JO, Stevenson J. "Food additives and hyperactive behaviour in 3-year-old and 8/9-year-old children in the community: a randomised, double-blinded, placebo-controlled trial." *Lancet*. 2007 Nov 3;370(9598):1560-7.

You can download a full copy of this publication at www.feingold.org. Feingold encourages parents to print that page and share it with their pediatricians, many of whom are unaware of this change of position.

Since there is solid evidence proving that some food additives can cause behavior problems in children, and since autism families appear to be sensitive to foods and chemicals in general, they should be avoided whenever possible. See FEINGOLD PROGRAM for more information.

FOOD COLORING

Although many food-sensitive children need to avoid artificial coloring, there are occasions when you want to color foods. Our ancestors used various fruits, vegetables and edible flours to make natural food colorings. Jay Berger, from Allergy Grocer*, has compiled ideas for making natural food coloring:

Natural Food Color Options

Use freshly puréed fruits with strong colors like strawberries or carrot juice for flavor and/or color (you may need to reduce or eliminate other liquids in the recipe). Purée & strain fruits of seeds before use. For richer colors, use concentrated fruit and vegetable juices.

- Blue-Purple: blueberries, purple grape juice, blackberries, blackberry juice.
- Red-orange: paprika
- Green: puréed, cooked spinach (thawed frozen spinach works great)
- Pink: cranberry juice, raspberries, red currants, strawberries
- Red: pomegranate juice, or boiled, unsalted red beets (grinding in the blender or food processor won't affect flavor).
- Rich brown: decaf instant coffee granules
- Yellow, gold, & orange: small amount of turmeric powder, yellow mustard powder, curry powder, annatto powder, carrot juice (final color depends on amount used).

There are also companies that make colors and flavorings out of natural ingredients (for example, www.naturesflavors.com). Read the ingredients of each color carefully to make sure it is appropriate for your child. Most are GF, but not all, and some may contain other ingredients you are avoiding.

*Allergy Grocer (formerly Miss Roben's) is an online store for individuals with all types of food allergy and intolerance. www.allergygrocer.com.

FOOD STORAGE

Plastic containers and bags are convenient, but for those avoiding chemicals, plastic may not be the best way to store leftovers. Consider switching to wax paper bags, and glass. Pyrex makes covered glass bowls, bakeware and storage containers that are widely available. Unlike plastic, glass containers withstand heat and cold, and do not stain or retain food odors. You can also find old fashioned glass containers at thrift shops, garage sales and flea markets.

It is especially important not to microwave food in plastic, because harmful chemicals can leach into the food. See also BISPHENOL.

FORMULA (See INFANT FORMULA)

FREE-RANGE (See MEAT, EGGS)

FRENCH FRIES

French fried potatoes are often the favorite food of children on the autism spectrum. Fries are the ideal food for getting picky children off gluten during the initial withdrawal stages of the diet, although they should not be a staple in any child's diet, and can be especially troublesome to children who must avoid starches and sugars.

Recently, McDonald's® acknowledged that their fries contain derivatives of wheat and milk. Fast-food fries may also be soaked in sugar water or MSG before they are frozen. Some frozen fries may have a hidden coating of wheat starch to keep them from sticking during preparation. If you use frozen fries at home, avoid those with spice powders, which may contain MSG, gluten and milk. These do not necessarily have to be listed in the ingredients, so check with the manufacturer, or make your own fries.

To make fries, cut potatoes into the desired shape and size, and remove excess moisture with a paper towel. If you don't own a deep-fryer, fill a small saucepan with cooking oil (not olive oil), heat until a small piece of potato dropped into the oil immediately begins to sizzle, and then lower some fries into the saucepan with a metal slotted spoon (to avoid splashing). Cook until golden, then use the spoon to remove the fries and drain them on a paper towel. Salt them immediately (if your child craves salt, use plenty of high-quality sea salt) and serve hot. You may also want to try frying parsnips (peel and slice into "chips") or sweet potatoes, both of which are nutritious and high in fiber.

NOTE: Many parents have reported that their children limit themselves to a specific brand of fries or potato chips. The brand in question almost always contains traces of casein, gluten, or both. If this describes your child, investigate the ingredients. When switched to a safe brand, or to homemade fries, the food repertoire will usually expand (see PICKINESS & FOOD ADDICTION). Do not hesitate to call the manufacturer whenever you are in doubt, and ask whether they can guarantee that the food is gluten and casein free.

FRUCTOSE

Fructose is a monosaccharide (an easily-digested simple sugar) found in many foods, especially fruits and root vegetables. Because it does not cause a rapid rise in blood sugar, it was once thought that fructose was a good substitute for sucrose (granulated sugar). It is now believed, however, that fructose contributes to a rise in triglycerides in the blood, a risk factor for heart disease.[70] There is also evidence that excess fructose consumption triggers insulin resistance, leading to type 2 diabetes. A typical can of soda pop has 23 grams of fructose, and because it is cheaper to produce than sugar, high-fructose corn syrup has been added to almost all processed food available today (see CORN SYRUP). Fructose has shown to be a problem for those battling GI yeast and fungal infections.

While natural fructose is allowed on SCD, powdered or liquid fructose is not.

---

[70] Bantle, John, et al. "Effects of dietary fructose on plasma lipids in healthy subjects." *American Journal of Clinical Nutrition* 72.5 (2000):1128-1134.

FRUIT

Fruits are considered to be healthy foods for many reasons. They contain vitamins, fiber, and some phytonutrients that your body needs for optimal health. However, for those battling yeast and bacterial problems, high-sugar fruits such as grapes or bananas are often problematic. In fact, a negative reaction to bananas might be a sign that there are issues with yeast and bacteria, which should be tested for and treated.

If you are going to include fruit in your special diet, aim for those with lower sugar, such as avocados, berries, green apples, pineapple, grapefruit and kiwi (note that kiwi is very high in oxalates). For those who do not tolerate many fruits, be sure to supplement with a daily dose of Vitamin C.

GARLIC

Garlic, widely used for cooking, is said to have antibiotic and antifungal properties and to lower blood cholesterol levels. In modern naturopathy, garlic is used as a treatment for intestinal parasites, digestive problems and fungal infections such as thrush.[71]

GASTROINTESTINAL FLORA (See GUT FLORA)

GASTROINTESTINAL ILLNESS (See BOWEL DISEASE AND AUTISM)

GASTROINTESTINAL TRACT (GI TRACT)

Sometimes called the gut, the GI tract consists of the mouth, pharynx, esophagus, and stomach (upper GI tract), and the intestines and anus (lower GI tract). The major functions of the GI tract are ingestion, digestion, absorption, and defecation (see DIGESTION).

GELATIN

Gelatin, used as a thickener in many foods, is gluten and dairy free. Only unflavored gelatin is allowed on the Specific Carbohydrate Diet™.

GENETICALLY MODIFIED ORGANISMS (GMO FOODS) (See also ORGANIC FOODS)

One of the most controversial advancements in science today is the ability to combine DNA molecules into genetically modified organisms (GMO) or genetically engineered organisms (GEO). Genetic engineering has been used in modern agriculture to make crops resistant to pests and herbicides, to improve nutritional value, and to increase yield and shelf life. There have been clear benefits to this process, but there are also some alarming concerns that have emerged over the past few years, including harm to other organisms, cross-pollination with conventional plants, and the spread of new "superweeds" and "superpests."

One of the primary concerns is the potential for new food allergies in people who are already allergic to one or more foods. It seems logical that mixing genes from different food sources could increase the risk of additional food allergies, and this has proven to be the case. In one study, a gene from the Brazil nut, when transferred to soybeans, was shown to trigger an

---

[71] Daniel Zohary and Maria Hopf, *Domestication of plants in the Old World, third edition* (Oxford: University Press, 2000), p. 197

allergic response in people with allergies to nuts.[72]

There is some debate over whether there is sufficient evidence of allergic reaction to new varieties of plant foods already on the market. However, the possibility certainly exists. And if such a thing is taking place, it will be very hard to contain: GMO plants tend to cross-pollinate with non-GMO plants. The rapid spread of pollen from GM rapeseed (canola) has made it nearly impossible to grow non-contaminated rapeseed in Canada today.

Researchers at Michigan State University have received an EPA (Environmental Protection Agency) grant to find ways to determine the allergenic potential of GMO crops before they're released into the human or animal food chain. Until then, you may want to choose non-GMO foods, when possible, for children prone to allergies.

GHEE (See also BUTTER)

Ghee or clarified butter, is made through a careful process of heating and straining (also called rendering). This process removes most of the water and milk solids from the butter, leaving a semi-solid, golden colored product.

Ghee is virtually casein free, and can be consumed on a casein free diet. Still, ghee is one product that is probably safer when store bought, because it can be hard to get all the milk solids separated. Look for an organic brand that is labeled 99.9% protein free. Many groceries now carry ghee (look in the ethnic foods aisle) or you may need to shop in an Indian grocery. You can also order it online.

However, if you cannot find commercially prepared ghee, you can make it at home. Simmer ½ pound of unsalted butter in a small saucepan until all of the water evaporates, and there is a residue of milk solids at the bottom. You will know when the water is gone because the ghee will stop bubbling, and take on a rich, yellow color. This may take 20-60 minutes, so keep an eye on it. If you continue cooking it after this time, the ghee will turn brown and take on a slightly more pronounced, almost caramelized flavor (this rich, darker version is delicious when used in baking, but less versatile for cooking eggs or other savory foods).

When this is done, line a metal strainer with a heavy-duty paper towel or two thinner ones (use unbleached paper towels, if you can find them). Some people find that straining through a paper coffee filter works best, but be sure to buy filters that contain no dioxins (they are usually brown). Carefully pour the hot liquid through the strainer into a glass or stainless steel container with a tight-fitting lid. If you notice any solid particles in the container, strain it again. The liquid should appear as pure as possible.

Ghee melts quickly when heated, is soft at room temperature and solid when cold. Ghee will keep for a relatively long time in a cool place, and almost indefinitely if frozen. It is delicious melted on popcorn, lobster, and other foods. Keep in mind that ghee contains virtually no water. When replacing butter in baking, you will need to increase the amount of liquid - add about 1 tablespoon of water per ¼ cup ghee. Ghee has a much higher smoking point than plain butter, so it can be used for frying.

GI TRACT (See GASTROINTESTINAL TRACT)

---

[72] Nordlee JA, Taylor SL, Townsend JA, Thomas LA, Bush RK. "Identification of a Brazil-nut allergen in transgenic soybeans." *N Engl J Med.* 1996 Mar 14;334(11):688-92.

GLIADIN

Gluten is made up of gliadin and glutenin. Those with celiac disease and gluten allergy react to the gliadin fraction of the gluten protein.

GLUCONO DELTA LACTONE

Glucono delta lactone is a gluten and dairy free additive produced by the fermentation of rice-derived glucose, and found in some commercial baked goods. Because it is an acid, it reacts with baking soda to release carbon dioxide, allowing dough to rise. Glucono delta lactone is non-toxic, soluble in water, and fully metabolized in our bodies.

GLUTAMATE/GLUTAMIC ACID (See EXCITOTOXICITY, MONOSODIUM GLUTAMATE)

GLUTAMINE (L-GLUTAMINE)

Glutamine is an amino acid used for several biochemical functions, including immune function. It is said to help heal and maintain the cells lining the small intestine, so it may be helpful for those concerned about gut healing and health. It is the most abundant amino acid in the body, but is often deficient in those under stress or illness.

Foods rich in glutamine include meats, fish, eggs, dairy products, cabbage, beets, beans, raw spinach, and raw parsley. It can be purchased online, or anywhere that sells nutritional supplements. Be sure to check ingredients for potential allergens.

GLUTATHIONE (GSH)

Glutathione is an antioxidant that protects cells from toxins such as free radicals (see DETOXIFICATION).

GLUTEN

Gluten is a protein found in members of the grass family including wheat, spelt, barley, rye and triticale. Gluten can also be found in products derived from these grains, such as malt, grain starches, hydrolyzed vegetable/plant proteins, textured vegetable proteins, soy sauce, grain alcohol, some natural flavorings, and some of the binders and fillers commonly found in vitamins and medications (see below). In their pure form oats do not contain gluten, but commercial oats are almost always contaminated with wheat (see OATS).

Gluten, like corn, can be found almost everywhere in the typical American diet. The avoidance of gluten is critical for those with celiac disease, since an immune reaction to gluten causes intestinal damage and disease.

Gliadorphin (also known as gluteomorphin), a peptide resulting from the incomplete breakdown product of gluten, is a known opioid, and has been identified in the urine of some individuals with autistic or behavioral disorders (see OPIOID EXCESS). This could theoretically explain why the complete avoidance of gluten has been beneficial to many with autism.

Avoiding Gluten: This can be a challenge for two reasons. One is that it takes some time to become familiar with the rules of the diet, and the lifestyle changes that are involved. The other problem has to do with getting your child on board; many children with autism will eat only wheat-based foods, such as bread, muffins, pretzels, crackers, noodles and breaded chicken or fish (nuggets and fish sticks). At first, it may be hard to persuade a child to try anything new (see PICKINESS & FOOD ADDICTION).

However, most people get the hang of a gluten free diet in a week or two, and many good substitutes are now available for traditional wheat products. There are commercially available gluten free breads at many supermarkets and all health food stores (see BREAD). Crackers without wheat or gluten are also widely available, made from grains, rice and even nuts. If your child likes pasta, there are many excellent gluten free alternatives; they come in different shapes and sizes and can be used in any recipe.

Gluten free baking, with a little practice, is an economical way to prepare your family's favorite baked goods at home (see COOKING & BAKING).

It is a good idea to accustom your child to meat, fish and chicken prepared simply, either baked, broiled or grilled. However, many children start the diet eating only breaded, fried "nuggets." You can still serve these, but you will need to make your own breading out of acceptable cereals, flours or ground nuts. Most commercially prepared and fast food versions are unacceptable.

Be aware that ingredients change in prepared foods, and that what was acceptable six months ago may not be so anymore. It is a good idea to learn to read labels, and to call companies for information whenever you are unsure about an ingredient or food.

When you are avoiding gluten and polysaccharides, it is important to know where the 'hidden' sources of gluten can be. For example, most children on these diets are allowed coconut and dried fruits, but many brands contain small amounts of gluten. Look for fruits that have no sulfites (added to preserve color and retard spoilage), especially if phenols are a problem. Be aware that raisins sold in canisters may have traveled down a conveyor belt that was dusted with flour to prevent the fruit from sticking together. Because the flour is not an 'ingredient' it does not have to be listed on the package.

Many foods are labeled "wheat free," but that does not mean they are gluten free. When in doubt, call the manufacturer. Almost all packaged foods have a toll-free number, or a website with contact information on the label. Find out whether they can guarantee that the product is free from gluten. If it's not, make sure to let them know that this will affect your decision to use the product.

"Hidden" gluten can also be found in some unexpected places, such as the glue on envelopes, Dixie® cups, ground spices (some use flour to prevent clumping), appliances, fast food fryers and tropical fish food. See also CHEWING GUM, CROSS CONTAMINATION, LIP BALM, MEDICATION, and SKIN CARE PRODUCTS.

Foods and Ingredients That Always Contain Gluten:

Barley
Barley Grass (can contain seeds)
Barley Malt
Beer
Bleached Flour
Bran
Bran Extract
Bread Flour
Brewers Yeast
Brown Flour
Bulgur (Bulgar Wheat/ Nuts)
Bulgur Wheat
Cereal Binding
Chilton
Club Wheat
Common Wheat
Couscous
Dextrimaltose
Durum wheat
Edible Starch
Einkorn
Emmer
Farina
Farina Graham

Filler
Flour
Fu
Germ
Graham Flour
Granary Flour
Groats
Hydrolyzed Wheat Gluten
Hydrolyzed Wheat Protein
Hydrolyzed Wheat Starch
Kamut
Malt
Malt Extract
Malt Flavoring
Malt Syrup
Malt Vinegar
Matzo Semolina
Mir
Pasta
Pearl Barley
Rice Malt (if barley or Koji are used)
Rye
Seitan
Semolina
Semolina Triticum

Shot Wheat (Triticum aestivum)
Small Spelt
Spelt (Triticum spelta)
Spirits (Specific Types)
Sprouted Wheat or Barley
Hydrolyzed Wheat Protein
Strong Flour
Suet in Packets
Tabbouleh
Teriyaki Sauce
Textured Vegetable Protein - TVP
Triticale
Udon
Unbleached Flour
Vegetable Starch
Wheat Flour Lipids
Wheat Germ
Wheat Grass (can contain seeds)
Wheat Nuts
Wheat Protein
Whole-Meal Flour

Foods and Ingredients That Often Contain Gluten:

Breading
Broth
Canned soups
Coating mixes
Communion wafers
HVP
Imitation Bacon
Imitation seafood
Marinades
Pastas
Rice Syrup
Roux
Sauces

Self-basting Poultry
Thickeners
Artificial Color
Caramel Color
Coloring
Dextrins
Flavoring
Food Starch
Glucose Syrup
Gravy Cubes
Ground Spices
Maltodextrin
Maltose
Miso

Modified Food Starch
Modified Starch
Monosodium Glutamate (MSG)
Mustard Powder
Natural Flavoring
Shoyu
Smoke Flavoring
Soba Noodles
Soy Sauce
Starch
Stock Cubes
Vitamins

GLUTEN & CASEIN FREE DIET ("THE GF/CF DIET")

A gluten and casein free diet is, quite simply, a diet without gluten or casein. Because these two proteins have shown to be the most problematic for people with autism spectrum and other chronic disorders, removing them is the basis for all of the diets mentioned in this book. Most of the people using a gluten and casein free diet have other food restrictions, based on individual intolerances or additional dietary principles.

Gluten and casein free diets have been used for people with autism and related disorders for many years, with numerous anecdotal reports of physical and behavioral improvements. Gluten and casein free diets began to gain widespread popularity in the 1990s, when the Internet made it possible for a large number of parents to compare notes and share information.

Overview of a Gluten and Casein Free Diet

Gluten-containing grains (wheat, barley, rye, spelt, kamut, and possibly oats)	Not allowed
Milk Products (milk, butter, cream, yogurt, cheese, casein, whey, etc.) and ingredients	Not allowed
Corn, Soy	May be problematic
Rice, Potatoes, Starches	Individual
Millet, Quinoa, Amaranth, Buckwheat, Teff	Individual
Eggs and Meat (incl. beef, lamb, fish, chicken, turkey)	Individual
Vegetables	Individual
Fruit, Juice	Individual
Sweeteners	Individual
Vinegar	Individual
Oils	Individual
Beans, Nuts, Seeds	Individual
Alcoholic Beverages	Beer not allowed
Coffee and Tea	Individual

Note: Certain *brands of foods* or *ingredients* are not allowed if they contain any amount of gluten or casein (see GLUTEN, DAIRY).

GLYCEMIC INDEX

In order to function, the brain must have glucose. To feed this requirement, the body converts all digestible carbohydrates into glucose. When glucose molecules pass into the bloodstream, the pancreas releases a hormone called insulin, which acts as a trigger that activates cells to absorb the glucose. All excess glucose is absorbed by muscle, fat and other cells, and then insulin levels return to normal.

The glycemic index ranks foods according to how rapidly their sugars are digested and released into the bloodstream. The concept of a glycemic index emerged in the 1990s, when researchers showed that some foods raised blood sugar faster than other foods, placing greater stress on the insulin system. That discovery led to concept of the glycemic load, which measures both a food's glycemic index and how much carbohydrate the food delivers in a single serving. Most fruits, vegetables, beans and whole grains have low glycemic loads, releasing their sugars into the bloodstream gradually, triggering only a moderate rise in insulin. When the same fruits are squeezed into juices, the glycemic load is greatly increased. A serving of orange juice has a glycemic load of 13, while the orange it came from measures only 5.

Most whole fruits, vegetables, beans and nuts deliver high quality nutrients and fiber without a high glycemic load. Whole grains have much lower glycemic loads than refined flours and grains. In contrast, starchy vegetables such as potatoes and corn have high glycemic loads, delivering a lot of sugar in a short period of time. It has been suggested that the glycemic index could be useful as a guide for foods to avoid when yeast is a persistent problem. For more information on glycemic index and glycemic loads, visit:

www.mendosa.com/gilists.htm
www.glycemicindex.com

GMO (See GENETICALLY MODIFIED ORGANISMS)

GOAT MILK (See MILK ALTERNATIVES)

GOAT YOGURT (See YOGURT)

GOING OFF THE DIET (See STOPPING DIETARY INTERVENTION)

GRAINS

Grains are grasses, also known as cereal crops. They are cultivated for their edible fruit seeds (what we think of as the grain itself). Grains are grown as a staple crop, and are a critical food source for much of the world. Grains provide complex carbohydrates when minimally processed. When refined (for example, to make flour) grains lose much of their nutritional value and fiber. However, whole grain flour tends to be slightly higher in oxalates. Some people do well with certain non-gluten grains, while some find that all grains are problematic.

Gluten Grains: wheat, rye, triticale, kamut, spelt, durum, semolina

Non-Gluten Grains: maize (corn), rice, sorghum, buckwheat, amaranth, quinoa, teff, millet, specially-grown oats (see OATS)

GUAR GUM

Guar gum is a vegetable gum made from the seeds of the guar plant. It is used as a stabilizer and emulsifier in many processed foods to prevent separation. It is commonly found in pickled foods, frozen foods, soft drinks and salad dressings. Guar gum can be used as a binder when baking with gluten free flours, but may have a laxative effect. Those who find this problematic usually prefer to use xanthan gum instead. Guar gum is not allowed on the SCD™.

GUT

The gut is another word for the gastrointestinal tract - especially the intestines.

GUT FLORA

Gut flora, also called "gastrointestinal flora," "intestinal microflora" or "intestinal microbiota," is the collection of thousands of different species of bacteria, yeast, and protozoa living in the gut - about a hundred trillion microorganisms altogether.

Mammals have a symbiotic relationship with these microorganisms, which perform a host of useful functions, such as preventing growth of harmful species and producing vitamins and digestive enzymes (see DYSBIOSIS, YEAST & FUNGUS).

GUT HEALING (See LEAKY GUT)

GUT PERMEABILITY (See LEAKY GUT)

HABITUATION

The process whereby the body adjusts to altered circumstances. In the context of the theory of OPIOID EXCESS, habituation refers to a process similar to that in morphine or heroin use. A standard dose of morphine will cause a much bigger response in a beginner than in a seasoned addict. The addict's central nervous system readjusts itself to the steady supply, and needs a much bigger dose in order to produce the same effect. When the drug wears off, the effect on the first-time user is also very different from that on the long-term user.

The opioid peptides from food are thought to act in the same manner. This is one of the reasons why the initial effect of a diet infringement can be very different from the long term effect of a steady intake: the body's sensitivity decreases over time. When the supply is withdrawn, the sensitivity will increase again. This phenomenon also effects the point of maximum effectiveness on the bell-shaped dose response curve: this point will move up or down as habituation increases and decreases.

HALLOWEEN (See HOLIDAYS)

HEMP (See SEEDS)

HERXHEIMER EFFECT (See "DIE-OFF" REACTIONS)

HOLIDAYS AND CELEBRATIONS

The inconvenience of dietary restrictions on special occasions can be minimized with a little advance planning. Here are a few tips that may help you get through holidays and celebrations:

Birthday parties: When your child is invited to a party, ask what will be served when you RSVP. Explain that your child is on a special diet, and that you will provide food for him. Whenever possible, bring it the day before so that it can be served with the rest of the food. Try to make your child's food as similar as possible to the rest of the party fare. If the party is being held at a restaurant, visit the restaurant and explain that you will need to provide food for your child. Bring it in advance if possible, and make sure that it is labeled with your child's name and the name of the party-giver. Be sure that your child has a standard answer to use if he is asked about his food. "I am allergic" is a response that even very small children can understand (see SOCIAL ASPECTS OF THE DIET). If you are able to make something that resembles a cupcake, keep a few in a large re-sealable bag in the school freezer, so your child isn't left out during classmates' birthdays parties at school. The Internet is a good source of recipes for cakes, cookies and other special occasion treats. There are also a number of cookbooks available for every dietary intervention mentioned in this book (see APPENDIX).

Parties: Whenever possible, host the celebration in your own home where you have control over ingredients (see COMPLIANCE). If you are celebrating at a friend's or relative's home, be sure that you contribute a few dishes that are safe for your child and that he will eat. If your hosts are willing, suggest some ingredient substitutions that would work in traditional recipes, such as using olive oil instead of butter on vegetables, making the mashed potatoes dairy-free, and making gravy with arrowroot starch instead of wheat flour. Children who like to feel involved can help you make something to bring.

Halloween: There are several ways to celebrate Halloween safely. First, instead of traditional trick or treating, you can host a party. If you are the host, you can make sure that all treats are safe. If your child wants to trick or treat, you can go to neighbors' homes in advance and provide candy or toys to give to your child when he rings their doorbell. Some parents keep treats at home and then do a "trade" when their children come home. Excessive sugar is never a good idea, so try to set the goodies aside and allow your child to pick out one or two per day. Visit a "dollar store" for an assortment of inexpensive toys and games that can be used in place of sugary treats.

Christmas & Hanukkah: Every family has their own food traditions, but there are few that cannot be modified to fit a special diet. Remember that stuffing can be made without bread, and pies and cakes can be made with acceptable grain or nut flours. Be sure that hams, turkeys and chickens are not injected or coated in flavorings or glazes, and buy free-range organic fowl if possible. There are even candy canes made without artificial colors and flavors. Try to emphasize the non-food aspects of the holidays.

Passover: This seven day Jewish holiday generally falls in April. Because wheat, barley, spelt, rye, oats and rice (and anything made from them) cannot be eaten during Passover, it is a time when many gluten free foods are available. Note that the exception to this is matzoh (made from wheat) and products made with matzoh meal or flour. Foods labeled "non-gebrokts" will be free of gluten flours, soy, corn and rice. There is no "hidden" gluten in Passover food; ingredients that are usually questionable (such as "flavorings" or "natural flavor") cannot contain gluten if they are Kosher for Passover. If you avoid dairy, look for labels that are marked with a U within a circle or have the word Pareve. KP designates that a food is Kosher for Passover.

Look for stores that have large kosher sections (e.g. ShopRite's Kosher Experience) and when possible shop in areas with large Jewish populations. Read labels carefully and note that any food listing "matzoh meal, matzoh flour or Passover cake flour" will contain gluten. Many Passover foods contain preservatives and other artificial ingredients that should be avoided when possible, or eaten only in very small amounts.

If you cannot find these foods as Passover is approaching, look for them online at www.mykoshermarket.com or www.kosher.com. If you do not know when Passover is, ask a Jewish friend or call a local synagogue. They may also be able to tell you the best place to find these foods. There is an excellent Passover food guide written by Nadine Gilder of Autism Educational Services. *The Gluten and Casein-Free Passover Guide* can be ordered for $34.95 at www.gfcfpassoverguide.com or by calling 732-473-9482.

Thanksgiving: Thanksgiving is traditionally a holiday that is centered around food. Many of the foods are heavy on the starch, but most can be modified to any special diet. Stuffing can be made with rice, or with gluten-free bread or grains. Since most small children do not like stuffing anyway, consider packing the inside of the bird with onions and lemons, and cook regular stuffing separately in a casserole. Pies can be made with special crusts or with no crust at all. In fact, your guests may agree that pumpkin custard made with coconut milk is as good as regular pumpkin pie. Look for a natural, organic turkey that has not been injected with chemicals or fat.

HVP (See HYDROLYZED VEGETABLE PROTEIN)

HYDROGENATED OILS AND FATS (See FATS & OILS)

HYDROLYZED VEGETABLE PROTEIN (HVP)

Hydrolyzed vegetable protein is produced by boiling vegetables, legumes or grains (such as corn, soy or wheat) in hydrochloric acid, then placing them in a neutralizing solution. The acid breaks down the protein into amino acids, including free glutamic acid (see MONOSODIUM GLUTAMATE/MSG), which is a flavor enhancer. Hydrolyzed vegetable protein is free of gluten and dairy, but those who have concerns about MSG should avoid it, as well as hydrolyzed yeast extract, autolyzed yeast extract, soy extracts, and "natural flavorings."

Hydrolyzed whey protein is a similar, dairy-based product.

IBS (See IRRITABLE BOWEL SYNDROME)

IMPLEMENTATION OF DIETARY INTERVENTIONS (See Part I)

IMMUNE SYSTEM ABNORMALITIES

It has been suggested that some basic immunologic defect is responsible for all of the newly-identified bio-markers for autism, such as increased vulnerability to OXIDATIVE STRESS (endogenous or environmental) and decreased capacity for METHYLATION[73] [74]. If such a defect leads to detoxification problems, these children could be significantly much more susceptible to factors like food allergy, chronic ear infections, viruses, bacteria, parasites, or exposure to environmental toxins and toxic metals (such as mercury, aluminum, tin, arsenic, cadmium, nickel, and lead).

Several studies have shown that there are differences between the immune systems of children with autism and those of neurologically typical children. These include a decrease in the number of T cells, a difference in lymphocyte function and fewer natural killer cells. This may make autistic children more susceptible to infection and it is possible that direct or indirect infection of the brain may cause autism in some children. In addition, children on the autism spectrum often have much lower levels of IgG, IgA and IgM antibodies (see IMMUNOGLOBULINS).

In a 2005 study, researchers at the UC Davis School of Medicine and the UC Davis M.I.N.D.

---

[73] James SJ, et al. "Metabolic biomarkers of increased oxidative stress and impaired methylation capacity in children with autism." *American Journal of Clinical Nutrition* 2004 80(Dec):1611-1617.

[74] James SJ, et al. "Metabolic endophenotype and related genotypes are associated with oxidative stress in children with autism." *Am J Med Genet B Neuropsychiatr Genet.* 2006 Dec 5;141(8):947-56.

Institute isolated immune cells from blood samples taken from 30 children with autism and 26 typically developing children. The cells from both groups were exposed to bacteria and viruses including tetanus and the MMR vaccine antigens, which should provoke T-cells, B cells and macrophages (important components of the immune system). Researches found clear differences between the immune response of children on the autism spectrum and normal controls. In response to bacteria, the researchers saw lower levels of protein molecules called cytokines in the group with autism. Cytokines carry messages between immune system cells and other systems, such as the nervous system, and are known to effect sleep, fever response, mood and behavior.[75] [76]

Children on the autism spectrum who have had recurring infections should be evaluated for immunodeficiencies, and those with eczema, chronic sinus symptoms, gastrointestinal problems or recurring respiratory infections should also be tested for IgE inhalant and food allergies.[77]

IMMUNOGLOBULIN (Ig)

Immunoglobulins (antibodies) are proteins produced by the white blood cells. They protect us from disease, by binding to foreign substances they encounter (antigens), such as viruses and bacteria. Each antibody is designed to recognize only one specific antigen. After the antibody has bound to an antigen, it is destroyed by the immune system. Immunoglobulins also play a role in allergies: sometimes they bind to antigens that are not necessarily a threat, and provoke an inflammatory response. There are many types of antibody; IgA, IgD, IgE, IgG and IgM are the most common forms. Low levels of IgA antibodies may predispose children to respiratory and gastrointestinal infections, and low IgE levels may lead to allergies.[78]

INFANT FORMULA

Most infant formulas are either milk-based or soy-based. In the autism spectrum population, either could present a problem.

There are several concerns about soy-based formulas for infants (see SOY). In addition to worries about soy protein allergy, soy formula is considerably higher in aluminum than breastmilk or other formulas, due to the mineral salts used in formula production. Soy protein-based formulas are not designed or recommended for pre-term infants.[79]

Hypoallergenic infant formulas such as Pregestimil®, Nutramigen®, and Alimentum® are called "extensively hydrolyzed" because they contain proteins which are partially broken down, intended to reduce or eliminate allergic reactions in babies who are allergic to soy or cow's milk

---

[75] Ashwood, P, J. Van De Water. "Altered cytkine profile in children with autistic spectrum disorder (ASD): Evidence for immune dysregulation." IMFAR presentation, May 2005.

[76] Goines, P, P. Ashwood, J Van de Water. "Autism Spectrum Disorders and the Immune System." *ASA, Environmental Health* 2006.

[77] El-Dahr, Jane. Defeat Autism Now! Conference Presentation, 2007.

[78] IBID

[79] American Academy Of Pediatrics Committee On Nutrition: "Soy Protein-Based Formulas: Recommendations For Use In Infant Feeding." *Pediatrics* Vol. 101 No. 1 January 1998, Pp. 148-153.

protein. Presumably, choosing one that is "whey-based" would be a better choice for children who are casein-intolerant.

Note that these products might contain corn starch, tapioca starch, corn syrup or other ingredients that your child might not tolerate, so check the labels. According to the FDA's division of regulatory guidance, you should not try to make your own infant formula at home, as you are likely to leave out some critical components necessary for your child's physical and mental development. However, the Weston A. Price Foundation's website has a recipe for homemade infant formula that they claim to be a healthy, safe alternative to commercial brands (see WESTON A. PRICE).

Be aware that some elemental or protein-hydrolysate formulas, which use cornstarch as an emulsifying agent, contain a substance called octenylsuccinic acid (OSA). This can lead to increased urinary levels of glutaric acid and 2-ketoglutaric acid.[80] These abnormal organic acid test results may confuse the interpretation of whether the child suffers from a genetic disease.

Neocate, an amino acid-based infant formula, is designed for babies with severe cow milk allergy and multiple food protein intolerance. Although the first ingredient is corn syrup, the proteins are broken down into their elemental amino acids. It is quite expensive, so talk to your doctor about whether it can be prescribed and covered by your health insurance.

Ultracare for Kids® by Metagenics is a rice-based nutritional drink for highly allergic children. It is used as a dairy-free source of calcium, and includes balanced essential fatty acids. It should not be used as an infant formula.

Some Defeat Autism Now! doctors suggest that babies who are not receiving breastmilk should have a hypoallergenic colostrum supplement added to their formula: ½ tsp twice daily, in an effort to provide some of the immune benefits that breastmilk would otherwise supply (see COLOSTRUM).

INFLAMMATION

Recent studies have shown that people on the autism spectrum may have abnormalities in their inflammatory response system, or IRS.[81] It has been suggested, for example, that cytokines (a product of the IRS) may cause some behavioral symptoms of autism such as social withdrawal, sleep problems and the need for sameness. Although there may be some benefit from the short-term use of steroidal anti-inflammatory drugs such as prednisone, the side-effects of such drugs (which are sometimes serious) may not justify the benefit.

Foods that can worsen inflammation include NIGHTSHADES, OXALATES, and saturated fats. Processed meats such as lunch meats, hot dogs and sausages containing nitrites have been associated with increased inflammation and chronic disease. Natural anti-inflammatory agents include vitamin D and omega-3 fatty acids (both are often deficient in those with autism). Quercetin, a compound in red onions, has strong anti-inflammatory properties. The phenolic

---

[80] Kelley RI. "Octenylsuccinic aciduria in children fed protein-hydrolysate formulas containing modified cornstarch." *Pediatr Res.* 1991 Dec;30(6):564-9.

[81] Croonenberghs J, Bosmans E, Deboutte D, Kenis G, Maes M. "Activation of the Inflammatory Response System In Autism." *Neuropsychobiology.* 2002;45(1):1-6.

compounds in brightly colored fruits, vegetables and berries can have anti-inflammatory properties,[82] but these may not be appropriate for some (see PHENOLS).

INFLAMMATORY BOWEL DISEASE (IBD)

Inflammatory bowel disease is a term used for several disorders, including Crohn's Disease, ulcerative colitis and enterocolitis. The exact cause of most IBD is not known, but some researchers suggest that it stems from a dysregulation of the mucosal immune system, which leads to excessive immune system responses to normal intestinal flora (see GUT FLORA).[83] Another theory takes the opposite position, that the immune system is normal but the composition of the gut flora is abnormal, which prompts an inflammatory response in the gut.[84]

INFRACTIONS

There are bound to be situations when gluten, casein or some other forbidden food is accidentally ingested. Generally, this is called an *infraction*. Sometimes, eating even a single bite of the wrong food can cause a profound reaction.

While mishaps can happen to anyone, it is important to understand which foods contain ingredients you are trying to avoid. If you believe your child's diet is free of gluten but it contains trace amounts, this can scuttle all of your efforts. Be sure that you are familiar with the names in ingredient lists, so you aren't fooled by the "dairy free" label on a cheese substitute that actually contains casein.

For some, reactions to gluten infractions happen as long as three days after the food was eaten, for others, the reaction occurs within an hour. It is common to see a child appear somewhat better immediately after an infraction, and then fall apart during the withdrawal period.

According to Dr. Kalle Reichelt, the effects of true opioid-type dietary infractions can sometimes be slow and insidious. He has found that opioid levels are significantly elevated by these infractions, regardless of the absence (in some children) of immediate and apparent reactions.

The answer to why some children react quickly to a dietary infraction while others show delayed reactions may be connected to the two-fold nature of problems with gluten and dairy. If opioid problems are responsible for autistic behaviors in some children, their removal could create a long-term effect. However, many children have an immune response to milk and/or wheat, which could create a noticeable short-term effect. Testing for food allergies (not just the "regular" IgE-type allergies, but blood testing for IgA and IgG intolerances as well) might shed some light on your child's individual situation (See ALLERGIES & INTOLERANCES).

Many professionals are not informed of the impact that IgG-mediated allergies can have on a person's mood and behavior, but for some parents, the effect is unmistakable..

"What happens when my son eats foods to which he has an IgG allergy? I'll share the more

---

[82] Santangelo C, Varì R, Scazzocchio B, Di Benedetto R, Filesi C, Masella R. "Polyphenols, intracellular signalling and inflammation." *Ann Ist Super Sanita.* 2007;43(4):394-405.

[83] Strober, W. "The fundamental basis of inflammatory bowel disease." *J. Clin. Invest.* 2007, 117:514-521

[84] IBID

spectacular reactions with you. Approximately three to four hours after ingestion, he becomes increasingly desolate. He will have crying fits, without being able to tell me why he's crying, his speech will slur, and his behavior will deteriorate to the point of screaming, violent tantrums. He will lose bladder control. Once when this happened, he ran through the house kicking every door and wall he could get his feet into. For at least a week after the infraction, he'll be spacey, have trouble with two-way communication, and write most of his letters and numbers in mirror script. And we have the GI issues - constipation, diarrhea, vomiting - which can also last one to two weeks.

Just ¼ of a banana will make him very giggly and silly within an hour. He will laugh hysterically and won't be able to stop. He'll get red ears. The next morning he'll wake up like a zombie, with big black circles under his eyes. You will not be able to have a two-way conversation with him (he'll monologue or script). His auditory processing is way off.

We were fortunate that we were able to afford the IgG testing. But if we hadn't been able to do this, I would have put my son on an elimination diet and would probably have teased most of his trouble foods out over time.

I never realized how much what he ingested was affecting him. He was a very irritable, cranky, obsessive-compulsive, sometimes violent child. Now when he's 'clean' he is very sweet, very affectionate, and very articulate. He is quite easygoing and adjusts to changes in the routine pretty well, but when his diet is compromised, we have 'Dr. Jekyll and Mr. Hyde' living in our home."

–Petra Smit

These reactions have been described by other parents. Slurred speech, "drunkenness," loss of bladder and/or bowel control, red ears, weepiness, tantrums, increased "stimming", vomiting and general spaciness have all been reported following infractions. Other children become aggressive, have OCD-type behaviors or have skin eruptions (rashes, hives, patches of eczema).

"After eating one chocolate chip cookie, our son was completely altered. Although he has been trained for over eighteen months, he had a bowel movement in his pants. He laughed hysterically over nothing. He began slapping himself and falling constantly. He also ran in circles and was completely non-compliant. At first, we were mystified and disheartened until I realized what had happened (the babysitter had given him the cookie). Luckily, after a few days he gradually returned to normal." -Shelley Ansaldi, reprinted from The ANDI News

"After 10 months on the GF/CF diet, our 14-year-old son was allowed to buy Poptarts® at school. This was an "oops" on the part of a new teacher. Within two hours he was agitated, ripping clothing and crying. Language diminished and he spent a week 'growling' all language, most of which was perseverative. He also became aggressive with his younger sister and me at home.

The growling has abated, but the affect is still variable. Aggression and perseveration have continued. This happened 9 days ago…how long before the effects wear off? There is one positive note—his teachers are now true believers! Any advice would be appreciated."

-Sue Loring, reprinted from The ANDI News

"My son has been on the diet for 6 months and we have seen some remarkable results. Last week at nursery school, he showed interest in another child's macaroni and cheese lunch. The director let him have some without consulting me, although she knows he is on this diet per doctor's orders. Since this event, he has completely changed. His behavior is even more severe than it was before his diagnosis at 2 yrs. old. All he does is line things up and hide in closets. He went from going to the community pool and playing with other children to screaming in the parking lot and refusing to go

near the pool. How long will these effects last?" -Lynn Zenone, reprinted from The ANDI News

There are many factors at play, such as the current condition of the gut, how much was ingested and how long the child was gluten and casein free prior to the incident. It generally takes about three weeks to get back to "baseline" after this type of incident, and there is little you can do but to wait it out. It is very rough on the family, but even rougher on the child because he probably feels terrible (physically and emotionally) and doesn't understand that it will pass.

After some time on the diet, when the gut has healed, the reaction to infractions is usually less dramatic.

If you are present when an infraction occurs, there are several things you can try which may ameliorate the situation. Give digestive enzymes as soon as possible. If there is an allergic reaction involved, you may want to give a dose of alcohol-free, dye-free Benedryl® or similar antihistamine. Available in most pharmacies, Activated Charcoal is used to absorb toxins if they are still in the digestive system, but it is unclear as to its usefulness during dietary infractions. (Do not give medicines or supplements until several hours have elapsed, as they may be neutralized by the charcoal.)

If such an incident does happen at school, you may want to obtain a written letter from the director of the school describing the diet infraction and the child's reaction, and stating that measures will be taken to ensure that this will not happen again. Copies of the letter should be given to anyone who, in future, will have responsibility for caring for and feeding your child.

Safe at School? A good rule of thumb: your child should never, ever be allowed to put anything in his mouth that was not provided by you. This means providing all lunches, snacks, food-based art supplies, and reinforcers, and having a serious conversation with every teacher, therapist, and bus driver who will supervise your child (see COMPLIANCE).

Common Mistakes: There are many foods that *sound* as if they contain gluten or wheat and do not (e.g. buckwheat). Unfortunately, there are even more foods that would seem to be gluten or dairy free, but are not. The most important step you can take to avoid mistakes is to learn how to read labels, to know what ingredients to avoid, and to check labels every time you buy a food, even if it has been acceptable in the past.

For some reason parents often assume that foods like Rice Krispies® or Krispix® will be "safe" because they are rice-based. Not so...both contain barley malt (a source of gluten). Others mistakenly believe that very heavily processed foods (such as Wonder Bread®) no longer contain gluten. Children who are fed even small amounts of gluten are never really "gluten free," so their parents cannot say with certainty that they did not benefit from the removal of gluten. See GLUTEN for lists of ingredients to be wary of.

It is also important not to be misled by the name of a product. "Millet Bread" can be made from millet and wheat flours. Rice cheese can (and usually does) contain dairy products such as sodium caseinate. Spelt, Kamut and Triticale are all varieties of wheat that are loaded with gluten, even though they can legally be called "wheat free."

Don't feed a child a food to which he is intolerant because you fear malnutrition or vitamin deficiency (for example, giving milk for calcium). All children on a limited or restricted diet should be taking vitamin and mineral supplements, and be under the care of a qualified nutritionist or dietician, so you can ensure that the essential nutrients are being provided.

INTOLERANCE (See ALLERGIES AND INTOLERANCES)

IRRITABLE BOWEL SYNDROME (IBS)

Also known as "spastic colon," this disorder may affect as many as 15% of all Americans, most of whom are never diagnosed. Some think it's normal to have only one bowel movement a week, while others run to the bathroom once or several times a day with loose stools or diarrhea. And yet, many sufferers do not realize that their collection of symptoms are even worth mentioning to their doctors, and may never seek a diagnosis. Even if they do, their doctors may dismiss the problem when test results come back normal.

IBS is a condition in which the colon is hypersensitive to triggers which can cause cramping, bloating, and pain. These triggers may slow down or speed up bowel motility, resulting in diarrhea, constipation, or alternating diarrhea and constipation. For some, this is a chronic problem, while others may have occasional bouts lasting days or weeks. Although IBS is a medical illness and not psychosomatic in origin, bowel function is affected by stress or depression, which can create a vicious cycle.

There are no consistently satisfactory medical treatments for this disorder. However, a 2007 study concluded that enteric-coated peppermint oil capsules have proven to be surprisingly effective at reducing IBS symptoms.[85] In addition, many people have gotten relief using a special diet described in the book *Eating for IBS*, by Heather Van Vorous.

According to Van Vorous, insoluble fiber (see FIBER), useful for other types of GI problems, tends to make IBS symptoms worse. But the symptoms can be greatly reduced by adhering to a very specific dietary regime which includes a steady supply of soluble fiber (such as acacia fiber, methylcellulose, guar gum, psyllium, cooked and peeled fruits, or starchy foods like white rice, oats, peas, beans, apples, citrus fruits, carrots, and barley), and restricts common triggers including dairy, meats and oily foods. IBS may explain why some people on a high protein, low starch diet become ill, experiencing extreme diarrhea or constipation.

Symptoms of IBS tend to emerge around puberty, and may be lifelong. Although many of our children don't fit into the IBS category, it's important to be aware of this condition, since childhood constipation may be a predictor of IBS in adulthood,[86] and because family members may also be affected. People with IBS have a 40% to 80% higher prevalence of migraine,

---

[85] Cappello G, Spezzaferro M, Grossi L, Manzoli L, Marzio L. "Peppermint oil (Mintoil) in the treatment of irritable bowel syndrome: a prospective double blind placebo-controlled randomized trial." *Dig Liver Dis*. 2007 Jun; 39(6):530-6.

[86] Khan S, et al. "Long-term outcome of functional childhood constipation." *Dig Dis Sci*. 2007 Jan;52(1):64-9.

fibromyalgia, chronic fatigue syndrome, depression, and obsessive compulsive disorder,[87] [88] [89] all of which have been observed to be common in families affected by autism. IBS is also often seen together with functional dyspepsia, gastroesophageal reflux disease, celiac disease, and lactose intolerance.[90]

You can find detailed information about eating for IBS at www.helpforibs.com. High-quality acacia powder and enteric-coated peppermint oil capsules can be purchased at www.helpforibs.com/shop.

JOWAR (See SORGHUM)

KAMUT

Kamut, like spelt, is a variety of wheat which contains gluten, and *is not suitable for those on a gluten-free diet*. For those with a wheat allergy who *do* tolerate gluten, kamut may be an acceptable substitute. Kamut and spelt more closely resemble the wheat grain that was grown and eaten by our ancestors before the grain was genetically modified to increase yield and pest resistance. It is speculated that these alterations to the original forms of wheat may explain why many modern people do not tolerate it.

KEFIR (See YOGURT AND KEFIR, PROBIOTICS)

KETOGENIC DIET

In the 1920's, doctors at Johns Hopkins Hospital in Baltimore began using an extremely high fat, low protein and carbohydrate diet to manage seizure disorders. They were inspired by reports from ancient times, that "fits" could be temporarily cured by fasting. This intervention lost popularity many years ago but resurfaced in the 1970's when Dr. John Freeman and nutritionist Millicent Kelly wrote a book on the use and management of the diet.[91] This diet is again being used at medical centers around the country to control intractable epileptic seizures in patients who do not respond to conventional drug therapy and are not good candidates for surgery.

In the ketogenic diet, fat becomes the main energy source for the body. When dietary fat is used for energy, "ketone bodies" are produced as a by-product of fat metabolism. It is believed

---

[87] Sperber AD, Atzmon Y, Neumann L, Weisberg I, Shalit Y, Abu-Shakrah M, Fich A, Buskila D. "Fibromyalgia in the irritable bowel syndrome: studies of prevalence and clinical implications." *Am J Gastroenterol.* 1999 Dec;94(12):3541-6.

[88] Cole JA, "Migraine, fibromyalgia, and depression among people with IBS: a prevalence study." *BMC Gastroenterol.* 2006 Sep 28;6:26.

[89] Masand PS, Keuthen NJ, Gupta S, Virk S, Yu-Siao B, Kaplan D. "Prevalence of irritable bowel syndrome in obsessive-compulsive disorder." *CNS Spectr.* 2006 Jan;11(1):21-5.

[90] Frissora CL, Koch KL. "Symptom overlap and comorbidity of irritable bowel syndrome with other conditions." *Curr Gastroenterol Rep.* 2005 Aug;7(4):264-71.

[91] *Epilepsy Diet Treatment : An Introduction to the Ketogenic Diet* by John M. Freeman, Millicent T. Kelly, Jennifer B. Freeman. Their followup book published in 2006 is entitled *The Ketogenic Diet : A Treatment for Children and Others with Epilepsy.*

that ketones inhibit seizure activity, though the precise mechanism by which this occurs is not understood. Between 50-75% of children put on this diet show considerable improvement.[92][93]

Despite the fact that all anti-seizure medications have the potential for serious side effects, doctors do not typically provide information about dietary intervention unless at least two of these medications have not worked. Even when medications dull the young patients into virtual insensibility, many doctors strongly discourage trying this diet if the seizures are under control.

There are several downsides to this therapy, however. Staying on the ketogenic diet requires perfect control of a person's dietary intake. Adverse side effects include constipation, vomiting, lack of energy and hunger. The diet may put stress on the heart or kidneys, and medical problems resulting from the diet have been reported. In addition, the diet is unpalatable and few patients are able to tolerate it long term. The use of a supplement containing medium-chain triglycerides (MCT) has been helpful in alleviating these effects.

Among other things, the ketogenic diet calls for the elimination of foods like starchy fruits and vegetables, bread, pasta, grains and sugar. With the help of an experienced dietician, it could be compatible with other dietary interventions for autism-related disorders.

KETOSIS

When the liver is depleted of stored glycogen (the form of glucose stored in the liver and muscles) during a low-carbohydrate diet, the body goes into a state of fasting to protect itself from starvation. After several hours, the body begins to burn ketones in order to derive energy from stored fats in the body. The breath of people in a ketotic state commonly smells of acetone (the ingredient in nail polish remover), or has a sweet smell similar to ethyl alcohol.

In some cases, ketosis is deliberately induced with a low-carbohydrate diet to treat medical conditions, such as epilepsy (see KETOGENIC DIET) or for weight loss.

In most cases, ketosis is a harmless condition, and one of the body's ways of metabolizing fat. However, if the concentration of ketones is too high, the breakdown of fatty acids can lead to a condition called *ketoacidosis*. In individuals with undiagnosed or untreated type 1 diabetes, a person can lapse into a diabetic coma which is called *diabetic ketoacidosis*.

KOSHER, KASHRUT (See also HOLIDAYS: Passover)

The body of Jewish laws governing what foods can be eaten, how they must be slaughtered, prepared and served is called *Kashrut*. Those who observe these laws are said to "keep kosher."

Although there are others, the main laws of kashrut are:

• Certain birds, fish, and animals may not be eaten at all.

• Of the animals that are allowed, certain parts of the animals may not be eaten.

• Animals must be killed in accordance with Jewish law.

---

[92] Neal EG, Chaffe H, Schwartz RH, Lawson MS, Edwards N, Fitzsimmons G, Whitney A, Cross JH. "The ketogenic diet for the treatment of childhood epilepsy: a randomised controlled trial." *Lancet Neurol.* 2008 May 2.

[93] A Freitas, J Albino da Paz, E Casella, M Marques-Dias, "Ketogenic diet for the treatment of refractory epilepsy: a 10 year experience in children." *Arq Neuropsiquiatr* 2007;65(2-B):381-384.

- Fruits and vegetables must be inspected for bugs.

- All blood must be drained from meat after slaughter.

- Meat cannot be eaten with dairy. (Fish, eggs, fruits, vegetables and grains can be eaten with either meat or dairy.)

It is useful to know something about kosher labeling, since a meat-based product is guaranteed to be milk free. When foods have been certified as kosher, they will be marked with a "K," or a "U" (sometimes circled or inside a star), or the symbol at right. If the product contains dairy, it will usually have a "D" or the word "Dairy" next to the kosher symbol.

You will also know that a product is dairy free if the package has the word "Pareve" or "Parev" near the certification symbol. This means it is a "neutral food" (neither meat nor dairy).

Some people contend that Kosher meat is safer and cleaner than conventional meat. Jewish law requires rigorous inspections, and kosher beef inspectors reject about 50 times as many animals as USDA inspectors do. Sick animals are never used for meat and the slaughtering process is considered to be humane.

This does not guarantee that kosher meat is always better for you. Although organic kosher meat is now becoming more widely available, most kosher animals are raised on conventionally-run farms, and may be given growth hormones and antibiotics. If you can find a local kosher butcher shop that can tell you where and how the meat has been treated, then it may be worth the extra expense.

For a detailed description of Kashrut visit www.jewfaq.org/kashrut.htm.

KUZU/KUDZU (See THICKENERS)

LACTIC ACID

A product of metabolism, lactic acid is found in every living thing. It is used in food processing as a preservative and to control acidity, and in some cases adds tartness to food. It is obtained by fermenting starch, whey, potatoes and/or molasses, but is usually safe on a casein free diet.

LACTASE

Lactase is the enzyme that breaks down the milk sugar *lactose* (see below).

LACTOSE

Lactose is a milk sugar that exists in varying quantities in most dairy products. Those who lack enough *lactase* have trouble digesting dairy foods. These lactose intolerant individuals usually suffer discomfort after eating them.

Lactose intolerance can be diagnosed with simple breath testing at the doctor's office, but the best test is simply to notice whether bloating, cramping, gas or diarrhea take place within a couple of hours after eating more than a small serving of dairy products.

About 75% of adults in most parts of the world suffer from lactose intolerance, since lactase production tends to decrease after age five. Northern Europeans are more likely to tolerate lactose, perhaps because of the historical prevalence of dairy in their diets. Low production of lactase may develop as a secondary condition in people already suffering from other gastrointestinal diseases such as celiac disease or enteritis.

Aged cheeses, yogurts, and sheep and goat milk have reduced quantities of lactose, but usually will cause a reaction in sensitive people. Some gut flora, such as *Lactobacillus*, convert lactose (milk sugar) into lactic acid. Those with lactose intolerance may find that this probiotic, when properly colonized in the gut, can help them to better tolerate dairy products.

Please note that lactose intolerance is not the same thing as milk allergy or casein maldigestion. Those conditions arise from reactions to the milk *protein*, not the milk sugar.

LAKANTO (See SUGAR SUBSTITUTES)

LEAKY GUT (See also ALLERGIES & INTOLERANCES, BOWEL DISEASE AND AUTISM, GUT FLORA)

In a healthy digestive system, there are small spaces in the lining of the gut; this lining will allow only tiny particles of proteins to migrate out into the bloodstream. If there is damage to the gut, its lining may become too *permeable* (which means porous or full of holes). Such a "leaky gut" may allow polypeptides (chains of amino acids) to pass through to the bloodstream, as well as incompletely digested foods and mycotoxins (toxic fungal waste products).

There are several theories to explain increased intestinal permeability:

- A chronic viral infection has established itself in the wall of the intestines, disrupting the gut-immune system, and weakening the integrity of the gut lining.

- The presence of excessive amounts of yeast and/or bacteria (either due to immune dysfunction, or resulting from it) has compromised the gut wall and increased its permeability. (This may especially pertain to those with very early or excessive use of antibiotics).

- A genetic predisposition to celiac disease, or another type of allergic reaction in the gut, results in an undiagnosed gluten (or other) intolerance, which flattens the intestinal villi and creates a celiac-like condition.

Other factors that could affect gut permeability include sulfation defects (see PHENOL SULFUR TRANSFERASE DEFICIENCY) and heavy metal toxicity. Further, when a person is under extreme stress, the body releases hormones such as adrenalin, opening the spaces in the gut wall for fastest uptake of energy.

A "leaky gut," *together with* a genetic or acquired enzyme deficiency, is the most likely combination of factors that could conceivably lead to an opioid excess. This could explain why not all people with leaky guts have autism.

Autism is what is referred to in medicine as a "final common pathway." In other words, children with autism may take several different roads to get there, but they will all end up in the same special education classroom. This is one reason why the treatment of autism has been so confounding: what works for one child may not work for another, even though they both display similar behaviors. However, a great number of these children seem to have symptoms of leaky gut, such as multiple food intolerances and poor nutritional absorption.

Most medical professionals with experience in the biomedical treatment of autism have come to the same conclusion: healing the gut is a top priority. They sometimes describe their gut-healing protocol as "the four Rs" - **Remove** (allergens, toxins, harmful microbes), **Replace** (deficient digestive enzymes), **Reinoculate** (with probiotics), and **Repair** (with nutritional supplements such as glutamine, vitamins A, C, and E, zinc, manganese, and amino acids).

LECITHIN

Lecithin is a natural component of plants and animals. It is used as an emulsifier to prevent separation in foods, and to retard spoilage. Commercial sources are usually derived from corn, seeds, soybeans and egg yolks, but most lecithin found in foods comes from soy. Because it contains no protein, it is usually tolerated even by those who react to other soy products.

LECTINS

Lectins are proteins, usually found in plant sources such as grains, legumes, nuts and beans. They bind to certain carbohydrates, and are mildly toxic. The lectin content can vary even in the same food, depending on how it was grown and processed. Soaking foods such as nuts and beans overnight may remove some of the lectins. Sprouting and fermentation may also be helpful.

LIP BALM

It's always a good idea to confirm with the manufacturer that all products touching your child's mouth are gluten free. If your child is sensitive to lanolin or other ingredients in lip balm, it is safe to use plain petroleum jelly. Some of the brands of lip balm you might also try are Badger Balm™, Burt's Bees™ (GF/CF, but contains lanolin) or Merry Hempsters Organic Hemp Balm™. Chapstick Brand™ has recently come out with a "Natural" balm that is free of common allergens.

LOD (See LOW OXALATE DIET)

LOTIONS & CREAMS (See SKIN CARE PRODUCTS)

LOW OXALATE DIET (LOD)

Did you ever eat rhubarb, and notice the way it stings your tongue? That's because it contains high levels of oxalates, which are tiny salts found in plant foods. Moderate amounts are not harmful for healthy individuals, but have been known to create problems for those with certain health conditions such as kidney stones, and in conditions where there is a loss of gut integrity, such as in gastric bypass surgery, some types of bowel disease including Crohn's and celiac, and in cystic fibrosis.

Theory: Autism Researcher Susan Owens suggested the LOD for autism in 2005 because of the leaky gut and gut inflammation in autism. She pointed out that oxalates from food in a healthy gut should pass through the body harmlessly bound to minerals like calcium, or else degraded ("eaten") by protective gut bacteria like *Oxalobacter formigenes*. If these minerals or microflora are deficient, unbound oxalate can be absorbed in the intestines, where it will travel through the gaps between cells and into the blood. From there, oxalates will end up in tissues of the body, worsening pain and inflammation throughout, and impairing many enzymes involved in energy metabolism and defense against yeast and dysbiosis. Oxalates can worsen sulfation issues, and greatly increase oxidative stress. Oxalates may be part of the reason why a host of problems arise from immune dysfunction, allergies, imbalanced microflora, mineral deficiency, and altered intestinal permeability (see LEAKY GUT).

Simple explanation: Foods high in oxalates should not be a problem for most healthy people. However, without certain minerals or the right sort of bacteria, the unbound oxalate can slip through gaps in the gut lining, and cause inflammation throughout the body. Oxalates from food, or that are secreted by the body, may also keep the gut from healing properly. Therefore, sharply reducing oxalates in the diet could speed up the process of healing a damaged gut.

Who might benefit: According to Owens, those who have done poorly on special diets based on nuts, or on grains and certain vegetables may be candidates for a trial of the LOD, as well as those who have steatorrhea (fat in the stool) or poor function of the upper intestine. Those with urinary issues, pain or stiffness, low energy, poor growth or skin issues that won't resolve may also benefit. Gluten-containing foods are often high in oxalates, which may explain why some people suffering from these symptoms find that they improve on a gluten free diet. Owens encourages those on LOD to stay or become gluten free, since gluten may also have the effect of increasing gut permeability.

Some parents have had success combining principles from the Low Oxalate Diet and the Specific Carbohydrate Diet™ or Body Ecology Diet to promote the fastest healing for inflamed tissue.

Testing: Testing for high oxalates is now being offered on some Organic Acids tests. However, initial clinical data suggests that urine testing is not predictive of success on this diet - some of the best responders are patients who had very low levels of oxalate in their urine before starting the LOD. This may be due to a problem in the kidney's ability to excrete oxalate, stemming from the sulfation problems common in autism.

What to do: Owens advises starting the diet by first cutting back the very high oxalate foods, then slowly moving to lower oxalate foods one food at a time until the oxalate count is below 40 mgs per 2000 calories, per day. *The Low Oxalate Cookbook, Version II** contains extensive information on oxalate content per serving, and you can find a comprehensive food list with oxalate content and other food traits at www.lowoxalate.info/recipes.html. As with many autism treatments, an early worsening may be seen as a good sign, but if the negative symptoms are severe, you should decrease the rate at which you are lowering oxalates, and use some recommended supplements. After the "detox process" is finished, which can take from a couple of months to a couple of years, then higher-oxalate foods can be cautiously added back into the diet one by one.

What to expect: Progress on the LOD usually occurs only after the body starts the cyclic process of freeing up oxalate from tissues. Those who had previously been eating a very high oxalate diet are most likely to suffer from a regression in the first stages of the diet, as built-up oxalates are released from the body. This usually involves some very obvious negative symptoms after a few days, such as diarrhea, urinary discomfort, behavioral changes, upper respiratory congestion or skin rashes. Parents sometimes refer to this as "the dump."

If this diet is helpful, you may notice (between "dumps") improvements in the areas of physical comfort, complex thinking, sociability, speech, gross and fine motor skills, energy, loss of stiffness, and skin problems such as eczema. Your child may be willing to eat foods he avoided before, and may stop craving high oxalate foods. He may have an increase in appetite, and a child with delayed growth may suddenly have a growth spurt.

If there is no change for the better or worse after two weeks on a very low oxalate diet, assuming that the guidelines for supplements are being followed, then this diet will probably not be helpful.

Although it may be necessary to continue to restrict foods that are very high in oxalates, Owens notes that this diet is not meant to be a lifetime program for autism. After some time on the LOD, when healing has taken place and symptoms of ill health have improved, it should be possible to increase the amount of oxalate in the diet without ill effects.

"We have been GF/CF for about 5 years and last fall tried the Specific Carbohydrate Diet™, which didn't work out well for my son. He was having mouth pain (gums), bad leg pain, back pain, and penile pain (very bad). After a couple weeks I talked with his Defeat Autism Now! Doctor and he thought it was related to oxalates. After starting the diet there was an immediate decrease in his penile pain. The other pains seemed to decrease a lot too.

We have been on the LOD for a little over three months now. The gum pain and back pain are still present at times though not to the same degree - I think they tend to pop up more when he is "dumping" more. Now I have to say he actually looks different physically. He looks healthy for the first time in years. He no longer has dark circles under his eyes, his skin looks terrific (he has had eczema issues forever), the little white bumps that have been under his eyes for the last 4 years are actually starting to go away, and his eyes no longer have that glazed-over drunken look to them. The only thing I can attribute all of this to is the diet. That is the only big change we have made in the last few months. I just wanted to let everyone know all of the positives we are seeing and even though it is hard initially, I think sticking with it is definitely worth it."

-Mary Muscarella

Status: Although initially skeptical about "yet another diet," some physicians have noted improvements in their patients on the LOD, and have been recommending a trial period on the diet for certain individuals with inflammation and/or GI symptoms. There are over 2000 members in the "Trying Low Oxalates" online support group.

Concerns: During the "dumping" period, one may notice a temporary worsening or onset of urinary issues like penis pain, redness, urinary frequency or urinary urgency. There might be unusual skin rashes, including *livedo reticularis*, which is an inflammation of blood vessels that makes them show up vividly in the skin, like a road map. Oxalate crystals can cause gum problems, so if teeth begin to feel loose, one should slow down and increase antioxidant protection. There might also be an onset of diarrhea, including sandy stools and stools with black specks. If these symptoms occur, or if your child appears to be in any discomfort, consult your doctor.

In some children, previous infections may reappear, such as streptococcus along with a syndrome known as PANDAS. Why this happens is unknown, but it has been theorized that some of the bacteria was trapped by oxalate crystals and later liberated when the crystals broke down.

High-Oxalate (** very high)

- Almonds**
- Amaranth
- Beans
- Beets (greens & root)**
- Bell pepper (green)
- Berries
- Bran
- Buckwheat
- Carob
- Carrots
- Celery
- Chard**
- Chicory
- Chili peppers
- Cinnamon (½ tsp. ground)
- Citrus peel
- Cocoa/Chocolate
- Collards
- Cumin
- Currants (red)
- Dandelion greens
- Eggplant
- Escarole
- Figs
- Ginger (1 tbsp)
- Gooseberries
- Graham crackers
- Grapes Concord
- Green beans
- Hazelnut
- Kale
- Kamut
- Kiwi
- Leeks
- Mustard Greens
- Nuts
- Okra**
- Olives
- Orange peel
- Parsley
- Parsnips
- Peanuts**
- Pecans
- Plums (purple)
- Pokeweed**
- Popcorn (4+ cups)
- Potatoes (white & sweet)
- Raspberries**
- Refried beans**
- Rhubarb
- Rice milk
- Rutabagas
- Sesame seeds**
- Sorrel
- Soy**
- Spinach**
- Star fruit**
- String beans
- Sweet potatoes**
- Swiss chard**
- Tahini**
- Tamarillo
- Tangerines
- Tapioca
- Tea (not herbal)
- Tomatoes (canned)
- Turmeric
- V-8 Juice
- Wheat flour
- Wholegrain flours
- Yams**

Low-Oxalate (* may be medium)

- Alfalfa sprouts
- Aloe vera juice
- Apple juice
- Apples, peeled
- Apricot (one)
- Asparagus*
- Avocado
- Bacon
- Bananas*
- Barley, cooked
- Basil, fresh (1 tsp)
- Beef
- Black-eyed peas
- Bok choy
- Broccoli*
- Brussel sprouts*
- Cabbage
- Cantaloupe
- Catsup
- Cauliflower
- Cherries
- Chives
- Cider
- Cilantro
- Coconut
- Corn*
- Cornstarch (1 tbsp)
- Cranberries
- Cucumbers, peeled
- Dill (1 tbsp)*
- Eggs
- Endive
- Fish
- Flax seed
- Fruit juices without berries (4 oz)
- Gelatin, unflavored
- Ginger ale
- Grape juice (red and white)
- Grapefruit*
- Grapes green
- Honey (1 tbsp)
- Honeydew
- Horseradish
- Ketchup
- Kohlrabi*
- Kumquat
- Lamb
- Lemon/lime
- Lettuce
- Lychee
- Mangoes
- Maple syrup
- Marjoram
- Margarine
- Mayonnaise
- Meats/Poultry
- Melons
- Milk/dairy
- Mung bean sprouts
- Mushrooms*
- Mustard
- Nectarines
- Nutmeg
- Oils
- Onions*
- Orange
- Oregano, dried (1 tsp)
- Papaya
- Passion fruit
- Peaches*
- Peas
- Pepper (white)
- Peppermint
- Pickles
- Pineapple
- Pistachios
- Plums
- Potatoes (white)*
- Pumpkin*
- Pumpkin seeds
- Radishes
- Raisins, golden
- Red currant juice
- Rosemary
- Rice (white)
- Rice (brown)*
- Rye
- Sage
- Salt
- Seafood
- Squash
- Strawberries
- Sunflower seeds (1 oz)
- Tarragon
- Tea, herbal
- Thyme
- Tomatoes (fresh)
- Turnips, turnip greens
- V-8 Juice
- Vanilla
- Vegetable oils
- Vinegar
- Water chestnuts
- Watercress
- Watermelon
- White flour (¼ cup)
- Wild rice
- Wine
- Zucchini

116

Keep in mind that these "dumping" symptoms shouldn't show up in someone unless they have had an oxalate problem. These bad periods tend to be followed by resolution of earlier symptoms, as well as in global improvements.

A further concern is that some people are prone to constipation on the LOD, possibly a result of the reduced amount of fiber from vegetables and whole grains. Calcium supplements (see below) can also be constipating to those who are sensitive to them. Owens suggests trying different types of calcium, switching to magnesium citrate, or else using a combination of the two (magnesium tends to be helpful for constipation - you can adjust the proportions until you hit the right balance). Ground flax seeds are relatively low in oxalates compared to other seeds; they are a good source of fiber, and may be helpful in treating constipation.

Supplements: High doses of probiotic supplements or cultured foods are recommended before starting this diet, because they can help degrade oxalates. Total intake of vitamin C should not exceed 250 mg/day because it can worsen an oxalate problem in the body. It was once thought that calcium was also problematic, however, studies have shown it is important to provide enough calcium orally (preferably calcium citrate) to bind to the free oxalate in the gut and form calcium oxalate, which can pass through the body without being absorbed. This should be taken without vitamin D, about ten minutes before meals.

Other supplements are recommended, or should be avoided, so read through the guidelines at www.lowoxalate.info/faqs.html.

Support: To get support for this diet, join the online support list at www.yahoogroups.com/group/Trying_Low_Oxalates.

*The Vulvar Pain Foundation has published two excellent cookbooks filled with low-oxalate recipes, and comprehensive lists of food oxalate levels. You can order them from www.wellnesshealth.com, or check out www.vulvarpainfoundation.org, telephone: (336) 226-0704.

LUTEIN

Lutein is a carotenoid that is found in spinach and kale, as well as egg yolk, and darkly colored fruits and vegetables. Foods high in lutein tend to be on the list of high-oxalate foods, and many are high in phenols. This may help to explain why it was once hypothesized that lutein was a problem food component in autism.

MACROBIOTICS

Macrobiotics is a dietary program based on grains, brown rice, vegetables, beans, and fermented soy. Followers of the macrobiotic approach believe that food and food quality powerfully affect health, well-being, and happiness. Principles include the avoidance of processed and refined foods, preparing foods in certain ways, and chewing food thoroughly to aid digestion. If you decide to incorporate some of the principles of macrobiotics to your family's diet, be sure that your child's nutritional needs are being met, and remember that recommended foods containing gluten should be avoided. There are several good books and websites devoted to macrobiotic diets, and information can also be found online at www.macrobioticcooking.com.

MALT

Malt is a barley product, and must be avoided by those on a gluten-free diet. Even a small quantity will affect results and cause elevated urinary peptides.

MALTASE

Maltase is a gut enzyme that breaks down the disaccharide maltose.

MANNITOL (See SUGAR SUBSTITUTES)

MEALS AND SNACKS (See also SCHOOL LUNCHES)

Providing healthy meals and snacks doesn't have to be a daunting task. For those following a gluten and casein free diet, most families serve meat and vegetables every night, alternating a grain with potatoes as a side dish. For those on the Specific Carbohydrate Diet™, you can omit the starches, and perhaps add a fruit.

Below are some ideas, many of which are suitable for a starch-free diet.

Breakfasts: Protein should be included in breakfast whenever possible, to keep your child alert and keep blood sugar levels stable. For children who do not like traditional breakfast foods, or cannot eat them, leftovers from dinner make a fine breakfast. If eggs are tolerated, there are many ways to prepare them. They can be boiled (soft or hard), fried, scrambled or made into an omelette or fritatta. Gluten free or nut bread makes very good toast; you can even make "toad in the hole" by removing a round from a slice and frying the egg in the middle.

French toast made with appropriate bread can be served with nitrite/nitrate free bacon or sausages. Pancakes or waffles made with appropriate flours also make a good breakfast. Serve them with fruit, jam, real maple syrup, honey, or with fresh berries on top. When making pancakes, waffles or muffins, add extra egg or protein powder to increase the nutritional value. You can also add calcium powder, which will add nutrients but will not change the flavor or texture. If a child is simply not a "breakfast person," consider using a well balanced protein bar. Be sure to find one that is high in protein but low in sugar.

Lunches: (See also SCHOOL LUNCHES)

Falafels can be made from a mix (for example, Authentic Foods) and served with hummus and fresh vegetables. Falafels are high in protein and easy to prepare and eat. They can be made ahead and frozen.

If your children will eat salads, top them with grilled chicken, bacon, sunflower seeds and a dressing they like. Add as many fresh vegetables as you can. If necessary, grate or chop the vegetables so they are less noticeable, or purée them and mix with the dressing.

Sandwiches can made with appropriate breads. If you want to limit starches, you can make roll-ups with ham, turkey, smoked salmon, or a thinly-cooked omelette. Or get your butcher to slice cold cuts in ½" slices, and cut them into sticks.*

Soup or stew makes a very good lunch, and if your child likes it, it is an excellent medium in which to hide puréed vegetables. Make homemade broth when possible (see BROTH).

***Note:** When buying sliced meats a the deli counter, ask the butcher to clean the blade before preparing your order; bologna and other luncheon meats may contain ingredients that you are trying to avoid. Use only cold cuts without added ingredients, which are not preserved with nitrites or nitrates. Some cold cuts are coated with MSG; you can ask to read the label before ordering.*

Dinners: Dinners do not have to be fancy to be nutritious and acceptable for any of the diets described in this book. Roasted chicken, grilled burgers and other meats or fish are all appropriate. If your child refuses any meat or fish that has not been breaded, use gluten free crumbs or nut flour. If possible, use increasingly lighter coatings until you are merely sautéing the food in olive or another healthy oil. Add a cooked vegetable to the meal and a salad, and you have a dinner acceptable to all diets.

If starch is allowed, potatoes, rice or other grains, or even gluten free pasta will round out the meal nicely. Gluten free pasta comes in many shapes, and when cooked properly, is almost identical to wheat-based pasta. Serve macaroni with homemade meatballs and an appropriate sauce, or layer lasagna noodles in a baking dish with meat, sauce, and vegetables. Again, cooked and puréed vegetables can be easily hidden in both meatballs and sauces. You can even substitute vegetable-thickened meat broth for tomato sauce when necessary.

For those who can't have starch, spaghetti squash can be dressed up as regular spaghetti. You may be surprised to find that your child will be willing to try this, especially after some time on a starch free diet.

When eggs are tolerated, savory pancakes can be made with diced ham, finely-chopped vegetables or other healthy foods, and they make a great family meal.

One-pot meals are especially easy. Stews and stir-fries can be made simply, and provide leftovers for the following day. Examples include lamb stew with carrots and potatoes, fish soup with rice and vegetables, diced sausage or chunks of lamb with cabbage and onions and boiled potatoes, Asian stir-fry, or mild Indian or Thai curries. For a treat, try sausages or hot dogs with beans, served with sauerkraut or homemade cultured vegetables. (Use sausages and hot dogs that are made without fillers, artificial ingredients or preservatives.)

Asian markets often carry spring roll wrappers made of rice. These are hard when purchased but become pliable after soaking briefly in warm water, and have a chewy texture. You can fill them with lettuce, scrambled eggs, shrimp or chicken and serve them fresh with a dipping sauce, or fill them with seasoned meat or vegetables and bake them in the oven (these are crunchy and easy for children to pick up). Many spring roll wraps are made of wheat, so read the label carefully.

Lettuce wraps are also easy to make and fun to eat. Sauté ground meat with salt, pepper, garlic and other seasonings. Drain the fat, then serve it with tomatoes, onions, salad dressing, and salsa. Spoon the meat and vegetables into the middle of a large lettuce leaf and roll up from one end, tucking in the bottom halfway.

Desserts: Dessert has become an everyday occurrence instead of a treat for special occasions. The easiest solution is to simply skip dessert, or serve fresh fruit. "Real" desserts become a treat when they are limited to special occasions such as birthdays and holidays. For those times when you choose to serve a sweet other than fruit, there are some you can buy or make:

- Brownies served with fresh berries or bananas (from scratch or a gluten free mix)

- Rice Dream "ice cream" (avoid flavors with pieces of cookies or cake)

- Sorbet, widely available in many flavors, most of which are free of gluten and casein

- Candy-coated nuts (nuts tossed in a frying pan with oil and melted sugar)

- Homemade pumpkin custard, made with coconut milk

- Apples fried in margarine, sugar and cinnamon can be served with non-dairy "ice cream"

- Nut butter balls with ground nuts, honey and calcium powder or powdered milk substitute

Snacks: Divide appropriate foods into portions so that healthy snacks are readily available between meals. Using individual wax bags or small containers, portion out small servings of chips, cashews, rice cakes, or other appropriate snack foods. Small bags of carrots, celery, broccoli or cucumber sticks (put ½ teaspoon of water in each bag) can be stored in a refrigerator bin.

Keep fruit washed and easily accessible. Children usually like "finger food," so an apple corer that cuts wedges can be handy for apples, pears, and even cucumbers or zucchini.

For more ideas, see www.gfcf-diet.talkaboutcuringautism.org/gfcf-in-10-weeks.htm

MEASLES (See VACCINES)

MEAT

Meat is a complete protein, and a great source of amino acids. Although some children are sensitive to certain meats (beef is a common allergen), there are many choices, including chicken, turkey, beef, ostrich, buffalo, and lamb.

Some chicken feed contains trace amounts of arsenic, and Defeat Autism Now! doctors report that impaired detoxification is often a problem for our children. Consider buying free-range, organic chicken. Those who have seen the appalling living conditions for most chickens will tell you that it is worth the extra money.

Whenever possible, look for grass-fed, free-range beef. Studies show that grass-fed beef contains far less saturated and trans-fat, with significantly higher levels of healthy fats (omega-3) and essential fatty acids.[94] Grass-fed beef usually costs more, so some families address the problem by eating red meat less often, or using less meat and more vegetables in soups, stews or stir-fry. You will probably notice how much better grass-fed beef actually tastes, and if the studies are correct, the health benefits are well worth the difference in price.

MEDICATION (See also ANTIBIOTICS)

When medication is prescribed for your child, it's important to remember to ask the doctor for a preparation that is free of lactose, gluten, wheat starch, and other fillers. If this is not

---

[94] Dannenberger D, Nuernberg G, Scollan N, Schabbel W, Steinhart H, Ender K, Nuernberg K., "Effect of feeding systems on omega-3 fatty acids, conjugated linoleic acid and trans fatty acids in Australian beef cuts: potential impact on human health." *Asia Pac J Clin Nutr.* 2006;15(1):21-9.

possible, ask them to call in or send the prescription to a compounding pharmacy, which will prepare and send the medication to you, usually overnight (see COMPOUNDING PHARMACIES).

MELATONIN (See also SLEEP DISORDERS)

Melatonin is a naturally occurring hormone that regulates sleep and wakefulness. Over-the-counter melatonin supplements have long been the "drug of choice" for the parents of disabled children with sleep disorders, and recent studies have borne out their usefulness.[95] [96] [97] Significantly positive results from melatonin use were found in neurotypical children, as well as children with autism and ADHD. In one study of 107 autistic children taking 5 mg of melatonin at bedtime, sleep disorders were found to have completely resolved in 25% of the subjects. No increase in seizures or other side effects were found - even for those on psychotropic medications. This indicates that melatonin can be a safe and effective supplement for children with sleep disorders, especially when used in conjunction with "sleep hygiene" (strategies for promoting regular sleep).

> **NOTE:** When nutritional supplements like melatonin prove to have medical value, pharmaceutical companies will typically create and market "analogs" (synthetic versions of the drug which can be patented). It's important for consumers to be aware of this practice, and help protect the availability of the low-cost, natural versions of these supplements.

New research indicates that melatonin, a powerful antioxidant, is a versatile treatment for individuals under oxidative stress, partly due to its ability to neutralize free radicals.[98] It also appears to have other potential health benefits, such as regulating the immune system's response to pathologies such as infection, inflammation, autoimmunity and possibly cancer.[99] [100] See also OXIDATIVE STRESS.

MERCURY (See also VACCINES)

There has been increasing concern over the possible correlation between autism and mercury toxicity. Mercury (Hg in the periodic table) is one of the most toxic substances on earth. Since some people react poorly to levels of exposure that would be relatively safe for others, several chronic illnesses, including autism, are being blamed on increasing levels of mercury in the environment.

---

[95] Smits MG, Nagtegaal EE, van der Heijden J, Coenen AM, Kerkhof GA. "Melatonin for chronic sleep onset insomnia in children: a randomized placebo-controlled trial." *J Child Neurol.* 2001 Feb;16(2):86-92.

[96] Van der Heijden KB, Smits MG, Van Someren EJ, Ridderinkhof KR, Gunning WB. "Effect of melatonin on sleep, behavior, and cognition in ADHD and chronic sleep-onset insomnia." *J Am Acad Child Adolesc Psychiatry.* 2007 Feb;46(2):233-41.

[97] Andersen IM, Kaczmarska J, McGrew SG, Malow BA. "Melatonin for Insomnia in Children With Autism Spectrum Disorders." *J Child Neurol.* 2008 Jan 8.

[98] Kücükakin B, Gögenur I, Reiter RJ, Rosenberg J. "Oxidative Stress in Relation to Surgery: Is There a Role for the Antioxidant Melatonin?" *J Surg Res.* 2008 Jan 10.

[99] Reiter RJ, Tan DX, Manchester LC, Pilar Terron M, Flores LJ, Koppisepi S. "Medical implications of melatonin: receptor-mediated and receptor-independent actions." *Adv Med Sci.* 2007;52:11-28.

[100] Carrillo-Vico A, Guerrero JM, Lardone PJ, Reiter RJ. "A review of the multiple actions of melatonin on the immune system." *Endocrine.* 2005 Jul;27(2):189-200.

Many of the symptoms and patterns of immune dysfunction in the autism population are consistent with those of mercury toxicity, and evidence for a connection is increasing:

- A study of baby hair found that excretion of mercury among autistic infants was significantly reduced relative to controls.[101]

- A study examining the level of mercury, lead, and zinc in baby teeth found that children with autism had similar levels of lead and zinc as typically-developing controls, but more than twice the level of mercury.[102]

- Urinary porphyrin levels (a marker for heavy metal toxicity) are significantly higher in autistic children than in controls.[103]

- Proximity to environmental mercury release is a predictor of autism prevalence.[104]

Most importantly, children who undergo heavy metal detoxification (see CHELATION THERAPY) have been reported by their parents and physicians to demonstrate remarkable improvements in health and behavior.

Everyone is exposed to some toxins and toxic metals. Increased levels of these toxins in autistic children may be attributed to inherent problems with detoxification and oxidative stress, in addition to excessive exposure. It is unclear whether metal detoxification problems are the cause or effect of their overall health concerns, or part of a vicious cycle.

Mercury and Seafood: As long as there is reasonable doubt on this issue, it is prudent to avoid foods that are high in mercury. Fish and shellfish have a natural tendency to accumulate and store methylmercury, a highly toxic organic compound. Predatory species of fish, such as shark, swordfish, king mackerel, albacore tuna, and tilefish contain higher concentrations of mercury than others, since they absorb and retain most of the mercury burden of the smaller fish they consume. Because methylmercury has been found to be particularly toxic to unborn or young children, the U.S. EPA (Environmental Protection Agency) and FDA (Food and Drug Administration) have recommended that women who are pregnant (or plan to become pregnant within the next one or two years), as well as infants and young children, avoid eating more than 6 ounces (one average meal) of fish per week.

Although the FDA characterizes shrimp, catfish, pollock, salmon, and canned light tuna as low-mercury seafood, an article in the Chicago Tribune reported that tests have found that up to six percent of canned light tuna may contain high levels.[105] This varies by location and the

---

[101] Holmes AS, Blaxill MF, Haley BE. "Reduced levels of mercury in first baby haircuts of autistic children." *Int J Toxicol.* 2003 Jul-Aug;22(4):277-85.

[102] Adams JB, Romdalvik J, Ramanujam VM, Legator MS. "Mercury, lead, and zinc in baby teeth of children with autism versus controls." *J Toxicol Environ Health A.* 2007 Jun;70(12):1046-51.

[103] Nataf R, Skorupka C, Amet L, Lam A, Springbett A, Lathe R. "Porphyrinuria in childhood autistic disorder: implications for environmental toxicity." *Toxicol Appl Pharmacol.* 2006 Jul 15;214(2):99-108.

[104] Palmer RF, Blanchard S, Wood R. "Proximity to point sources of environmental mercury release as a predictor of autism prevalence." *Health Place.* 2008 Feb 12.

[105] "FDA tests show risk in tuna", Chicago Tribune, January 27, 2006.

122

origin of the fish. The Monterey Bay Aquarium has an excellent seafood guide that shows which fish are safe in different parts of the country. It also has downloadable regional "pocket" guides.[106] More information can be found at www.gotmercury.org, including an online calculator that can help gauge your mercury intake from seafood.

*Note: only wild caught Alaskan salmon is low in mercury. Farm raised salmon should be avoided.

Mercury and Dairy: It appears that a milk-based diet may also play a major role in the inability of mammals to excrete mercury, raising the question of whether dairy foods could be partially responsible for the onset of autism. Studies have shown that three different diets fed to adult female mice (high protein synthetic diet; standard rat chow diet; milk diet) dramatically changed the rate of fecal excretion of mercury. The mice on the milk diet had significantly slower excretion of mercury than those on the other diets.[107]

METABOLIC DISORDERS (See RELATED AND CO-EXISTING DISORDERS)

METALLOTHIONEIN

Metallothioneins are polypeptides thought to help regulate the proper function of essential elements zinc and copper, and to neutralize the harmful effects of toxic elements such as mercury. The Pfeiffer Treatment Center, after comprehensive testing of a large number of autism spectrum patients, has determined that most exhibit evidence of a metallothionein (MT) dysfunction, which would result in some of the classic features of autism. They propose that autism results from a defect in MT functioning, followed by an environmental insult. After adjusting the biochemistry of these patients using nutritional supplements, they report certain improvements. See THE PFEIFFER CENTER for more information.

METHYLATION (See also OXIDATIVE STRESS)

Methylation is the process of attaching compounds called "methyl groups" to other chemicals in the body, in order to regulate them. Methylation is necessary for several biochemical functions, including the elimination of metals from the body (see DETOXIFICATION). Impaired methylation can lead to oxidative stress, which is the harmful condition that occurs when the body has an excess of free radicals, a decrease in antioxidant levels, or both. A number of children on the autism spectrum have been found to have impaired methylation.

MIGRAINES

Research on headaches has shown that many migraines are triggered by hyper-sensitivities, often to foods. The most common offenders are dairy products, wheat, eggs, soy, corn, citrus, caffeine, beef, yeast and red wine. Highly refined foods, particularly those containing additives and preservatives such as MSG, are also common migraine triggers. Elimination diets have been used successfully to determine migraine triggers, and many headaches can be avoided if these trigger foods are removed from the diet.

---

[106] Go to www.mbayaq.org/cr/seafoodwatch.asp to learn which fish are safe in your area, and to download a printable pocket guide.

[107] Rowland, I.R., Robinson, R.D. and Doherty, R.A. "Effects of Diet on Mercury Metabolism and Excretion in Mice Given Methylmercury: Role of Gut Flora." *Archives of Environmental Health* V39, 401-408, 1984.

MILK AND DAIRY

Milk consists of 87.4% water, 3.5% protein, and between zero and 3.7% fat. We all grew up with the idea that milk is a healthy food, and are naturally reluctant to take it out of our children's diets. But is it really good for everybody?

All mammal mothers feed their infants milk, but humans are the only mammal that ingests the milk of an unrelated species, and continues to do so long after weaning. This may be why dairy is one of the eight foods to which those with food allergies most frequently react[108] (see ALLERGIES & INTOLERANCES).

Because mammals have not evolved to continue drinking milk past weaning, many adults do not produce enough lactase (the enzyme that digests the milk sugar lactose) to consume dairy products without experiencing gastrointestinal discomfort. Most mammals in the world feed exclusively on mother's milk only until their birth weight has tripled; in humans, this occurs at approximately one year of age. At that time, the decrease in the enzyme lactase begins. By the age of five, many people cannot drink milk or eat dairy products without some degree of intestinal discomfort. In some cultures the population is nearly 100% lactose intolerant, and everywhere this inability to digest milk sugar is the most common cause of diet-related intestinal symptoms.

Symptoms of lactose intolerance include bloating, pain, gas and/or diarrhea within a couple of hours of eating dairy. Although lactase enzymes can be helpful, the overall feeling of discomfort motivates most lactose-intolerant people to avoid it altogether.

Many children react to milk proteins such as casein or whey from an early age. For others, the problems start when a faulty digestive system allows partially digested proteins to cross the gut wall (see LEAKY GUT). Those children prone to sinus and ear infections may need to avoid milk because it makes mucus thicker and harder to drain.

Even if a child has no problems with the sugars or peptides found in milk, there are ample reasons to reconsider its use. The vast majority of dairy cows in this country are fed growth hormones to increase production. Although the FDA and Monsanto (manufacturer of the hormones) assert that the milk is safe, there may still be reason for concern. Cows given hormones have a higher rate of infections such as mastitis, which means that in addition to hormones, the milk will inevitably contain pus and traces of the antibiotics used to treat the infected cows.[109] Another problem with milk includes Juvenile (type I) diabetes. This lifelong, life-threatening disease strikes one in every 500 children, and more than 90 studies have now implicated milk as a major cause. A review concluded that cow's milk exposure could increase the risk by 1.5 times.[110] One theory for this is that children sensitive to bovine albumen produce antibodies that also attack insulin-producing cells in the pancreas.

---

[108] According to the Food Allergy & Anaphylaxis Network, eight foods account for 90% of all food allergies. These include milk, egg, peanut, tree nuts (walnuts, cashew etc), fish, shellfish, soy and wheat.

[109] *RACHEL'S Hazardous Waste News* #381 (1994) Environmental Research Foundation Annapolis, MD 21403.

[110] HC Gerstein, "Cow's milk exposure and type I diabetes mellitus. A critical overview of the clinical literature." *Diabetes Care,* Vol 17, Issue 1 13-19.

Although most American children get their required calcium and vitamin D from milk, there are many other sources for these vital nutrients. Therefore, pediatricians who insist that milk is necessary for good health are misinformed. Many perfectly healthy children do very well without it. In fact, many cultures consider cow's milk unfit for human consumption. Cows have evolved to produce milk that is most beneficial to its intended recipients: calves. The milk of every type of mammal has striking differences in composition, with variation in the contents of fats, protein, sugar and minerals. Each evolves to provide optimum nutrition to the young of its own species.

Although milk is rich in calcium, it may not be the best way to obtain this mineral. Cow's milk contains 1200 mg of calcium per quart, compared to 300 mg per quart of human milk. Despite this difference, studies have shown that nursing infants absorb more calcium than those fed cow's milk based formulas.[111] This seems to be due to the fact that cow's milk is much richer in phosphorus, a mineral that can combine with calcium in the intestines and prevent its absorption. (This is another reason to avoid drinking soda pop, which is extremely high in phosphorus.) Finally, research has shown that cow's milk protein intolerance (CMPI) is associated with a very high frequency of multiple food intolerance and allergic diseases.[112]

We all know that growing bones and teeth need calcium, but most of us have no idea where else to get these important minerals. Green vegetables such as kale, collards and bok choy are excellent sources of calcium, with the added benefit of being low in oxalates (spinach, though high in calcium, should be avoided if oxalates are a problem). Certain fish, like salmon and perch, are also good sources of calcium, but take care to buy fish that is not high in mercury or other environmental toxins. A mere tablespoon of molasses contains 172 mg of calcium (as well as iron), so if yeast is not a big problem it is a good choice for sweetening baked goods. Some nuts, beans, and seeds (like sesame seeds) are rich in calcium, but they should be ground for best absorption. Calcium fortified orange juice is equivalent to a glass of milk, although it is very high in fructose (fruit sugar). Finally, if a child will not eat enough non-dairy sources of calcium, there are many good supplements available (see SUPPLEMENTS). Because vitamin D is required to properly absorb calcium, a good supplement will contain both.

With all these problems, why would anyone want to feed their children dairy products? First, it is hard to fight back years of thinking that milk is "the perfect food." The necessity of milk is perpetuated by every advertising medium currently in use, so it is certainly understandable that most parents believe that it is their duty to feed their children as much cow's milk as possible. Despite all the celebrities who sport "milk mustaches," dairy is not necessary for good nutrition, and can actually be harmful for some children.

How to Avoid Dairy: Removing dairy from the diet is not as difficult as it sounds, but you need to understand a few basic principles. First of all, you must remove *all* sources of dairy. This includes obvious sources such as butter, cheese, cream cheese and sour cream, but it also includes some "hidden" sources. There are several packaged foods that surprisingly contain some form of milk protein, such as canned fish and bread. Even soy and rice cheeses generally contain some form of casein or sodium caseinate. It is imperative that you learn to read and understand labels, and that you continue to check them each time you buy a food. Food

---

[111] Oski, Frank A, MD 1996 *Don't Drink Your Milk*. Teacher Services, Inc.

[112] Iacono G, Cavataio F, Montalto G, Soresi M, Notarbartolo A, Carroccio A. "Persistent cow's milk protein intolerance in infants: the changing faces of the same disease." *Clin Exp Allergy* 1998 Jul;28(7):817-23.

manufacturers often switch out ingredients due to price or availability, so a once-trusted item must be considered suspect until you have double-checked the ingredients. In many cases, food manufacturers are allowed to use up old food labels even if minor changes have been made in the ingredients. If you think you see a reaction to a food that formerly produced no problem, call the company to verify that the ingredients listed are indeed correct. If not, you can inform them that you will no longer be able to use the product, and that you will be sharing this information with others who have the same dietary requirements. Customer feedback will sometimes persuade them to revert to an older recipe.

Foods to Avoid (always contain dairy):

Cheese (all types)	Evaporated milk	Cream
Butter	Condensed milk	Sour cream
Skim milk	Milk chocolate	Cottage cheese
Whole milk	Yogurt	Goat's milk
Buttermilk	Kefir	Sheep's milk
Powdered milk	Ice cream/Ice milk	

Foods to Be Wary Of (often contain dairy):

Baked goods (even if GF)	Candies	Mashed potatoes
Bologna	Cakes/cake mix	Nougat/caramel/toffee
Broth (canned)	Chewing gum	Pudding/custard mixes
Candy	Chicken broth	Scrambled eggs
Canned foods	Creamed vegetables	Soy cheese
Salad dressings	Margarine/buttery spreads	Tuna fish (canned)

Ingredients to Avoid:

Albumin*	Lactalbumin	Milk Solids
Butter oil	Lactic Acid	Rennet
Casein/Caseinates	Lactoglobulins	Whey
Lactose	Milk Protein	

*May contain milk

Keep in mind that "non-dairy" does not mean milk-free. It is a term the dairy industry invented to indicate less than .5% milk by weight, which could mean fully as much casein as whole milk.

MILK ALTERNATIVES

Most parents like to use a milk substitute for cooking, baking and drinking, and most of our children expect or demand something white in a bottle, sippy cup or glass. The following can be found in gluten and dairy free varieties. If you have other restrictions, some may not be acceptable.

Rice Milk: Widely available, rice milk can be used as a drink or for cooking or baking. It is acceptable on most gluten free diets, but it's usually not a first choice for our population. Rice milk is relatively high in sugar, not recommended when restricting carbohydrates, and the unsweetened types tend to be unpalatable for drinking. Rice Dream™ is usually available at the supermarket, but this brand of rice milk is processed with barley enzymes, so there is some concern over whether it will cause a reaction in individuals highly sensitive to gluten. Rice Milk can be made at home by finely blending cooked rice and water. It is not appropriate for use with monosaccharide diets such as the SCD™.

Nut Milk: Almond and other types of nut milk are available at health food stores and many grocery stores, and are good for cereals, smoothies, hot drinks, baking, and yogurt making. Some brands may have added maltodextrin (often wheat or barley derived) so read labels carefully. Unsweetened varieties are available for use with restricted carbohydrate diets. Nut milk can be used for monosaccharide diets such as the SCD™, but only if it is unsweetened and contains no additives - unfortunately, most commercially available brands do contain soy and/or carageenan. Therefore, many families prefer to make nut milk and nut yogurt themselves (see NUT MILK, YOGURT for recipes).

Potato Milk: In the 1990's, an American company called Vance's Foods developed a product called DariFree™, hoping fill the need for a milk alternative without rice or soy. Since then, potato milk has been used successfully by many families due to its pleasant taste and low sugar content, visual resemblance to milk, vitamin, mineral and calcium content, and high tolerability. It has a creamy, milk-like color and texture due to the addition of an inert mineral used as a coloring agent (see TITANIUM DIOXIDE), so you may notice that your child's stools are lighter in color when using this product.

Because it contains starch, potato milk is not suitable for the Specific Carbohydrate Diet™. DariFree™ is available by mail-order: 1-800-497-4834, or at www.vancesfoods.com/darifree.htm. In Canada, English Bay Dairy-Free™ (www.englishbaydairyfree.com) is a comparable product, although not vitamin-enriched. Unlike regular milk, potato milk does not contain fat, which small children need for proper development, so be sure that your child is getting enough healthy fats, such as olive oil, fish oil, and flax seed oil.

Coconut Milk: Coconut milk is widely available, and is delicious in smoothies, puddings, sauces, and curries. It can be diluted to reduce the fat content, and light versions are available. Unlike many milk substitutes, it is not fortified with vitamins and minerals. If you make your own coconut milk you can use the leftover coconut meat in yogurt, puddings or shakes, or to thicken sauces. If unsweetened, it should be acceptable on most restricted carbohydrate diets.

Soy Milk: Although widely available, soy milk is generally not a good option. Unfortunately, many children on special diets are intolerant to soy (for an explanation, see SOY). Soy milk is not appropriate for use with monosaccharide diets such as the SCD™.

Goat, sheep, and other types of animal milk: Many people have heard that goat milk is a good substitute for cow's milk. There is some truth to this: some types of milk protein may be better tolerated than others, and lactose levels may vary between different types. But goat milk is not an appropriate milk substitute for children with IgE-mediated cow's milk allergy,[113] and those sensitive to casein will have problems with any kind of mammalian milk – possibly even human breastmilk. Since cow's milk has a fairly high A1 betacasein content, opioid effects might be much more noticeable than with other types, but casomorphin will still be present in those consuming goat's milk, human milk, mare's milk, etc.[114]

According to Dr. Kalle Reichelt, "Ovine (goat) milk contains the exact sequence for casomorphine 1-8 as cow's milk. It is however, in a different position in the casein chain and with different neighbors. It is conceivable that it may be split in different ways, but I have seen no evidence that this is so."[115]

> *"If your kids are reactive to cow milk and goat milk, you want to be really careful with any 'mammal milk'. I did a trial of sheep's milk and water buffalo yogurt - unfortunately, I didn't exactly get the effect I was looking for. I decided that my boys most likely do not tolerate any dairy that comes from a mammal (which would certainly explain their issues while I was breastfeeding them)."* -Petra Smit

There is some concern that even after some time on a GF/CF diet, each dietary infringement raises the sensitivity of the opioid receptor sites, and it is theorized that this could allow these children to react adversely to all kinds of opioid exposures, including the body's natural endorphins. For that reason, exposures to milk and gluten should probably be limited to those which are accidental, not deliberate.*

We have no way of knowing when the gut is fully healed, which children can begin to tolerate dairy, and which cannot. Those with a milk allergy (IgE or IgG) should continue to avoid it altogether. It is unclear whether dairy would be safe for every child after some period of time, or whether there are some children for whom it will never be safe. Hopefully, future research will clarify this issue.

For more information on dairy-free living, there's a very good book called *Raising Your Child Without Milk* by Jane Zukin.

NOTE: Do not give milk products in any form to children with a known milk allergy.

MILK - "A2"™

Different strains of dairy cattle produce milk containing predominantly one of two types of casein, either A1 or A2 beta casein. Friesian cows produce mostly A1 milk while Jersey and Guernseys produce milk with mostly A2 beta casein. Most dairy herds have a mix of breeds and milk is also combined during bottling, so most milk contains both forms of beta casein.

---

[113] Bellioni-Buscinco B. Allergenicity of goat's milk in children with cow milk allergy. *J Allergy Clin Immunol.* 1999 Jun;103(6): 1191-4.

[114] Marletta, D., Bordonaro, S., Guastella, A. M., Falagiani, P., Crimi, N., D'Urso, G. Goat milk with different S2-casein content: analysis of allergenic potency by REAST-inhibition assay. *Small Ruminant Research*, 2004.

[115] Pers. comm.

Dr Keith Woodford, Professor of Farm Management at Lincoln University in New Zealand, has studied the connection between consumption of A1 milk and serious health conditions. According to Woodford, "Wherever we have a country that has high intake per capita of A1 milk... we have high levels of type 1 diabetes and heart disease. Wherever the milk is low in the A1 beta casein, high in the A2 beta casein we have low level of the type 1 diabetes."

The cows for A2 milk must be specially bred and a number of farmers in Australia have converted their herds to produce this virtually pure A2 milk. In 2002, a New Zealand businessman and a research scientist started the A2 Corporation (www. a2corporation.com), using DNA testing to create herds of cattle that produce A2 Milk™ only. They claimed that their Guernsey, Jersey or Friesian Holstein variety of cows produce the A2 protein that humans have been drinking safely for thousands of years, and that the newer A1 protein from other breeds is responsible for increased rates of heart disease, diabetes, chronic illness, and autism.

While critics argue that there is not enough evidence to support the health claims of A2 Milk™, some dairies in New Zealand have begun using DNA testing kits purchased from the A2 Corporation to determine which cows produce this protein, and since April 2003, have been marketing milk that contains only 0.1% A1 beta-casein. Consumers of this milk claim health benefits, including reduced tantrums in autistic children, but dairy industry spokesmen are pressuring health authorities to investigate these claims and perhaps even limit the distribution of this milk. Clinical trials will be needed to determine whether A1-free milk can reduce the risk of diabetes and heart disease. Although it may be slightly better tolerated by some than regular milk, A2 milk is not recommended for those who are allergic or sensitive to casein.

At this time the product is not available in North America.

MILK, FROM GOATS AND OTHER MAMMALS (See MILK ALTERNATIVES)

MILK, RAW (See also BUTTER, RAW)

Dr. Joseph Mercola, a well-publicized doctor of alternative medicine, believes that the pasteurization process turns casein into a dangerous molecule that can further precipitate brain injury in autism. He writes: "Many autistic children are cautioned to avoid milk, however they actually need to avoid pasteurized milk. Raw milk is fine for autism."[116]

Based on the limited amount of data available at this time, one must respectfully question whether it is safe to say that "raw milk is fine for autism." That would be like saying "peanuts are fine for autism." Autism is not a single entity, and one size treatment does not fit all. Some of our children may never be able to tolerate even a trace of dairy, in any form.

If we assume that raw milk products will be tolerated by some, the question that arises is: what are the supposed benefits of raw milk? What does raw milk provide that pasteurized milk, or milk avoidance, does not?

Claims are made that pasteurizing milk destroys vitamin B12 and B6, kills beneficial bacteria and promotes pathogens. Raw milk left out will simply sour, while pasteurized milk will rot without the beneficial bacteria to keep putrefactive bacteria under control.

---

[116] www.mercola.com

Farmers who produce raw milk tend to feed their cows grass instead of grain, and this leads to a higher content of conjugated linolenic acids (CLA), beta carotene and retinol, and lower cholesterol content in the milk.

In addition, some sources indicate that the butyric and rumenic acids in milk are anticarcinogenic, and that mid to short length fatty acids are antihypertensive. Proponents of raw milk believe that raw milk and butter helps gut healing by creating a nesting ground for beneficial bacteria in the GI tract, when given in combination with a rich source of these bacteria.

The naturally occurring enzymes in raw milk, such as lipase and proteinase, may also help with digestion and reduce symptoms in intolerant individuals. Fermentation (culturing into yogurt or kefir) and storage of raw milk may lead to partial degradation of whey and casein proteins.

Over the years, we have heard many reports by those on a GF/CF diet trying dairy products in various forms, and these reports have been, unfortunately, mostly negative. Of course, the outcomes might have been different with raw milk, or with a healthy gut ecology. Effects of dairy can be delayed and diffuse, so care is needed if you decide to test it. Although bacterial infections from unpasteurized milk are quite rare, if you decide to try raw dairy products be sure to use only products from an established dairy that you know and trust. Reputable dairy farmers should be willing to provide information on the testing of their herd and products for pathogens. Most testing is performed weekly.

For information on raw milk, visit www.realmilk.com. For a well-documented argument in favor of the sale of raw milk by the Natural Milk Coalition of Canada, visit: www.magma.ca/~ca/rawmilk/submission.htm.

MILK SUBSTITUTES (See MILK ALTERNATIVES)

MILK, BREASTMILK (See BREASTFEEDING)

MILK, FOR INFANTS (See INFANT FORMULA)

MILLET

Until recently, millet was used mostly as birdseed in the United States, but it is actually a very old grain used in much of the world. It is versatile and gluten free, and can be used as a side dish, a porridge or ground into flour. Millet flour has a slightly bitter flavor, so it is frequently blended with other types of flour when used in baking.

MOLD, MOLDY FOODS

Some children who are battling yeast have a sensitivity to mold, and must avoid moldy foods. Packaged foods, especially processed meats, may contain mold built up during drying, smoking or curing. Vinegar, brine pickles and soy sauce (even if it is gluten free) may be problematic. So may ground nuts such as peanuts. Certain fruits (such as grapes) and fruit juices can also be moldy; some doctors advise limiting fruits to one peeled fruit per day when fighting a yeast overgrowth.

MONOSACCHARIDES

Monosaccharides are the simplest form of carbohydrate, consisting of a single molecule of sugar. Examples include glucose, fructose, galactose and ribose. *Disaccharides* (such as sucrose or table sugar) are made of two monosaccharides, and *polysaccharides* are made of more than two monosaccharides.

MONOSODIUM GLUTAMATE (MSG)

MSG is a food additive and "flavor enhancer," stimulating certain receptors in the taste buds to increase savory (meaty) flavors. Unlike salt, which can make food taste better, MSG makes *you* "taste" better.

Glutamate is an amino acid found naturally in the body and in protein-containing foods, such as cheese, milk, meat, peas, and mushrooms. Glutamate is necessary for nerve function, and in its natural form, is not harmful unless excessive amounts arc produced.

Monosodium glutamate, or "free glutamic acid" may be a cause for concern, however. Glutamic acid "freed" from protein by a manufacturing process, or even by certain types of fermentation, can cause adverse reactions in MSG-sensitive people. The MSG industry has issued statements indicating that MSG is no more harmful than the naturally-occuring glutamates in foods like fresh tomatoes. This is misleading, however. Processed foods like tomato paste and some aged cheeses may contain free glutamic acid, but a fresh tomato contains little or none.

In addition, hydrolyzed proteins (protein hydrolysates), often contain free glutamic acid, and are used to enhance the flavor of canned vegetables, soups, and processed meats. For this reason, FDA considers foods whose labels say "No MSG" or "No Added MSG" to be misleading if the food contains ingredients that are sources of free glutamates, such as hydrolyzed protein. Check ingredient labels for hydrolyzed vegetable proteins, hydrolyzed yeast, soy extracts, and "natural flavorings."

In many countries the ingredient might be called MSG or glutamate, but it is often listed simply as "flavor enhancer." In the EU additive code, MSG is identified as "E621." In the United States, under current FDA regulations, when MSG is added to a food, it must be identified as "monosodium glutamate" in the label's ingredient list.

In 1994, the FDA received a citizen's petition requesting changes in labeling requirements for foods that contain MSG or related substances. The petition asked for mandatory listing of MSG as an ingredient on labels of manufactured and processed foods that contain manufactured free glutamic acid. It further asked that the amount of free glutamic acid or MSG in such products be stated on the label, along with a warning that MSG may be harmful to certain groups of people. FDA has not yet taken action on the petition.

The FDA classifies MSG as a "generally recognized as safe" substance at "current levels of use" but acknowledged that "reactions of brief duration" might occur in some people. However, some studies found that certain individuals do have allergies and/or sensitivities to MSG, reported to cause a wide variety of symptoms such as migraines, nausea, digestive upsets, drowsiness, heart palpitations, mood swings, and seizures. Sometimes this is referred to as "Chinese restaurant syndrome," since MSG is commonly used in Asian foods.

In 1995 the FDA was presented with a comprehensive report reviewing all available scientific data. Among the report's key findings:

"An unknown percentage of the population may react to MSG and develop MSG symptom

complex, a condition characterized by one or more of the following symptoms: burning sensation in the back of the neck, forearms and chest, numbness in the back of the neck, radiating to the arms and back, tingling, warmth and weakness in the face, temples, upper back, neck and arms, facial pressure or tightness, chest pain, headache, nausea, rapid heartbeat, weak pulse, violent dreams, difficulty breathing in MSG-intolerant people with asthma, drowsiness, and weakness.

In otherwise healthy MSG-intolerant people, the MSG symptom complex tends to occur within one hour after eating 3 grams or more of MSG on an empty stomach or without other food. (A typical serving of glutamate-treated food contains less than 0.5 grams of MSG.) A reaction is most likely if the MSG is eaten in a large quantity, or in a liquid, such as a clear soup."

For those who are suffering from what they believe to be an MSG reaction, natural remedies that have been suggested include ibuprofen, magnesium, vitamin B6, gingko biloba, and CoQ-10. The amino acid taurine is said to be especially useful for neutralizing the negative effects of glutamate, and a 2006 study found that vitamin A relieved the oxidative stress induced by MSG in rats.[117]

MSG (See MONOSODIUM GLUTAMATE)

MULTIPLE FOOD SENSITIVITIES

The primary theory about why some people have multiple food sensitivities is that partially digested foods are leaking from the gut into bloodstream (see LEAKY GUT), thus triggering an immune reaction and sensitivity to those foods. So why is it that some of our children become so sensitive *after* removing problem foods?

"As the worst food offenders are removed you become aware of the minor offenders," says Arthur Krigsman, pediatric gastroenterologist. "It's like...you become more aware of the pickpockets when all of the murderers are in jail. Many, if not most foods, are going to cause a reaction, to different extents, as long as the tissue is sensitive and inflamed, and the gut immunity is compromised. Digestive enzymes are produced by intestinal villi. If they are damaged by disease or inflammation, the gut can't produce the enzymes it needs to digest foods. This may be why taking enzyme tablets could be useful in partially breaking down these foods that are triggering an immune response (see DIGESTIVE ENZYME TABLETS). In addition, bowel inflammation may result in malabsorption and rapid transit of foods through the bowel, both of which can reduce the amount of calories and nutrients absorbed."

Practically speaking, you can't remove all of the foods that cause problems. The stools will still tend to be abnormal, and the child's behavior is not going to be in top form. Our parents often report that their child is at his very best during the bowel prep for a colonoscopy, when restricted to clear liquids for 24 hours prior to the procedure."

According to Dr. Krigsman, the first step is to address any underlying gastrointestinal illness. Meanwhile, utilize the foods that elicit the smallest reaction, while taking great pains to ensure that the restrictions do not result in nutritional deprivation. He emphasizes that it is critical for these children to undertake these diets under the care of a certified nutritionist and to supplement when necessary for missing vitamins and minerals. See BOWEL DISEASE AND AUTISM, and COLONOSCOPY.

---

[117] Onyema OO, Farombi EO, Emerole GO, Ukoha AI, Onyeze GO. "Effect of vitamin E on monosodium glutamate induced hepatotoxicity and oxidative stress in rats." *Indian J Biochem Biophys.* 2006 Feb;43(1):20-4.

MULTIPLE SCLEROSIS (MS) (See RELATED AND/OR CO-EXISTING DISORDERS)

NAET®

NAET® stands for Nambudripad's Allergy Elimination Technique (www.naet.com). It is an allergy treatment program developed by Dr. Devi S. Nambudripad in 1983. Nambudripad claims that food intolerances can be cured, through "a blend of selective energy balancing, testing and treatment procedures from acupuncture/acupressure, allopathy, chiropractic, nutritional, and kinesiological disciplines of medicine." Foods are tested with a strength test, using the premise that if you become weakened while holding the food, you have an allergy or intolerance to it. According to practitioners, treatment can be achieved even through another person who is touching the subject and the food.

Parents who have written to us about their experience with NAET are divided between those who claim the technique did help with seasonal or food allergies, and those who believe the treatment was of no benefit at all.

Be wary of claims that this technique will "cure" your child, or allow him to successfully go off of a GF/CF diet without the return of autistic symptoms. And letters like the one we received below should also caution you to ask about the total cost of such a treatment before beginning.

> *"We went GF/CF the day that my son Tommy was diagnosed with autism, which eliminated his chronic diarrhea and tantrums. I also signed up for NAET with a chiropractor that specializes in "curing the food allergies found in the autistic child." The treatments were not covered by my insurance. The first consultation cost $160 and every follow up treatment an additional $60. We treated wheat, dairy, corn, eggs, soy, nuts, pollen, sugar, bananas, dust, mold, citrus, preservatives and television radiation before I finally called a "time out." After a month of going back every 3 days, my bill had reached the $1,000 mark. To top it off, my son still showed allergic symptoms to all of the foods we had supposedly treated!*
>
> *The chiropractor then told me that sometimes allergies are not eliminated if you don't follow the long list of eliminations that need to be done in order…even if your child is not showing an allergy to them. That long list meant a $60.00 payment for each item, whether Tommy was allergic to it or not." -Leslie Kohler, reprinted from The ANDI News*

"NATURAL FLAVORINGS"

Unfortunately, it is impossible to know what "natural flavor" in a list of product ingredients actually means. Federal regulations allow food manufacturers to call almost *anything* a natural flavor. Often, natural flavors are harmless, and contain no hidden gluten or casein. You cannot be sure, however, and if you are dealing with food allergies or other sensitivities, a "natural flavor" could lead to a serious dietary infraction. So beware of items with this imprecise label, and be sure to check with manufacturer for specific ingredients. If the person answering the phone can't answer the question, ask to speak with a supervisor or avoid the food. To find out what you can do to make better labeling a requirement, contact the Vegetarian Legal Action Network at www.enviroweb.org/vlan.

NIGHTSHADES (Solanum)

Tomatoes, potatoes, peppers, eggplants, and tobacco are from the nightshade family, They are of concern because they contain a chemical alkaloid called solanine, which is suspected of

 causing inflammation in some people. Parents of allergic children sometimes report that nightshades can result in a stuffy nose, headache or other physical discomfort. Unless your autistic child is high-functioning enough to describe his symptoms, it may be difficult to tell whether he has a problem with these foods. If you suspect a nightshade allergy, remove them for two weeks. Then serve a dish rich in tomatoes, eggplant, and peppers (which seem to cause the most discomfort). A typical reaction will appear in the next 1-4 days, manifesting as fatigue, brain fog, and frequently, joint pain and stiffness or behavioral problems. Some claim that nightshade foods will fuel protozoa and other harmful parasites, but the main reason why some people try to avoid them is because of allergy or intolerance. It has been suggested that nightshades may also be a problem for those with fibromyalgia or joint pain.

NOURISHING TRADITIONS (See also FATS & OILS, WESTON A. PRICE)

Nourishing Traditions[118] is described as "a full-spectrum nutritional cookbook with a startling message: animal fats and cholesterol are vital factors in the human diet, necessary for reproduction and normal growth, proper function of the brain and nervous system, protection from disease and optimum energy levels." This book includes information on how to prepare grains, and the health benefits of bone broths and enzyme-rich lacto-fermented foods. Author Sally Fallon is the President and Treasurer of the Weston A. Price Foundation.

NUTS (See also PEANUTS)

When tolerated, nuts are a great food, providing fats, fiber, and protein. Unfortunately, many of our children can't eat nuts because of allergies or their high oxalate content. Ground nuts often contain mold. For those with poor digestion, nuts may be difficult to digest.

Nuts are among the most common allergens, but if your child is allergic to peanuts, which are actually a legume, ask your doctor to test for a tolerance to tree nuts, such as almonds, brazil nuts, cashews, hazelnuts, hickory nuts, macadamia nuts, pecans, pine nuts, pistachios and walnuts.

Tree nuts may also be better tolerated by those with a mold allergy: foods growing on the ground, such as peanuts, are more likely to contain mold. Pistachios and macadamia nuts are sometimes more easily tolerated by those with food sensitivities.

NOTE: if there is a known allergy to one kind of nut or legume, do not experiment with giving your child other nuts unless under the supervision of a physician (see ANAPHYLAXIS).

Finely ground almonds (and other nuts) can be used in baking cakes and cookies instead of flour: grind your own nut flour, or purchase it from health food stores or online companies such as www.nuts4you.com or www.kingarthurflour.com.

When tolerated, almonds may be the key for those with constipation. If they are problematic for those with loose stools, try blanching the almonds (place in boiling water for 1 minute, then drain), and removing the brown coating before eating. Soaking raw nuts for twelve hours prior to cooking will also make them easier to digest, and thus more nutritious.

For variety, and to reduce the risk of developing a new allergy, rotate nut butters made from a

---

[118] Fallon, Sally with Mary G. Enig, PhD (1991, 2001). *Nourishing Traditions: The Cookbook that Challenges Politically Correct Nutrition and the Diet Dictocrats.* New Trends: Washington, D.C.

variety of nuts and seeds which are known to be safe for your child.

NUT MILK & NUT YOGURT (See also MILK ALTERNATIVES, PROBIOTICS)

Nut milk and nut yogurt are alternatives to dairy-based milk and yogurt. Both are easy and inexpensive to make at home, and taste good. They can be made from a variety of nuts, and you can experiment with adding your favorite sweetener and flavorings. Nut yogurt contains far more beneficial bacteria than you can get from a capsule, and has a mild, pleasant flavor.

To make nut milk, soak nuts overnight. Combine in a blender with cold water (1 part soaked nuts and 2 parts water), at low and then high speed for 10 to 15 seconds. Then strain and serve.* If you want to, you can sweeten the milk with anything appropriate for your family's diet (e.g. rice syrup, vegetable glycerin, ground dates, stevia or honey). Some nuts have a slight sweetness on their own, and the addition of fruits for a smoothie may add all the flavor and sweetening needed. The residual nuts can be saved and used in muffins or as a filler in meatballs or meatloaves. If unsweetened, or sweetened with honey, nut milk is perfect for monosaccharide diets such as the SCD™.

The general principles for making nut yogurt are as follows: Puree two cups nuts with four cups of hot water (macadamia nuts work well). Strain through a fine sieve* and cool to 110° F, then stir in yogurt starter (you can easily find it online). Keep it in the yogurt maker for about 24 hours. It will separate somewhat, but don't throw away the liquid - it is rich in probiotics. You can drink it, or stir it back in to make a yogurt smoothie. The leftover nut solids can be used in place of grated coconut in cookies and puddings. You can also find an excellent recipe for nut yogurt online, at www.pecanbread.com/recipes/almondyogurt.html.

Nut milk and yogurt are not appropriate for the Low Oxalate Diet, since they contain a great deal of soluble oxalate.

*Note: A "nut milk bag" makes it easy to squeeze out the liquid when making nut milk and nut yogurt. You can order one at www.purejoyplanet.com.

NUTRASWEET® (See ASPARTAME)

NUTRITION (See also PICKINESS AND FOOD ADDICTION, SUPPLEMENTS)

Some critics have claimed that "gluten free diets are nutritionally unsound," or "gluten free diets contain too many starches and sugars." A gluten free diet is a diet free of gluten, and that's all it is. When you additionally remove corn, it's still a gluten free diet. When you additionally remove complex sugars, it's still a gluten free diet. If your child eats nothing but rice cakes and potato chips, or nothing but lamb and broccoli, he is on a gluten free diet. The "SCD™" is a type of gluten free diet, and so is the "BED."

Unfortunately, there *are* a lot of autistic children walking around on a "potato chip and rice cake diet." This is usually the result of extreme pickiness, multiple food sensitivities or sensory issues. It may be understandable, but as caregivers, it is our job to make sure our children are getting the nutrients they need. Good nutrition is necessary for health. And it is possible to make sure your child gets it, even if it involves sensory integration therapy, creative cooking or sometimes, a little "tough love."

In the chart on the following page, you can get an idea about why today's children are growing up with a different nutritional package than their parents' (chart reprinted by permission from the Feingold Association).

What the child growing up in the U.S. in the 1940's got:	What the child growing up in the U.S. today gets:
White toothpaste	Multi-colored toothpaste, perhaps with sparkles
Oatmeal	Sea Treasures Instant Oatmeal (turns milk blue)
Corn flakes	Fruity Pebbles™
Toast & butter, jam	Pop Tarts™
Cocoa made with natural ingredients	Cocoa made with artificial flavoring, & some with dyes.
Whipped cream	Cool Whip™
No vitamins (or perhaps cod liver oil)	Flintstone vitamins™ with coloring & flavoring
White powder or bad-tasting liquid medicine	Bright pink, bubble-gum flavored chewable or liquid medicine
Sample school lunch: Meat loaf, freshly made mashed potatoes, vegetable. Milk, cupcake made from scratch.	Sample school lunch: Highly processed foods loaded with synthetic additives, no vegetable. Chocolate milk with artificial flavor.
Sample school beverage: Water from the drinking fountain	Sample school beverage: Soft drink with artificial color, flavor, caffeine, aspartame, etc.
Candy in the classroom a few times a year at class parties.	Candy (with synthetic additives) given frequently.

Most of us would never allow a "typical" child to live on a diet of flavored yogurt, gummy bears, and pretzels. And most of us were sent to bed without supper once or twice for refusing to eat what was served to us. With autistic children, however, there is a small but real risk that the child will refuse to eat for several hours, or longer. This is the fear that makes us believe that there is nothing we can do to change the situation, but it is always unfounded. All of these children can, and most will expand their diets once all traces of gluten have been removed, and their parents take a stand.

There are six basic things a person needs from food: water, protein (including all of the essential amino acids), carbohydrates, fats, vitamins, and minerals (including iron & calcium). In addition, food contains certain phytochemical substances and antioxidants which have been found to be important for immune function and disease prevention.

Certain deficiencies have been frequently noted in autistic children, especially (but not limited to) calcium, zinc, magnesium, iron, and vitamins C, B6, and B12. In addition, there can be mild to serious shortages of a range of essential amino acids and fatty acids[119] (see AMINO ACID DEFICIENCIES). This may be due to restricted diets, a self-limiting child, and/or enzyme deficiencies resulting in poor absorption of vitamins and minerals. This is why the use of supplements and digestive enzyme tablets are crucial while the child is being moved toward a healthy digestive system and a greater variety of foods.

Children on very limited diets (for example, chicken, sunflower oil, potato, rice, sesame seeds,

[119] Arnold GL, Hyman SL, Mooney RA, Kirby RS "Plasma amino acids profiles in children with autism: potential risk of nutritional deficiencies." *J Autism Dev Disord.* 2003 Aug;33(4):449-54.

136

calcium-enriched beverages) *who are being adequately supplemented* have had excellent results on nutritional blood tests. However, systematic approaches to reducing starches and increasing vegetables will get you to the goal of a varied and nutritious diet, and some very effective behavioral techniques have been developed to do just that (see PICKINESS AND FOOD ADDICTION). Don't get stressed – just make it a goal like any of the other goals you have set for your child, and talk to your doctor about monitoring your child's nutritional status until you reach that goal.

Dietary Guidelines for Americans is published jointly every 5 years by the Department of Health and Human Services (HHS) and the Department of Agriculture (USDA). The *Guidelines* provide authoritative advice for people two years and older on the dietary habits that can promote health and reduce risk for major chronic diseases. The latest edition of the *Guidelines* is something that every parent should read.

If you have looked at earlier versions, you'll notice a few changes. Gone is the old food pyramid. While dairy (low fat) still figures prominently, there is a section on substitutions for milk products, and the need to choose alternate sources of the nutrients provided by milk, including potassium, magnesium, calcium, and vitamins A and D. Some other sound changes appear, including increased emphasis on fruits and vegetables and a big decrease in the acceptable amount of sugar.

For more information and a copy of these guidelines, go to www.health.gov/ DietaryGuidelines

---

NYSTATIN (See ANTI-FUNGAL TREATMENTS)

O.A.T. (See ORGANIC ACIDS TEST)

OATS

Oats are a species of cereal grain. Although they do not technically contain gluten in their pure form, they are almost universally problematic for the gluten-free population. This has been attributed to contamination of many oat products with wheat, rye and particularly barley.[120] Gluten free oats are now available; these are tolerated by many with celiac disease and gluten intolerance, but appear to cause a reaction in others. A 2008 study showed that a small number of gluten-sensitive patients display a specific small intestinal T cell response to oat peptides that cannot be explained by contamination with other cereals.[121] According to the authors, *"Oats could form a potentially useful part of a gluten-free diet, but patients require careful advice and monitoring, backed by robust gluten-assay techniques."* If you decide to try oats, be sure you buy those which are designated gluten free, and watch closely for any reaction.

OBSESSIVE COMPULSIVE DISORDER (OCD) (See RELATED AND/OR CO-EXISTING DISORDERS)

---

[120] Dickey W. "Making oats safer for patients with coeliac disease." *Eur J Gastroenterol Hepatol.* 2008 Jun;20(6): 494-5.

[121] Ellis HJ, Ciclitira PJ. "Should coeliac sufferers be allowed their oats?" *Eur J Gastroenterol Hepatol.* 2008 Jun; 20(6):492-493.

ODORS, UNUSUAL

Parents occasionally report unusual odors in their autistic spectrum children. Sometimes these reports are of strange breath or skin, but more often it refers to urine or stool. "Fishy" breath, or urine that smells of acetone, mothballs or maple syrup could be a side effect of certain supplements, or it could be a reason for concern. Sweet-smelling urine may be a warning sign of diabetes. Sweet-smelling breath or breath smelling of acetone (as in nail polish remover) may be a warning sign of KETOSIS. Strange smells may also signal a nutritional deficiency or a metabolic disorder, so it is important to talk to your doctor if you notice a strange smell that persists.

If the breath smells like fish, it may be due to cod liver oil supplementation. Try switching to a different brand, and make sure to store CLO in the refrigerator to maintain freshness after opening. Here's a report that we received from a parent:

"My son has been greatly helped by inositol (a component of lecithin) for his digestion of fats and proteins. When he doesn't get it he has screaming fits, night waking, and fishy breath."

A fishy body odor can come from trimethylamine (TMA), a breakdown product of carnitine in the gut. For some people it is a result of a metabolic disorder called Trimethylaminuria, while for others it is merely a side effect of taking carnitine supplements. If the odor is being caused by carnitine supplementation, the doctor may want to reduce the dosage.

A mothball (napthalene) smell in the stool or urine of autistic children has occasionally been reported. There are a few theories about the origin of the naphthalene smell – abnormal gut flora, "die-off," detoxification, a metabolic disorder, a dysfunctional glutathione transferase, herbal or nutritional supplements, food dyes, etc. "Sister" chemicals may have similar smells or that may be metabolized into naphthalene first cousins. However, to date, reports of this indicate that it is temporary and benign.

An odor of maple syrup in the urine could be caused by the metabolic disorder "maple syrup urine disease" (MSUD). This is a disorder of branched-chain amino acid metabolism. Changes in diet and gut flora could theoretically result in a temporary episode of this metabolic abnormality, but any odor of maple should be investigated.

NUTRASWEET® (See SUGAR SUBSTITUTES)

OLDER CHILDREN (See ADULTS/OLDER CHILDREN)

OMEGA-3 & OMEGA-6 FATTY ACIDS

Omega-3 and omega-6 fatty acids are "essential fatty acids" (also called polyunsaturated fatty acids (PUFAs). They are "essential" because the body cannot produce them, so they must be taken in through the diet. The omega-3 fatty acids are important components of nerve cell membranes and help nerve cell communication. These are highly concentrated in the brain, and appear to be involved in memory and learning.

Doctors treating autistic children report that supplementing omega-3 fatty acids has a mood elevating and stabilizing effect. For reasons that are not yet fully understood, individuals with autism seem to have difficulty converting essential fatty acids from foods into the forms necessary for important biochemical reactions.[122] Preliminary results of a study at the Children's Center at the University of Medicine and Dentistry of New Jersey indicate that some children with autism are unable to metabolize key fatty acids, which help the body to fight the inflammation that causes damage to the brain and other organs.[123] The potential treatment would consist of a combination of fatty acids tailored to individual children.

A deficiency of omega-3 fatty acids, or an imbalance between omega-3 and omega-6 fatty acids, has also been correlated with ADHD and mental health problems, including depression and bipolar disorder. A preliminary study has shown that omega-3 fatty acids (compared with placebo) improved symptoms of hyperactivity and stereotypy. And studies are underway to examine whether they also play a role in schizophrenia.[124] [125] [126] [127] [128]

In addition, research indicates that omega-3 fatty acids reduce inflammation and help prevent risk factors associated with heart disease, cancer and arthritis.

A healthy diet should consist of twice as many omega-6 fatty acids as omega-3s, and it is important that this balance be achieved. Grains, meat, milk, eggs, and corn oil all contain omega-6 EFAs. The best sources of omega-3 EFAs come from fatty fish such as cod, tuna, halibut, mackerel, herring, trout, sardines, and salmon, as well as other marine life such as algae and krill. Eggs, canola oil, nut oils and walnuts also contain omega-3 EFAs.

Unfortunately, the typical American diet contains too many omega-6 fatty acids and too few omega-3 fatty acids. One reason for this may be that the meat from grain-fed cattle now contains far more omega-6 than omega-3 fatty acids (a good reason to consider switching to free-range, grass-fed beef), and another is the reduced consumption of fish. Since most fatty fish are also high in mercury and other heavy metal contaminants, many doctors now suggest that we add a fish oil supplement to our children's diet (See COD LIVER OIL).

OPIATES & OPIOIDS (See also OPIOID EXCESS, OPIOID PEPTIDES)

In medical terminology, "opiates" are any of the narcotic alkaloids found in opium, including heroin and morphine. An "opioid" is a chemical substance that has a morphine-like action in

---

[122] Tsalamanio, E., et al. 2006. "Omega-3 Fatty Acids: Role in the Prevention and Treatment of Psychiatric Disorders." *Current Psychiatry Reviews* 2(2):215-234.

[123] New Jersey Star Ledger, 2007 Feb 18.

[124] Amminger GP, Berger GE, Schäfer MR, Klier C, Friedrich MH, Feucht M. "Omega-3 fatty acid supplementation in children with autism: a double-blind randomized, placebo-controlled pilot study." *Biol Psychiatry*. 2007 Feb 15;61(4):551-3.

[125] Arnold, LE, Kleykamp, D., Votolato,N, Gibson RA, Horrocks, L. "Potential link between dietary intake of fatty acid and behavior: pilot exploration of serum lips in attention deficit hyperactivity disorder." *J. Child Adolesc Psychopharmacol*. 1994: 4(3): 171-182.

[126] Burgess J, Stevens, L, Zhang W, Peck L. "Long-chain polyunsaturated fatty acids in children with attention deficity hyperactivity disorder." *Am J Clin Nutr*. 2000; 71(supple):327S-330S.

[127] Sinn, N and Bryan, J, "Effect of Supplementation with Polyunsaturated Fatty Acids and Micronutrients on Learning and Behavior Problems Associated with Child ADHD," *Journal of Developmental & Behavioral Pediatrics*. 28(2):82-91, April 2007.

[128] Stoll, AL, Severus WE, Freeman MP, et al. "Omega 3 fatty acids in bipolar disorder: a preliminary double-blind placebo-controlled Trial." *Arch Gen Psychiatry*. 1999:56(5): 407-412.

the body. However, the terms are frequently used interchangeably.

The main effect of opiates and opioids is pain relief. They may be hallucinogenic and are known to be highly addictive. They affect hormones and hormonal regulation, and cause side effects such as constipation. Endogenous opioids (those manufactured by the body) are known to play an important role in motivation, emotion, attachment behavior, sexual behavior, the response to stress and pain, and appetite.

OPIOID EXCESS

The "Opioid Excess Theory" holds that the incomplete breakdown products of gluten and casein proteins can disrupt sensory input and affect behavior (see OPIOID PEPTIDES). The word "excess" refers to the opioid peptides that survive the digestive process, and can be found, intact, in the urine. High levels of these "escapees" in the urine suggests that a number of them are likely to have made their way to the central nervous system.

History of the Opioid Excess Theory: In 1966, F.C. Dohan proposed that a genetic defect made schizophrenics incapable of completely metabolizing milk and grains.[129] He also advocated the removal of these proteins for children with "behavioral disorders," including autism. In 1979, neuroscientist Jaak Panksepp noted the similarity between traits shown by autistic children and the effects of opioid drugs (such as morphine). He proposed a mechanism by which people with autism might have elevated levels of opioids which occur naturally in the central nervous system of humans.[130]

The drug-like symptoms of autism noted by Panksepp include:

*   Self absorption – being "in one's own world"
*   Inappropriate affect – giggling or crying for no reason
*   Stereotyped behavior, e.g. rocking, "stimming"
*   Bizarre preoccupations
*   Gastrointestinal problems
*   Insensitivity to pain

At around the same time, Swedish researcher Christopher Gillberg found elevated levels of endogenous endorphin-like substances in the spinal fluid of children with autism. Intrigued by these findings, Norwegian physician Karl Reichelt was reminded of previously published work suggesting that diet could be implicated in some cases of schizophrenia. He set out to look for evidence of opioids in autistic children, choosing to study urine samples, which could be collected with minimal disruption to his young subjects.

Reichelt found highly elevated urinary peptides in this study group, and his work was later replicated by Paul Shattock at the University of Sunderland in England, and then by American Robert Cade, MD, at the University of Florida. Reichelt began recommending the removal of gluten and casein from the diets of autistic children as early as 1981. Later, Shattock and his colleagues, as well as the Norwegian scientists, wrote extensively on their findings throughout

[129] Dohan, F.C. (1966) "Cereals and Schizophrenia, data and hypothesis." *Acta Physiologica Scandinavica*, 42, 125-132.

[130] Panksepp J. "A Neurochemical Theory of Autism." *Trends in Neurosciences* 1979: 2: 174-177

the 1990's; In 2000, Cade published similar findings.[131] [132] [133] [134] [135]

Why Gluten and Casein? Both proteins, when partially digested, have opioid characteristics. Gluten breaks down to gliadorphin, (sometimes called gluteomorphin) while milk is broken down into casomorphin.[136]

Some question whether the opioid excess theory has validity. Consider the following points:

- One of the symptoms of opiate use is contracted (small) pupils while under the influence of opiates, and dilated (large) pupils during the withdrawal period. These pupil changes are frequently observed in autistic children during dietary infractions. Habitual morphine users may have somewhat enlarged pupils even after a period of abstinence, and this has been noted also in autistic children, sometimes for months after starting the diet.

- Constipation, self-absorption, and insensitivity to pain are hallmarks of both autism and opiate use.

- The addiction to gluten and dairy-containing foods can be quite pronounced, often eaten to the exclusion of every other type of food. Children placed on a gluten and dairy free diet have been reported to drink foundation makeup or school glue, or to lick the backs of stamps in order to satisfy their cravings for these foods.

- When gluten and dairy are removed from a child's diet, the physical and emotional withdrawal response can be extreme. Simply avoiding certain foods should not cause the kind of discomfort we see in children first starting the diet.

- Because these peptides decrease in the urine of patients consuming a gluten-free diet, it is reasonable to conclude that they have a dietary origin.[137]

The "DPP-4 Connection:" DPP-4 (Dipeptidyl peptidase-4) is a special peptidase - an enzyme whose job it is to break down certain peptides in our digestive system. It is the only peptidase that can break apart peptides, including opioid peptides, that have proline as the second amino

---

[131] Shattock, P, Whiteley, P. (2002) "Biochemical aspects in autism spectrum disorders: updating the opioid-excess theory and presenting new opportunities for biomedical intervention." *Expert Opin Ther Targets*. 2002 Apr;6(2): 175-83.

[132] Knivsberg A-M., Reichelt K.L., Lind G. & Nodland M. "Probable Etiology and Possible Treatment of Childhood Autism." *Brain Dysfunction* 1991 4: 308-319.

[133] Reichelt K.L., Hole K., Hamberger A. et al "Biologically Active Peptide-Containing Fractions in Schizophrenia and Childhood Autism." *Advances in Biochemical Psychopharmacology* 1981 28: 627-643.

[134] Shattock P., Kennedy A., Rowell F, & Berney T.P. "Role of Neuropeptides in Autism and their Relationship with Classical Neurotransmitters." *Brain Dysfunction* 1990 3: 328-345.

[135] Shattock, Paul & Paul Whiteley "The Use of Gluten and Casein Free Diets with People with Autism." 1995, 2006. Publication of the Autism Research Unit, University of Sunderland, UK.

[136] Whiteley, Paul, Jacqui Rodgers, Dawn Savery, Paul Shattock "A Gluten-Free Diet as an Intervention for Autism and Associated Spectrum Disorders: Preliminary Findings," *Autism*, 1999 Vol. 3, No. 1, 45-65.

[137] Ek J, Stensrud M, Reichelt KL. "Gluten-free diet decreases urinary peptide levels in children with celiac disease." *J Pediatr Gastroenterol Nutr* 1999 Sep;29(3):282-5.

A protein is like a necklace strung together with different colored beads. Amino acids are like the beads in the necklace. If each color represents a different kind of amino acid, then you could say that the pattern of colors determines the type of protein it is.

Proteins are broken down in the body by digestive enzymes: think of these as pairs of scissors. The enzymes chop the necklace into big pieces (polypeptides), then smaller pieces (peptides), then finally, individual beads (amino acids).

There are tight spaces in the lining of the gut wall, just big enough to allow these tiny beads into the bloodstream to provide nourishment, while keeping larger particles inside the digestive tract. If damage to the gut enlarges the holes (see LEAKY GUT), then undigested peptides can get into the bloodstream.

*With some peptides, this might not be much of a problem. However, certain peptides are known to affect the central nervous system and the brain. These are called **opioid peptides**.*

acid from either end. According to biochemist Jon Pangborn, Ph.D., some of the autism "diet responders" may not only be under the influence of opioids, even though these may be present in the urine. For those with weak DPP-4 digestion, opiate peptides that find their way into the bloodstream could lead to other consequences, such as immune dysregulation. Says Pangborn, "For some children, lesions and inflammation in the small intestine could be contributory problems." Some digestive enzyme tablets have been formulated to include this enzyme.

OPIOID PEPTIDES (See also OPIOID EXCESS)

Opioid peptides are short sequences of amino acids that mimic the effect of opiate drugs in the brain. Opioid peptides may be produced by the body itself, for example endorphins (the body's natural painkillers), or they can be absorbed from partially digested food, or possibly even from certain types of microbes. The effect of these peptides vary, but they all resemble opiates, and can bind to opioid receptor sites in the central nervous system and the gastrointestinal tract.

Opioid peptides from food have lengths of typically 4-8 amino acids. The body's own opioids arc generally longer. Opioid food peptides include casomorphin (from milk) and gliadorphin/gluteomorphin (from gluten). Rubiscolin (from spinach) has opioid properties, but unless your child is eating excessive amounts of spinach, this is probably not a concern. There is some evidence that there may be opioid peptides derived from soy.[138]

Opioid peptides of microbial origin include deltorphin I and II (fungal), and dermorphin (from an unknown microbe). These have previously been identified in very specific breeds of frogs and mollusks. However, amphibian skin peptides often correspond to hormones and/or neurotransmitters of mammals. Several researchers have searched for dermorphins and deltorphins in mammals, in the brain, gastrointestinal tract, and other organs, but have not been able to isolate and characterize them. If these peptides are potent enough to cause mischief even at undetectable levels, it could explain why some children respond more powerfully to antifungal and antibacterial treatments than to dietary interventions.

---

[138] Ohinata K, Agui S, Yoshikawa M. "Soymorphins, novel mu opioid peptides derived from soy beta-conglycinin beta-subunit, have anxiolytic activities." *Biosci Biotechnol Biochem.* 2007 Oct;71(10):2618-21.

ORAL ALLERGY SYNDROME

Oral allergy syndrome is a form of contact allergy to raw fruits and vegetables that is localized to the mucus membranes in and around the mouth. People with pollen allergies may experience this reaction when they eat foods that are related to different types of pollen. For example, a person with a birch allergy may react to apple, cherry, peach, and carrot. A person with a grass allergy might have trouble with tomato or kiwi; those with a ragweed allergy can react to melon, banana or tomato, and a mugwort allergy can result in problems with carrot or celery. These foods may not be problematic when they are cooked. Oral allergy syndrome affects approximately 50% of pollen-allergic adults and represents the most common adult food allergy.[139] Symptoms can include itching, tingling, or swelling in the lips, tongue, palate and throat. These symptoms are usually mild, and resolve promptly when the food is swallowed or removed. However, in a small subset of patients, this type of allergy to fruits and vegetables may progress to more serious systemic reactions.

ORGANIC ACIDS TEST (OAT)

An Organic Acid Test is a urine test, first developed to find inborn errors of metabolism (i.e. genetic defects causing metabolic or other disorders such as phenylketonuria). The OAT measures approximately 70 different biochemical compounds, including those that indicate an overgrowth of yeast and bacteria. This is a common test for patients with autism, and those suspected of having problems related to dysbiosis. An OAT will not tell you what strain of yeast is present in the urine and generally, *C. difficile* is the only strain of bacteria that is identified. This test can be done by Great Plains Laboratory or Metametrix, but the tests must be ordered by a doctor. Great Plains also offers a comprehensive panel that includes an OAT together with a stool test for yeast culture plus sensitivity, to test for yeast problems that have not responded well to antifungal treatments.

ORGANIC FOODS (See also GENETICALLY MODIFIED FOODS)

Organic foods are produced according to specific production standards, and certified according to specific, legally regulated standards. To be certified, the food and the farm it was grown on must pass rigorous tests, regulated by the US Department of Agriculture. "Certified Organic" crops must be grown without the use of conventional pesticides, artificial fertilizers or sewage sludge, and processed without ionizing radiation or food additives. Certified organic meat comes from animals reared without the routine use of antibiotics and without the use of growth hormones. In most countries, organic produce cannot be genetically modified. Note that all "certified" organic food is organic, but not all organic food is certified. This, in part, has led to the increasing popularity of locally grown food over organic food.

Although organic food is more expensive, it is recommended because even a careful washing of produce will not eliminate pesticides and other toxins from fresh produce. Additionally, because standard crops are no longer routinely rotated, the soil in which they grow is not replenished with nutrients.

If purchasing organic food is a financial hardship, try to prioritize organic foods which are not peeled or boiled. An even better solution is to buy from your local farmer at organic farmer's markets. This not only ensures your food to be pesticide free, but it supports the family farm, your regional water source, and local economy. It also saves on fuel used for shipping foods

---

[139] Nowak-Wegrzyn A. Sampson H. "Adverse Reactions to Foods." *Med Clin N Am* 90 (2006) 97–127.

long distances. If you have property, consider planting fruit trees and a garden; you will have toxin-free produce and your children will learn valuable lessons about sustainable living.

OXALATES (See LOW OXALATE DIET)

OXIDATIVE STRESS (See also METHYLATION)

Oxidative stress is caused by the normal byproducts of metabolism, or the result of environmental and lifestyle insults like cigarette smoke and pesticides. It can damage cells, and cause premature aging and disease.

Oxidative stress appears to be an important factor in the cascade of health problems seen in autistic and related disorders. Dr. Jill James, of the University of Arkansas for Medical Sciences, found an increased vulnerability to oxidative stress and a decreased capacity for methylation in individuals with autism. [140] [141] Oxidative stress can be counteracted by the avoidance of factors that are poisonous to the body, and by eating antioxidants foods like blueberries or taking supplements like melatonin and glutathione (see ANTIOXIDANTS).

PALM OIL (See FATS & OILS)

PARENTS MAGAZINE

In February, 2000, Karyn Seroussi published a widely-read article about autism and diet in *Parents Magazine*. A handy resource for parents educating others about the diet, it is available online at www.autismndi.com. Click on "We Rescued Our Child From Autism," bottom right.

PASSOVER (See HOLIDAYS)

PASTA

For those who tolerate flour, there are some very good gluten free pastas on the market today. These are usually made from rice, corn, or quinoa, or a combination of these grains. Rice pasta usually comes in various shapes and types, including lasagna noodles, and corkscrews that include powdered vegetables.

Rice pasta should be cooked in lots of water with a few drops of oil, to prevent it from sticking or becoming gummy. If cooking simultaneously with a pot of wheat pasta, keep the gluten pot on the front burner to avoid dripping into the GF pot. Avoid mixing up the stirring spoons. To reheat, rinse with warm water and drain well.

PEA PROTEIN POWDER (See PROTEIN)

PEANUTS (See also NUTS)

The peanut is not a nut, but a legume plant that grows underground. It is related to other legumes, such as peas, beans and lentils. Peanuts are flavorful and high in protein and fat.

---

[140] James SJ, Cutler P, Melnyk S, Jernigan S, Janak L, Gaylor DW, Neubrander JA. "Metabolic biomarkers of increased oxidative stress and impaired methylation capacity in children with autism." *Am J Clin Nutr.* 2004 Dec; 80(6):1611-7.

[141] James SJ, et al. "Metabolic endophenotype and related genotypes are associated with oxidative stress in children with autism." *Am J Med Genet B Neuropsychiatr Genet.* 2006 Dec 5;141(8):947-56.

144

Nuts and legumes are among the most common allergens. Peanuts, especially, are well-known to cause severe or life-threatening allergic reactions (see ANAPHYLAXIS). Studies show that there has been a sharp increase in peanut allergies over the last 5-10 years, particularly in children, in many parts of the world. The increased use of soy (also a legume) for infants may explain this phenomenon for some. Increased incidence of peanut allergy has also been linked with raising children in an antibacterial environment, increased antibiotic use, vaccinations, genetically modified food, and food pesticides.

According to the Food Allergy & Anaphylaxis Network (www.foodallergy.org), if your child has a peanut allergy, you should keep the following in mind:

- Many different nut butters are produced on equipment used to process peanut butter. Additionally, most experts recommend that peanut-allergic patients avoid tree nuts.

- Studies show that most allergic individuals can safely eat peanut oil, but *not* cold pressed, expelled, or extruded peanut oil - sometimes represented as "gourmet oils." If you are allergic to peanuts, talk to your doctor about whether or not you should avoid peanut oil. *Arachis oil* is peanut oil.

- African, Chinese, Indonesian, Mexican, Thai, and Vietnamese dishes often contain peanuts or are contaminated with peanuts during the preparation process. Additionally, foods sold in bakeries and ice cream shops are often in contact with peanuts.

- Many brands of sunflower seeds are produced on equipment shared with peanuts. "Mandelonas" are peanuts soaked in almond flavoring.

Although once considered to be a lifelong allergy, recent studies indicate that up to 20 percent of children diagnosed with peanut allergy outgrow it. (This should be determined only under the supervision of your physician or allergist.) Additionally, because peanuts grow on the ground, they can contain a great deal of mold, and may need to be avoided by those who have a mold allergy.

PEPCID (FAMOTIDINE)

Famotidine is a histamine-2 receptor blocker, widely prescribed (and now available over the counter) primarily for the treatment of heartburn, peptic ulcer disease and gastroesophogeal reflux. Recent reports indicate that it may be an effective treatment for certain symptoms of schizophrenia (e.g. loss of interest in others, decreased attachment).[142] Because individuals with autism show similar deficits, some researchers have theorized that famotidine might also be useful in treating the social symptoms in autism. Histamine serves as a neurotransmitter and neuromodulator in the brain.

When H2-receptors in the brain are stimulated in animals, spontaneous activity and exploratory behavior decrease; blocking the H2-receptors would therefore be expected to reverse this inhibition.[143]

---

[142] Linday LA, "Oral famotidine: a potential treatment for children with autism" *Medical hypotheses* 1997, vol. 48, no.5, pp. 381-386.

[143] *Med Hypotheses* 1997 May 48:5 381-6.

PEPTIDES

Peptides are the breakdown products of proteins, comprised of short chains of AMINO ACIDS. See also OPIOID PEPTIDES.

PEPTIDUREA

Peptidurea literally translates to "peptides in the urine." This refers to the finding of abnormal breakdown products of proteins (peptides) in unusually high amounts, in the urine of patients with autism or related disorders. See OPIOID EXCESS.

PERMEABILITY, INTESTINAL (See LEAKY GUT)

PERVASIVE DEVELOPMENTAL DELAY (PDD) (See RELATED AND/OR CO-EXISTING DISORDERS)

PFEIFFER TREATMENT CENTER

The Pfeiffer Treatment Center is a not-for-profit outpatient facility for children and adults, specializing in the evaluation and management of biochemical imbalances, which may be associated with symptoms of mental illness or developmental, learning and behavior disorders.

Patients are screened for biochemical imbalances with a comprehensive medical history, physical exam and lab analysis. Based on these findings, their practitioners prescribe vitamins, minerals, amino acids and fatty acids based on each patient's unique chemistry.

According to their patient information, their child and adult patients report that nutritional treatment for these imbalances has resulted in notable improvements in behavior disorders, depression, learning and attention disorders, schizophrenia, and autism spectrum disorders. For more information: www.hriptc.org.

PHENOLS (See also PHENOL SULFUR TRANSFERASE DEFICIENCY)

Phenols are substances found in several foods, especially brightly colored fruits and vegetables. For many years, parents have noted that their very sensitive children do best on what is known as "the white diet," meaning low-phenol foods like white rice, potatoes, chicken, etc. This is probably a result of problems with a biochemical process called SULFATION.

Highly Phenolic Foods:	almonds	coffee	peppers
	apples	cucumbers/pickles	plums
	apricots	currants	prunes
almonds	bananas	red grapes/raisins	tangerines
apples	berries (all)	ketchup	tea
apricots	cherries	nectarines	tomatoes
bananas	chili powder	oranges	wine
berries (all)	cider and cider vinegar (apples)	paprika	vinegar (grapes)
cherries		peaches	oil of wintergreen (methyl salicylate)
chili powder	cloves		

Phenols may also be found in commercial foods that list "natural or artificial flavors," "natural or artificial colors" or preservatives (see FEINGOLD PROGRAM).

PHENOL SULFUR TRANSFERASE (PST) DEFICIENCY

Research by Dr. Rosemary Waring of the University of Birmingham has shown that children on the autism spectrum have a deficiency in phenol sulfur transferase (PST), impairing the body's ability to rid itself of toxins.[144]

During detoxification, toxins are transformed into harmless substances and excreted. The body often accomplishes this transformation by adding a molecule to the toxin. This process is called *conjugation*. Sulfate conjugation is such a process, used to transform many chemicals including environmental toxins, drugs, and neurotransmitters. For sulfate conjugation to occur, there must be a sufficient amount of an enzyme called phenol sulfur transferase. If there are an insufficient number of sulfate ions, detoxification will be impaired.

If the PST system is dysfunctional, harmful substances can build up. In addition, some important neurotransmitters may not be properly metabolized, and other metabolic processes can be disturbed by phenolic compounds. PST is also vital to the sulfate conjugation of phenols (see PHENOLS). This is important because phenolic compounds are nearly everywhere in the foods we eat and the juices we drink. They are in household chemicals and even in freshly cut grass.

The proteins lining the gut are normally sulfated, and they form a protective layer over the surface of the gut wall. If sulfation is deficient, proteins can stick together causing gaps in the gut wall. In other words, a PST deficiency may contribute to intestinal permeability (see LEAKY GUT).

Symptoms of PST deficiency include red face, red ears, dark circles under the eyes, hyperactivity, aggressive behavior, head-banging, self-injurious behavior, inappropriate laughter, insomnia, headache, diarrhea, lethargy, excessive thirst, and night sweats. One way of checking to see whether phenols could be a problem is to feed your child a fair quantity of red grapes and see if you notice anything odd - especially red cheeks or ears shortly after eating.

For some, supplementing with sulfur-containing amino acids such as taurine and cysteine, or with MSM (methysulfonylmethane), may be helpful, but it is difficult to add sulfate to the body through supplements, because sulfate ions are not easily absorbed through the gut. However, they can be absorbed through the skin, which can explain why some parents have found that regular epsom salt baths are helpful (see EPSOM SALTS).

Those with PST deficiency may exhibit significant improvements by reducing the amount of phenolic foods in the diet. Although phenols are fairly common, it is possible to avoid foods and additives that are highly phenolic (see PHENOLS). Biochemist Jon Pangborn, Ph.D. discourages the use of enzyme products intended to destroy phenols, because some phenols, such as tyrosine, are essential to human life. He believes that such a product could invite a metabolic disorder, especially for autistic individuals who may have problems with tyrosine inadequacy.

---

[144] Alberti A, Pirrone P, Elia M, Waring RH, Romano C., "Sulphation deficit in 'low-functioning' autistic children: a pilot study." *Biol Psychiatry.* 1999 Aug 1;46(3):420-4.

PHYTIC ACID

Phytic acid is a substance common in plant cells, particularly seeds, nuts and grains. It acts as a storage compound for phosphates in these plants. Because it can block the uptake of important minerals such as calcium, magnesium, iron and zinc, it is sometimes called an "anti-nutrient."

Cooking and baking destroys about half of the phytic acid in whole grains. Breaking down the phytic acid in nuts and seeds makes the nutrients more available and improves digestion; this can be done by sprouting, or by soaking in water or a slightly acidic solution of water with a few added drops of lemon juice.

PICA

Pica is a term that describes an appetite for non-food substances such as wood, soil, chalk, cardboard, etc., or for edible but unusual substances such as flour or raw potatoes. Pica is usually diagnosed when symptoms persist for more than a month, at an age where eating such objects is considered developmentally inappropriate. Pica is seen in all ages, particularly in pregnant women and small children, but especially among children who are developmentally disabled.

Research suggests that many afflicted with pica suffer from a nutritional deficiency, but it is unclear whether inappropriate foods are eaten because of the deficiency, or the deficiency is caused by the inappropriate items ingested. Defeat Autism Now! Doctor David Berger, MD suggests testing a child's mineral levels in the red blood cells (not just in serum/plasma). He reports that zinc and selenium are the minerals most commonly deficient in his patients with Pica, and that supplementation usually proves to be beneficial.

Pica and iron deficiency are also associated with a decrease in the activity of dopamine, an important neurotransmitter.

Children with pica sometimes eat dangerous substances (e.g. paint chips) and may require periodic screenings for lead or other toxins.

PICKINESS & FOOD ADDICTION

Many parents will swear that their mealtimes feel more like a prizefight than a family dinner. Small children are often picky eaters, but children on the autism spectrum can take pickiness to extremes. These children are sometimes called "self-limiters." Even when parents recognize the potential benefits that can result from dietary intervention, they may hesitate to remove some of the few foods that their children will eat.

Self-limiting children often eat fewer than five different foods; the list generally includes foods like milk, yogurt, bread, chicken nuggets and fries. These foods contain gluten, casein or both. It is probable that such children are limiting themselves to foods to which they have a physical addiction (see OPIOID EXCESS).

All of these children can (and most will) expand their diets once all traces of gluten have been removed (see NUTRITION).

Common Reasons for Pickiness: Self-limiters are choosing foods that support a very real addiction. Going for a few hours without gluten or dairy may cause sensations of pain and discomfort. Those who have been put on a "GF/CF diet" that retains traces of gluten or dairy may continue to narrow their food choices until they are down to just one or two foods. A classic example is a child who started out with several foods, and is now eating just one, such as a specific brand of store-bought fries or potato chips. It is highly likely that these contain traces of gluten from the manufacturing process, and the child is sensitive enough to notice the difference. When switched to homemade fried potatoes, the food repertoire may quickly expand.

Eating is a very different experience when one of your senses is disrupted. Children on the autism spectrum often have severe disturbances in several of their sensory channels; this dysfunction renders them unable to process sensory information, and affects the way they experience food. If olfaction is overly acute, ordinary cooking smells may be seem disgusting. For others, an insensitive nose may mean that food simply is not appetizing. Foods of particular textures or temperatures may be intolerable.

If texture seems to be the limiting factor, introduce new foods that are similar in texture to foods that are already accepted. If a child only eats crunchy foods, look for crunchy gluten and casein free foods. If they refuse to chew, you can make puddings, purées and even "yogurt" from appropriate ingredients.

Some parents find that their children will not even try a new version of a favorite food. This may be due to the characteristic "need for sameness" common to children on the autism spectrum. For these children it will be important to try to approximate the appearance of their favorite foods as closely as possible.

Here are some ideas for increasing the number of foods in the diet:

- Study the favored brand of chicken nugget and make yours look exactly the same in size, shape and color. You can go to your child's favorite fast food restaurant and ask for some of the nugget envelopes or boxes (most store managers will give them to you if you ask - if they are reluctant, offer to buy them).

- If a child is a confirmed 'milkaholic,' a similar technique may be needed to introduce an acceptable substitute. There are several excellent milk substitutes on the market that provide the required vitamins and calcium, but if your child won't drink them, he may not be getting the nutrition he needs. When first making the switch, try adding just a tiny bit of milk substitute to the milk carton. Each day, increase the proportion until there is no milk at all. For the truly stubborn, a little milk-free chocolate syrup may be the shortest route to a successful switch. The flavoring can then be slowly phased out to minimize sugar in the diet.

- One woman reported that her child only ate muffins, so for the first few weeks, she made chicken muffins, pork muffins and beef muffins, including puréed vegetables in the batter.

- Let your child help you cook; following a recipe and taking pride his participation may induce her to taste the result.

- Introduce a new food when he is especially hungry.

- "Run out" of the foods that he is used to having, and explain that the new food is all there is.

- Introduce foods in a new environment, such as at Grandma's house.

- Use peer pressure. Serve other children the food, and reluctantly tell him he can try a little if he really wants to.

> "A highly-preferred food is not always a troublemaker, but for any adult or child with a chronic complaint, the following question frequently fingers the culprit: 'Is there any food that you would consider to be your favorite, or that you would miss if you did not eat it every day?' Cravings tend to apply in two situations: carbohydrates and food allergies."
>
> -Defeat Autism Now! Doctor Sidney Baker, MD

For severe tactile issues, it may be necessary to work with an occupational therapist trained in sensory integration dysfunction. These professionals work slowly and gradually to increase the child's tolerance of many textures, temperatures and smells. They can desensitize the child's lips and mouth, which will allow them to eat a more normal diet. For more information, or to find an OT in your area, write to the American Occupational Therapy Association at P.O. Box 31220/ Bethesda, MD 20824-1220 or visit www.aota.org.

Feeding the Self-Limiting Child by Susan Wallitsch

Whether switching to GF/CF, SCD™ or any new dietary intervention, parents are often faced with children who simply refuse to eat. I think we are all biologically compelled to feed our children, which makes it extremely difficult to continue to offer foods that a child refuses to eat. It is also heart-rending at times, to steadfastly withhold food that we know our child wants. These factors are probably responsible for most failures to give dietary interventions a proper trial.

I speak from experience, because I too have a child who refused many new food items. Fortunately we worked with Toni Haman, a wonderful behavioral specialist. Toni convinced us that forcing a reluctant child to eat will make the avoidance problem worse. She devised a method to introduce a new food very gradually, and it worked very well for my family. The process involves a very slow acclimation to the food in distinct stages. The steps are:

1. The food is present in the room with the child for a short time.
2. The child is shown the food (nothing else is asked of the child).
3. The child is asked to touch the food (nothing else).
4. The child is asked to pick up the food.
5. The child is asked to hold the food near his mouth.
6. The child is asked to hold the food near his mouth and touch it with his tongue.
7. The child is asked to put the food in his mouth and then allowed to spit it out

immediately.

The child should have the food in his mouth for 10 to 20 trials at this step. The child will either begin to tolerate eating the food or if the child continues to spit the food out, the food is probably really aversive to the child and a new food should be started.

Do the steps in order and only one at a time. Stay with each step until your child is comfortable with it and tolerates it well. Only then move to the next step. Each step may take several days. Each time you present the step and your child complies, provide lots of rewards (hugs, tickles, even a small amount of a permitted food, whatever your child loves) and praise.

Use gentle prompting, but never force a child with the food introduction program. Do the step you are working on 3 to 6 times over the course of a day, but never all in a row. Work on one food at a time. For example, if you are introducing steak, cook a portion and cut it into small, bite sized pieces. Freeze the cut up steak and thaw only the amount you need for the program that day. This way you are not cooking (and wasting) a lot of food. This program is much easier if your child is able to do non-verbal imitation.

Another tip for introducing a food like meat is to make it very flavorful and soft to chew. My son first ate stews and roasts prepared in the crock pot because they were so tender and moist. His favorite is roast beef. There are many recipes online and in various cookbooks. My son was a very limited eater. With lots of experimenting to find his favorite flavors and textures we were able to expand his diet remarkably. He now loves to hang out in the kitchen with me and we are going to start to teach him to cook as part of his home program. It may seem impossible now, but keep with it and you will be rewarded with a child who eats well.

Susan Wallitsch has extensive experience counseling other families about autism interventions.

Here is a similar, more detailed behavioral approach. Again, this is a process that should not be rushed, and may take several weeks to complete:

1. Eat the food next to the child and comment "this ___ is yummy." (Be sure you have your child's attention and he is watching you eat the new food.)

2. A friend of the child or a highly reinforcing person eats the food next to the child and comments "this ___ is yummy."

3. In home therapy time, school, and down time, have the therapists/parents take a picture of the desired food and talk about it. Do therapy or sort foods into similar categories. Move from pictures to actual whole bananas and other fruits during therapy and play activities.

4. Put a small amount of the food on a separate plate **next to your child's plate.** Point to it and discuss. Eat some off the plate and comment "this ___ is yummy."

5. The first big step: put the food **on your child's plate.** He/she does not eat the food, but

has to tolerate the food being on the plate. Tell your child "you don't have to eat the ____. It just needs to be on your plate during your meal."

6. Next big step: put the same food on your child's plate and during the meal your child needs to **touch the food**. Tell your child "you don't have to eat the ____, it just needs to be touched with a finger during your meal."

7. Really big step: put the same food on your child's plate and during the meal your child needs to **pick up the food**. Tell your child "you don't have to eat the ____, it just needs to be picked up once during your meal."

8. Now we are moving: put the same food on your child's plate and during the meal your child needs to **pick up and put the food on the lips**. Tell your child "you don't have to eat the ____, it just needs to be picked up and put on the lips during your meal."

9. Next, put the same food on your child's plate and during the meal your child needs to **pick up and put the food on the tongue**. Tell your child "you don't have to eat the ____, it just needs to be picked up and put on the tongue during your meal."

10. Last step – **putting the smallest piece in the mouth** and finally **swallowing the food.**

Note: it is possible that there will initially be little chewing. Work with your child to chew as the final step.

All I can say is WOW! The difference has been amazing— she is eating. Although she did not care too much about dairy foods, when I first removed gluten Sarah basically went on a food strike. I did not worry too much, since she continued to nurse well, but she ate virtually nothing else for about ten days. Then, once she started eating, she began to accept more foods within just a few days. Now, the change in her diet is amazing. She is eating GF chicken nuggets, broccoli, GF/CF pizza and Canadian bacon. She will now accept three different kinds of juice. She even ate the Breakfast "Cookies" (from Special Diets for Special Kids II*) and sucked down half a bottle of her toddler formula! I am thrilled.*

-Heather Madden, reprinted from The ANDI News

There has been a great deal of emphasis on the strictness and firmness that parents must show their children during the difficult withdrawal and transition from their favorite foods. But it's worth mentioning that from the child's point of view, this will probably mean several days of real discomfort. Listening to whining and crying can be upsetting, but remind yourself that it's probably a good sign, and that it will pass. Be patient, and make him as comfortable as possible. Do not give in and allow him a "treat." This will only prolong the addiction and discomfort.

Note: *If your child refuses to eat, make sure he is getting plenty of liquids. Consult a doctor or nutritionist if you need help or advice. An occupational therapist specializing in sensory and eating issues may be helpful.*

PIZZA

Pizza is probably the food that older children on special diets miss the most. For very sensitive children, it can be hard to come up with something that looks or tastes even remotely like it. For others, you may be able to come up with a reasonable substitute. Gluten and casein free pizza dough is easy to make or buy (check the Internet for recipes or pre-made crusts). For those on SCD™, there are recipes for crusts made of nut flour. Some commercially prepared sauces are acceptable, or you can make your own. Vegetables make good toppings, though there are no really good "cheeses" for those avoiding dairy and soy. Most cheese alternatives contain casein. As an alternative to pizza, you can also bake a fritatta in an oiled pie pan using beaten eggs, chopped onion, garlic, and meatballs, salami or bacon. Drizzle with sauce, and cut into wedges. Sometimes just calling it "pizza" is enough to help your child feel included.

PLAYDOUGH

Playdough can and will end up in your child's mouth, so at home or school, make sure that the only dough in sight is gluten-free. Volunteer to be the school "playdough parent" if necessary. A gluten free recipe:

Place 1 cup finely-ground white rice flour,* 2 tsp cream of tartar, ¼ cup salt, 1 tsp xanthan gum, and 2 TBSP vegetable oil in a blender. With the blade running, slowly add approximately ½ cup of boiling water through the feed tube until the mixture forms a ball. Add water a spoonful at a time until the dough is soft and firm. Add natural food coloring if desired. If you don't have a food processor, this can be mixed by hand. Let cool and knead until silky, lightly dusting the kneading surface with more flour if necessary. Store in a tightly-sealed container. Refrigeration isn't necessary but will keep it fresh longer.

*Note: for a softer, smoother end result, look for "sweet rice flour" at your local Asian market or natural foods store.

PREGNANCY & INFANCY

Mothers of ASD children have special concerns when it comes to preparing for the birth of another child. Research suggests that these disorders begin with a genetic predisposition, but are triggered by an environmental factor (either in utero or in infancy). Therefore, it is sensible to try to minimize this concern by reducing maternal exposure to known environmental toxins, as much as possible, during pregnancy and breastfeeding (see ENVIRONMENTAL TOXICITY).

If a pregnant woman has a mouth full of "silver" fillings, or eats lots of fish, it is possible that this could impact the child's chances of developing neurological problems (see MERCURY). If you decide to avoid fish, remember to supplement your diet with a good, clean source of cod liver oil, which is an excellent source of Omega-3 fatty acids.

If you are planning a pregnancy, consider testing your heavy metal load beforehand (for example, with a DMPS challenge and urine testing). If your levels of mercury, lead, aluminum, etc. are high, detoxification treatment could be something to discuss with your doctor.

Another concern is early antibiotic use, so it might make sense to avoid using them for your child when not absolutely necessary (as for non life-threatening ear infections, etc.). If they must be used, consider adding probiotic supplements or cultured foods. Your pediatrician should be willing to prescribe nystatin as a precaution whenever antibiotics are prescribed.

Donna Gates (see BODY ECOLOGY DIET) describes an ideal birth process, in which nature goes through a systematic process of establishing the correct microflora in the intestines of the baby:

"Shortly before birth, the cervix starts to dilate, and the microflora in the mother's body invades the sterile environment that the baby has lived in during the pregnancy. The baby is born with a small amount of microflora in place, and is nourished by colostrum, which is high in fats, antibodies, and most importantly, the correct microflora to prepare the baby to properly digest and assimilate breastmilk. It also is the beginning of the establishment of the baby's immune system. We now know that most of the body's immune cells are actually located in the gut, and healthy microflora are an integral part of keeping the immune system strong.

But for various reasons, this process is disrupted in our modern world. Mothers of children with autism may themselves be suffering from unresolved fungal infections, passing unhealthy flora along to the baby. If the baby's immature immune system is unable to cope with environmental toxins or vaccines, it could theoretically be weakened, allowing the unhealthy flora to proliferate. Sugars in baby formula could encourage the growth of intestinal fungus in babies who are not breast-fed. Worst of all, with each course of antibiotics (for example, for birth complications or ear infections), the microflora needed to establish a healthy and functional gut is wiped out. The fungus has free reign to take over the gut, causing inflammation and a "leaky gut" that allows incompletely digested foods and mycotoxins (toxic fungal waste products) to pass into the bloodstream."

Some women choose to go gluten and dairy free during pregnancy and nursing, especially if an older child has responded well to dietary intervention. Calcium and other nutrient supplementation may be necessary, so let your doctor knows that you are on a non-dairy diet. When the baby is born, breastmilk is usually best, but again, the mother's diet should be gluten and dairy free (see BREASTFEEDING, INFANT FORMULA).

Most Defeat Autism Now! doctors advise against giving milk products to the younger siblings of autistic children for at least two years (aside from a hypoallergenic infant formula, if tolerated, for the first year).

PRESERVATIVES (See FOOD ADDITIVES)

PROBIOTICS (See also DYSBIOSIS, GUT FLORA, YEAST & FUNGUS)

Probiotics are beneficial bacteria and yeasts that live in our digestive tract, aid in digestion, synthesize vitamins (folic acid and other B vitamins), and inhibit the growth of toxic microbes, viruses, fungi, yeast, and parasites. Therefore, one of the most common (and safest) treatments recommended by doctors and nutritionists is supplementation with these live microorganisms to restore the balance of helpful intestinal flora, especially after a course of antibiotics.

Different strains of *Lactobacillus* and *Bifidobacterium* are among the most common types of probiotic bacteria. These are widely available as supplements, and have shown to be helpful in restoring a healthy balance of gut flora.* A particular strain of *Lactobacillus*, "Lactobacillus GG," has a documented ability to adhere to the intestinal mucosa and colonize the intestinal tract. It assists in controlling overgrowth of harmful bacteria including *E. coli* and *salmonella*, stimulates the body's natural immunity, and effectively treats yeast overgrowth, viral gastroenteritis, diarrhea/constipation, intestinal health, and antibiotic-associated diarrhea. It has also been implicated in preventing allergy-related illnesses: studies found that it could reduce symptoms of the atopic eczema/dermatitis in food-allergic infants.[145]

"Lactic acid bacteria" such as *Lactobaccillus* are used for making yogurt because their main function is to convert lactose (milk sugar) into lactic acid (this creates the characteristic tart flavor). Those with lactose intolerance may find that this probiotic, when properly colonized in the gut, can help them to better tolerate dairy products.

When using probiotic supplements, it is often wise to rotate brands; this may nourish a broader diversity of beneficial bacteria. And these supplements are said to survive better when taken with a full glass of water between meals (without food). Probiotic supplements should always be stored in the refrigerator.

Keep in mind that you can swallow billions of cells of a beneficial strain like *L. acidophilus*, but if they don't "implant" themselves in the gut lining, they won't do any good. Even the highest quality probiotics won't implant in some individuals, probably due to abnormal intestinal pH or a hostile environment in the gut. Diarrhea and constipation will also make it hard for them to colonize. This is why it's important to address all of the various aspects of intestinal dysfunction such as enzyme deficiency, allergens, viruses, parasites, etc.

Note: Look for a high-quality, high-potency brand that doesn't contain dairy or other allergens. A brand that is slightly less expensive may be far less effective.

PROPRIONIC ACID (PPA)

Propionic acid is a short chain fatty acid sometimes used as a food preservative. However, because propionic acid also exists as a by-product of certain gut flora, the results of a recent study may shed some light on the role of gut bacteria in autism.

The study found that some types of autism may involve altered PPA metabolism. Infusions of PPA in adult rats produced (reversible) repetitive behaviors, abnormal motor behaviors, hyperactivity, and the progressive development of certain types seizures, suggesting that this compound has effects on the central nervous system, and may be associated with some autistic behaviors. In addition, biochemical analyses of the rats showed an increase in oxidative stress markers and a decrease in glutathione and glutathione peroxidase activity, also observed in

---

[145] Viljanen M, Savilahti E, Haahtela T, Juntunen-Backman K, Korpela R, Poussa T, Tuure T, Kuitunen M. "Probiotics in the treatment of atopic eczema/dermatitis syndrome in infants: a double-blind placebo-controlled trial." *Allergy.* 2005 Apr;60(4):494-500.

autistic individuals.[146]

PROTEIN

Protein is a complete source of amino acids, and an important part of our nutritional needs. When carbohydrates are combined with proteins, they are broken down more slowly, helping to stabilize blood sugar. Donna Gates (Body Ecology Diet) claims that carbohydrates and protein should not be combined, and that a meal should consist either of carbohydrates and vegetables, or proteins and vegetables. You may want to test these principles on yourself and your child, to decide which works best for you.

Families with food allergies often try to rotate animal proteins, including beef, chicken, turkey, lamb, buffalo, ostrich, venison and others (see MEAT).

Beans and nuts are also a good protein choice, if tolerated. If raw beans and nuts are soaked for twelve hours prior to cooking or eating, they will be easier to digest, and thus more nutritious.

If your child is not getting enough protein due to pickiness or food sensitivities, consider adding protein powder to their diet (see PROTEIN POWDER).

PROTEIN POWDER

If your nutritionist wants you to add protein powder to your child's diet, there are several available, including powders derived from soy, rice, eggs, and even peas (pea protein is available at www.kirkmanlabs.com). Protein powder can be added to drinks or baked goods, or sprinkled on food. Be sure to get a product that is guaranteed to be free of gluten, milk, casein and whey.

PUPILS, CHANGES IN SIZE

One of the symptoms of opiate use is contracted (small) pupils while under the influence of opiates, and dilated (large) pupils during the withdrawal period. These observations have been made about our children after eating gluten and casein (see OPIOID EXCESS). Habitual morphine users may have somewhat enlarged pupils even after a period of abstinence, and this has been noted also in autistic children, sometimes for months after starting a restricted diet.

PURINE AUTISM (See RELATED AND/OR CO-EXISTING DISORDERS)

QUINOA

Quinoa (pronounced "keen-wah") is a grain originating from the Andes in South America. It's called a "pseudograin" since it is not a grass, and flour is made from the ground seeds of the plant. It is a gluten-free product, although it may not be tolerated by some sensitive people. Quinoa flour can be useful as an alternative to rice or other flours in a rotation diet. It is not safe on the Specific Carbohydrate Diet™, but is usually one of the grains of choice on reduced carbohydrate diets. It is extremely high in oxalates. Quinoa may taste slightly bitter, but is frequently used in gluten-free cooking, especially in combination with other types of flour.

RAW BUTTER (See BUTTER, RAW)

[146] MacFabe DF, Cain DP, Rodriguez-Capote K, Franklin AE, Hoffman JE, Boon F, Taylor AR, Kavaliers M, Ossenkopp KP. "Neurobiological effects of intraventricular propionic acid in rats: possible role of short chain fatty acids on the pathogenesis and characteristics of autism spectrum disorders." *Behav Brain Res.* 2007 Jan 10;176(1): 149-69.

REACTIVE ATTACHMENT DISORDER (RAD) (See RELATED AND CO-EXISTING DISORDERS)

RECIPE CONVERSION (See COOKING & BAKING)

RECORD KEEPING

The best way to determine whether or not dietary (or any) intervention is working, is by keeping scrupulous records. This will make it much easier to understand and track reactions to foods. Keeping a food diary will be very helpful, but you should also document how your child is progressing with behavior, social interaction and language. You may want to take still pictures or video to document progress in language and table-work. Pictures can be pasted into a record book with notes, or if you use a digital camera you can upload photos to your computer and keep electronic records.

A useful method of checking on your child's progress is to use the "ATEC" (Autism Treatment Evaluation Checklist), at www.autism.com/ari/atec, before starting a new treatment. It takes just a few minutes to fill out this online form, and you can repeat the evaluation periodically to see whether your child's score has improved.

Allison Ditmars created a novel way to record her son's progress on the Low Oxalate Diet: a chart that her son could fill out to communicate about how he was feeling.

"When we first started using the chart, we would fill it out five times a day (school days it was usually three times). Seems like overkill, but at the time we were stalled in progress and my son always had a gray appearance.

Upon waking, after breakfast, lunch and dinner and again at bedtime I'd ask him to complete the chart. I ended up writing my observations on the back of the sheet (i.e. red cheeks, red ears, ashen color, behavior issues, confusion, poor coordination, hyperactivity, auditory processing difficulties etc.) mostly because at the time my son didn't have much to say except he was a "1" or "2" and that his body hurt. I will say though that he started becoming much more curious about how his body worked during this time and pored over anatomy books for awhile.

When we first started LOD we were able to use this chart to get an idea of what was going on during his "dumping." Mostly during that time my son circled his head and stomach. At one point he circled just one of his eyes. I should mention that the way he circles things is also significant. Darker and bigger means it hurts more, smaller and lighter circles means not as bad. (About 3-4 weeks into LOD he stopped circling anything on the body.)

We've actually stopped using the chart on a daily basis; there's nothing to complain about. Now, if he's sick or something is bothering him he just asks for the chart."

I AM FEELING

WHAT'S BOTHERING ME

5	GREAT
4	PRETTY GOOD
3	OK
2	NOT SO GOOD
1	BAD/SICK

DATE_____   TIME_____   NOTE:_____

Idcally, you should keep a log for the first few weeks or months of any intervention, not just diet. For a food diary, note mealtimes, foods eaten, behavior, physical symptoms, abnormal bowel movements, and sleep habits (see ROTATION DIETS).

RECOVERY THROUGH BIOMEDICAL INTERVENTIONS

"Will my child recover from autism?"

The Internet is filled with "recovery" stories after biomedical interventions - especially diet. But if you look more closely, what you will also notice are stories of small successes, of hope, of empowerment for the families of those affected. One parent described how his pediatrician discouraged him about trying the diet, for fear it would give him false hope. He replied, "Well, you are offering me *no* hope. Which option would you follow for *your* child?"

There is no formula to determine if your child is a candidate for "recovery." But there are some important things to consider when asking that question.

Does "recovered" mean that your child will be indistinguishable from his peers? That he would not receive a diagnosis of any kind of developmental disorder after being subjected to a battery of tests?

Now, ask yourself how many "normal" people you know, adults and children, who are "indistinguishable from their peers." The hyperactive child next door? Your best friend's anorexic daughter? Your sister's ex-husband with his "intermittent rage disorder?" Your boss, who denies that she drinks too much? Your uncle, who lives alone in a messy apartment with a computer, and a refrigerator containing nothing but baking soda and chocolate milk? Could any or all of these people benefit from some kind of treatment or intervention? Couldn't you describe them as having a disorder?

As parents, we never know what sort of child we are going to get. Sometimes the best parents end up with a child they never expected to raise, and don't know how to handle. Parenthood makes us exquisitely vulnerable the moment it begins. When parenting is a sorrow, it's hard not to let it wipe away all of the joys. Remember that worry will only drain you of the resources you need to move forward.

> *Don't spend too much time on grief for the child you dreamed of raising; make room for the child you have. Measure your success as a parent based on the process of raising your child, and not on the end result.*

Will your child recover from autism? If "recovered" means that your child would not receive a diagnosis of any kind of developmental disorder after being subjected to a battery of tests, the answer may be no. For the hyperactive child, the anorexic teenager, the angry ex, the hung-over boss, and the eccentric uncle, the answer may also be no.

And for some of you reading this book, the answer will be yes. But that does not mean your child will be "perfect" any more than any other child. Trying to have a perfect child, disabled or not, is a good way of driving yourself (and your child) completely nuts. Making "Full Recovery" your only goal, as the finish line is to a marathon runner, can be both motivating and devastating. So instead, let's stick to the goals that *all* parents aim for:

1.   To provide food, shelter, and a safe environment
2.   To give unconditional love and firm, consistent boundaries
3.   To respect your child for who he is, not for who you want him to be
4.   To look for resources, do research, and provide help when needed
5.   To nurture and forgive him when he falls short of his goals
6.   To nurture and forgive yourself when you fall short of your goals
7.   To help him be a comfortable and integrated member of your family
8.   To teach him to be independent, to the best of his abilities

If you know in your heart that you are working toward these goals, you will keep from seeing your child as a disappointment. *No child will want to meet your gaze if it is always filled with worry, fear and regret.*

RED CHEEKS (See ALLERGIES & INTOLERANCES, PHENOL SULFUR TRANSFERASE DEFICIENCY)

REFLUX

Gastroesophageal reflux (GER) is the actual term for is a common condition involving regurgitation, or "spitting up" of the contents of the stomach into the esophagus. Milk allergy and other food allergies have been strongly associated with GER,[147] [148] and removing milk (or milk and soy) from infant formula or a nursing mother's diet can improve this condition. According to the American Academy of Family Physicians, the prevalence of GER peaks between one to four months of age, and usually resolves by six to twelve months of age.

A more severe form of this disorder is called gastroesophageal reflux disease (GERD). In this case, the infant may have poor weight gain, signs of esophagitis, persistent respiratory symptoms, and neurological delays. GERD occurs in approximately one in 300 infants,[149] and is harder to treat after the infant is over a year old, so talk with your doctor if your child has excessive reflux and a failure to gain weight.

REGRESSION, AFTER STARTING DIETARY INTERVENTIONS

Parents often report physical and behavioral regression after initiating dietary intervention. This is typically a good sign, indicating that dietary intervention will ultimately lead to improvement. After all, if a food to which a person does not have an allergy or intolerance is removed, there should be no reaction at all. If the child has a drug-like "dependence" on the food (see OPIOID EXCESS) then the regression may be very similar to that seen when an addict goes "cold turkey." In addition to behavioral problems, some children experience fevers, gastrointestinal discomfort and other physical symptoms. This typically goes away within one to three weeks. If you see a regression, it is very important not to give the child the food because you are worried about his discomfort, as this will only prolong the problem. Further, giving in to the child will teach him that if he simply tantrums long enough, the "good" food will reappear.

REGRESSION, AFTER PROGRESS ON DIETARY INTERVENTIONS

Children sometimes make great progress soon after starting a special diet, but then regress a few weeks later. This may be due to an increased reliance on a food that has been substituted for foods that were eliminated. For example, heavy reliance on soy or corn after wheat has been eliminated may uncover a previously unnoticed intolerance, or trigger a new one. Another situation in which regression follows initial success is when yeast or other infections flourish due to an increase in carbohydrate foods (common when first transitioning to a new diet). It is nearly always necessary to fine-tune a diet to meet the needs of a particular child.

---

[147] Cavataio F, Carroccio A, Iacono G. "Milk-induced reflux in infants less than one year of age." *J Pediatr Gastroenterol Nutr* 2000;30(suppl):S36-44.

[148] Semeniuk J, Kaczmarski M. "Gastroesophageal reflux (GER) in children and adolescents with regard to food intolerance." *Adv Med Sci.* 2006;51:321-6.

[149] Behrman RE, Kliegman R, Jenso HB, eds. *Nelson Textbook of Pediatrics.* 16th ed. Philadelphia: W.B. Saunders, 2000:1125-6.

REGRESSION, AFTER GOING OFF THE DIET

Some parents have reported that after a successful and effective period of strict dietary intervention, homeopathy, chelation or other restorative treatments healed the immune system and resolved the gluten and casein problem. However, for a child with allergies, an enzyme deficiency or viral infection in the gut, diet may be the only solution currently available, and parents should tread carefully. Some have found that stopping the diet was followed by a few weeks of stability, followed by a regression, sometimes severe. When going off dietary intervention, it is prudent to continue to record what is eaten and any changes in behavior, bowel habits or physical appearance. See also INFRACTIONS, STOPPING DIETARY INTERVENTION IN A DIET RESPONDER.

RELATED AND/OR CO-EXISTING DISORDERS

Do children with Apraxia, Asperger's Syndrome, Attention Deficit Disorder, Auditory Processing Disorders, Bipolar Disorder, Dyspraxia, Expressive/Receptive Language Disorder, Obsessive Compulsive Disorder, Pervasive Developmental Disorder, Schizophrenia, Sensory Integration Dysfunction or Tourette's respond to dietary changes?

What about those with genetic or inborn metabolic disorders such as Down Syndrome, Adenylosuccinate Lyase Deficiency, Angelman Syndrome, Cerebral Folate Deficiency, Duplication of 15q11-q13 or 22q13 deletion, Fetal Alcohol Syndrome, Fragile X, MECP2-related disorders, Histidinemia, Landau-Kleffner Syndrome, Phenylketonuria, Purine Autism, Rett Syndrome, San Filippo syndrome, Smith-Lemli-Opitz Syndrome and Smith-Magenis Syndrome?

The answer is: sometimes yes, and sometimes no.

Some of the above are considered to be disorders on the autism spectrum, and some are often associated with autistic symptoms. If you took the same autistic child to six different doctors, he could be diagnosed with one or more of the above. Some professionals are reluctant to use the "autism" label, perhaps because they don't want to risk being mistaken, or they want to "spare" the family. Many parents report that some of their children with these diagnoses responded dramatically to the diet. Remember, dietary intervention will only benefit some of the symptoms in children with allergies, those with fungal or bacterial overgrowths, or in those whose behaviors are being caused by the abnormal breakdown of proteins.

Some children are vulnerable from birth. Those with allergies, auto-immunity, premature birth, multiple births, Rett or Down Syndrome, or other issues, may be more likely to succumb to a trigger that leads to autism. Quite simply, autism can be a "co-morbid" condition – that is, one distinct disorder often seen together with another.

Special diets will not reverse a true genetic disorder. But they may relieve the accompanying damage that certain foods can do to brain and nervous-system development. In other words, an allergic child with Down may significantly benefit from strengthening a weak immune system and removing food and other allergens, but there is probably little that can be done to resolve the underlying genetic disorder.

However, a child with Down *and autism* may experience a significant reduction in *autistic* symptoms after starting a special diet.

The following are just some of the disorders that:

- Are frequently seen in autistic individuals or their family members
- May sometimes be misdiagnosed
- Will often be remediated by dietary interventions.

Potential responders to special diets are by no means limited to those with these disorders.

Asperger Syndrome (also called Asperger's Syndrome): Asperger Syndrome, when correctly diagnosed, is in many ways distinct from "classic autism." However, there can be a great deal of overlap, both behaviorally and medically. As in the case of all disorders on the autistic spectrum, many children and adults diagnosed with Asperger have benefited from dietary interventions. Teens with AS can find peer support online at www.yahoogroups.com/group/aspergers-teens. Some members of this group are on special diets.

Asthma: Asthma is a chronic respiratory condition in which the airways constrict, swell and are lined with excessive amounts of mucus. Often, asthma attacks are triggered by allergens. It has been reported that children on the autism spectrum who were given multiple courses of antibiotics in their first few years of life are more likely to develop asthma than those who are neurologically typical.[150]

Attention Deficit (Hyperactivity) Disorder - AD(H)D: ADHD is the most commonly diagnosed developmental disorder in children. It is characterized by impulsiveness, inattention and (sometimes) hyperactivity.

Early claims that ADHD is caused by "naughtiness, bad parenting and too much television," have become obsolete. ADHD is now being recognized a distinct physiological entity, with many of the same biochemical markers as in autism (such as oxidative stress[151]). Like autism, prevalence has increased far beyond what can be explained by greater awareness and diagnosis. Because of these similarities, some doctors consider ADHD to be on the autism spectrum, and many children diagnosed with autism, or a related disorder such as Asperger's or PDD, also show signs of ADD or ADHD. In addition, ADHD seems to be remarkably common in siblings of children with autism. Children diagnosed with ADHD may be prescribed stimulant medication like Ritalin or Concerta, but many of them have been able to go "drug-free" with dietary and behavioral interventions.

Auditory Processing Disorders (APD): Auditory processing disorder is a term that describes a variety of problems with the brain that can interfere with processing information. Although people with APD can hear what people are saying to them, they may have difficulty understanding or interpreting it. APD is associated with dyslexia and other developmental disorders, including autism.

Bipolar Disorder (BD) (formerly Manic-Depressive Illness): Bipolar is a mood disorder defined by episodes of abnormally elevated mood (sometimes called "mania") and/or

---

[150] Bock, Kenneth, Cameron Stauth (2008) *Healing the New Childhood Epidemics: Autism, ADHD, Asthma, and Allergies: The Groundbreaking Program for the 4-A Disorders* Ballantine Books.

[151] Bulut M, Selek S, Gergerlioglu HS, Savas HA, Yilmaz HR, Yuce M, Ekici G. "Malondialdehyde levels in adult attention-deficit hyperactivity disorder." *J Psychiatry Neurosci.* 2007 Nov;32(6):435-8.

depressive episodes, or mixed episodes with features of both mania and depression. These episodes are normally separated by periods of normal mood, but in some patients, depression and mania may quickly alternate; this is called "rapid cycling." Some children with autism show a different pattern, in which mania alternates with aggression rather than depression. Mania usually manifests as extreme hyperactivity and inappropriate affect (often silliness) in these children. A number of parents have reported that symptoms of BD have improved significantly in children (autistic and non-autistic) placed on a gluten free, casein free diet.

Cerebral Folate Deficiency Syndrome (CFD): Cerebral folate deficiency is the name for any neurological syndrome associated with low folate metabolism.

> *"Typical features became manifest from the age of 4 months, starting with marked unrest, irritability, and sleep disturbances followed by psychomotor retardation, cerebellar ataxia, spastic paraplegia, and dyskinesia; epilepsy developed in about one third of the children. Most children showed deceleration of head growth from the age of 4 to 6 months. Visual disturbances began to develop around the age of 3 years and progressive sensorineural hearing loss started from the age of 6 years."[152]*

According to a recent study, a milk-free diet and treatment with folinic acid significantly reduced autoantibodies against the folate receptor.[153] In other words, milk can impair the body's ability to use folate, and avoiding it (as well as supplementing the diet with folate) can help to improve the situation.

Down Syndrome (DS): Based on a review of all available studies, George Capone, MD, Director of the Down Syndrome Clinic, and Attending Physician on the Neurobehavioral Unit at Kennedy Krieger Institute in Baltimore, estimates that 5-7% of children with Down's Syndrome have autism spectrum disorders, which is substantially higher than is seen in the general population. He suggests that the occurrence of trisomy 21 lowers the threshold for the emergence of ASD in some children. So, although the disorders are two separate entities, those with DS may be more sensitive to the environmental triggers that can cause autism.

In addition, a study found that people with Down syndrome have an astonishingly high incidence of celiac disease, of at least 7 percent.[154] Screening for the disease in 115 children with Down syndrome (using antigliadin, antiendomysial and antireticulin serum antibodies and an intestinal permeability test) resulted in a positive diagnosis in eight children. The study authors recommend screening all patients with Down syndrome for celiac disease.

Children with DS and autism who respond to dietary intervention show global improvements in their *autistic* behaviors. And there may be other benefits to changing the diet of all children with DS: because their immune systems have been shown to be more fragile than other children, identifying and treating allergies and correcting deficiencies in vitamins and minerals

---

[152] Ramaekers VT, Blau N. "Cerebral folate deficiency." *Dev Med Child Neurol.* 2004 Dec;46(12):843-51.

[153] Ramaekers VT, Sequeira JM, Blau N, Quadros EV. "A milk-free diet downregulates folate receptor autoimmunity in cerebral folate deficiency syndrome." *Dev Med Child Neurol.* 2008 Mar 19.

[154] George EK, Mearin ML, Bouquet J, von Blomberg BM, Stapel SO, van Elburg RM, et al. "High frequency of celiac disease in Down syndrome." *J Pediatr* 1996;128:555-7.

could lower their susceptibility to infection and disease.

Dyslexia: Although not usually closely identified with autism, those with dyslexia often share some symptoms such as visual perception deficits and auditory processing disorders. Researchers testing for opioid peptides have reported that they can identify a specific pattern of abnormal peptides in those with dyslexia, suggesting that a gluten and dairy free diet may be beneficial.

Epilepsy/Seizure Disorders (See EPILEPSY)

Fetal Alcohol Syndrome (FAS): Fetal Alcohol Syndrome is a birth defect that occurs in the children of some women who drink alcohol during pregnancy. It can lead to permanent central nervous system damage, but there are some treatments that can be beneficial. Autism is common in children with FAS, and many families report that dietary intervention, including supplementation, has been very helpful in treating the autistic symptoms. For comprehensive information about FAS, go to www.faslink.org. Under "Key Articles" in the left-hand column, click on "Nutrition" for an article by Diane Black, Ph.D., describing the success of a GF/CF diet for her three adopted children with FAS.

Fibromyalgia Syndrome/Chronic Fatigue (FMS/CFS): Fibromyalgia refers to a disorder involving chronic widespread pain, frequently in combination with chronic fatigue. Those with FMS/CFS commonly report improvements on gluten free diets, as well as elimination diets addressing allergies and food sensitivities. Nightshade foods may be problematic for some. People with Fibromyalgia Syndrome should strictly avoid MSG (see MONOSODIUM GLUTAMATE), with has been associated with symptom flare-ups.[155] It is also worth investigating whether a low oxalate diet can be helpful, since that diet has been rapidly gaining popularity among FMS sufferers.

Fibromyalgia is often seen together with other disorders such as IBS.[156] In one study, all of the subjects with FMS had an abnormal hydrogen breath test (an indicator of intestinal bacterial overgrowth), compared with 84% of subjects with IBS and 20% of control subjects.[157] This supports the theory that those with FMS can benefit from cultured foods and other sources of probiotics.

Environmental sensitivities, for example to smoke and perfume, have also been reported, and people with FMS/CFS may benefit from reducing their exposure to toxins (see ENVIRONMENTAL ILLNESS/ENVIRONMENTAL TOXICITY). Migraines are strongly associated with FMS.

---

[155] Smith et al, "Relief of fibromyalgia symptoms following discontinuation of dietary excitotoxins," *Ann Pharmacother.* 2001 Jun;35(6):702-6.

[156] García MD. "Functional digestive disorders and fibromyalgia." *An R Acad Nac Med (Madr).* 2007;124(3):479-90; discussion 490-4.

[157] Pimentel M, Wallace D, Hallegua D, Chow E, Kong Y, Park S, Lin HC. "A link between irritable bowel syndrome and fibromyalgia may be related to findings on lactulose breath testing." *Ann Rheum Dis.* 2004 Apr; 63(4):450-2.

Anecdotally, parents (especially mothers) of children with autism are reported to have a higher than average incidence of FMS/CFS.

Multiple Sclerosis (MS): Multiple Sclerosis is a progressive, inflammatory, autoimmune disease in which the immune system attacks the central nervous system. Some doctors recommend a gluten and dairy free diet for their patients with MS because significant increases were found for IgA and IgG antibodies against gliadin and gluten in MS patients versus controls, and IgA antibodies against casein were also significantly increased.[158] Other studies on the association between gluten intolerance and MS have had mixed results.

One possible trigger in adults could be a history of childhood vitamin D deficiency,[159] indicating that people living in northern climates should make sure that their children are not deficient in this vitamin.

Obsessive Compulsive Disorder (OCD) and Tourette Syndrome: OCD is an anxiety disorder characterized by recurrent thoughts (obsessions) and/or repetitive behaviors and rituals (compulsions). Repetitive questions or statements and some self-stimulatory behaviors may also be present. Tourette is part of a spectrum of tic disorders that may share some of these symptoms. Both can be seen in children on the autism spectrum. Now, emerging evidence associates some cases with a syndrome called "PANDAS,"[160] where the obsessive/compulsive symptoms are linked with an autoimmune reaction. This is induced by the antibodies from a childhood streptococcal (strep) infection.[161]

Although the reasons for this are unclear, there have been reports that dietary intervention (especially a gluten-free diet), can lessen symptoms of OCD and Tourette, even in people without autism.

Pervasive Developmental Disorder (PDD): PDD is generally considered to be synonymous with autism. As in the case of all disorders on the autism spectrum, many children diagnosed with Pervasive Developmental Disorder have benefited from dietary interventions.

Purine Autism: More than 30 years ago, Drs. Ted Page and Mary Coleman determined that abnormalities of purine and pyrimidine metabolism were common in children with autism and PDD, though no specific enzyme defect has been identified. Purines and pyrimidines are the building blocks of DNA and RNA. A number of cases have been reported in medical literature in which classic autistic symptoms are combined with an overproduction of purine compounds. Research is ongoing to identify the defect, and to explore possible therapies. There have been reports of dietary successes in children with purine autism and other metabolic disorders.

---

[158] Reichelt KL, Jensen D. "IgA antibodies against gliadin and gluten in multiple sclerosis." *Acta Neurol Scand.* 2004 Oct;110(4):239-41.

[159] Munger KL, Levin LI, Hollis BW, Howard NS, Ascherio A (2006). "Serum 25-hydroxyvitamin D levels and risk of multiple sclerosis." *JAMA* 296 (23): 2832-8

[160] Children who meet five diagnostic criteria are classified, according to the hypothesis, as having PANDAS stands for Pediatric Autoimmune Neuropsychiatric Disorders Associated with Streptococcal infections.

[161] Mell LK, Davis RL, Owens D. "Association between streptococcal infection and obsessive-compulsive disorder, Tourette's syndrome, and tic disorder." Pediatrics. 2005 Jul;116(1):56-60.

Pyroluria: Pyroluria is a proposed type of chemical imbalance, possibly genetic, that causes an excess of pyrroles in the blood. The theory behind pyroluria is that these substances bind to vitamin B6 and zinc, strip them from the bloodstream, and flush them out through the urine. Those with pyroluria usually exhibit some symptoms of zinc and B6 deficiencies, including poor stress control, nervousness, anxiety, mood swings, tension, episodic anger, and depression. Those diagnosed with autism, epilepsy, and other disorders may experience some relief when treated for pyroluria.

Approximately 20% of people with pyroluria have symptoms of autism. Pyroluria is treated by restoring vitamin B6 and zinc in efficiently absorbed forms. Additional nutrients which can help to control this balance include manganese, vitamins C and E, and cysteine. Copper and red/yellow food dyes should be avoided.

There have been reports of dietary successes in children with pyroluria, especially in combination with anti-yeast therapies and vitamin/mineral supplementation.

Reactive Attachment Disorder (RAD): Reactive Attachment Disorder is characterized by emotionally disturbed and developmentally inappropriate ways of relating to others. This can be accompanied by severe aggression or sociopathic behavior. RAD is sometimes diagnosed as autism, and vice versa. It has been thought that RAD is always caused by emotional trauma or abuse in early infancy, but there are emerging views that some cases may be genetic or biological. In other words, what causes a child to be emotionally dysfunctional may in part be the same pathological problem that caused the parent's abusive behavior.

In any case, there have been dramatic cases of children with RAD responding to dietary intervention, indicating that for some, these behaviors can be linked with a biomedical condition.

"We adopted my 6-year-old daughter from China when she was 6 months old, and over the years she was diagnosed (or misdiagnosed) with Reactive Attachment Disorder, PTSD, Anxiety Disorder NOS, Neurological Disorder NOS, ADHD, and Sensory Integration Dysfunction. She has blossomed into a totally different child via GF/CF/corn-free/egg-free/Feingold + supplements, etc.

RAD is the first thing that many adoptive parents and professionals think of when a post-institutionalized child is having behavioral & sensory issues, learning delays, etc. When my husband and I learned that other children with aggressive behavior had been helped via the diet, we started it the very next day. Within a couple of days our daughter's rage stopped and our warm, wonderful, loving little girl emerged! I never would have believed the dramatic, overnight changes had I not seen them with my own eyes.

Lily is now 95% recovered via diet and Defeat Autism Now!-based biomedical treatments. Her behaviors are fabulous. Our "finish line" is now purely medical.

I wrote all of this several hours ago and I am still crying. I can not even believe where we were at a year ago compared to where we are at today. It is an unbelievable miracle. Thank you, again. Not only for helping our family, but for all of your efforts over so many years. I can't even think about where we'd be today without your efforts and the help we've received." –Dawn R.

Rett Syndrome: Rett syndrome, which mainly affects girls, is a complex neurological disorder, usually classified as a pervasive developmental disorder, and attributed to a genetic defect. Although present at birth, it becomes more evident during the second year of a child's life.

Many have difficulty walking and have breathing irregularities including hyperventilation, breath-holding and air swallowing.

The condition has been thought to be irreversible, although Scottish researchers have recently had some success using gene therapy to reverse Rett symptoms in mice. However, there is some evidence that there could be benefits from dietary restrictions. Girls with Rett syndrome are prone to gastrointestinal and eating disorders[162] and up to 80% have seizures.[163] The level of IgA antibodies to gluten and gliadin proteins found in grains and to milk casein as well as the level of IgG to gluten and gliadin were compared in 23 girls with Rett syndrome and 53 controls, and highly statistically significant increases were found for the Rett population.[164]

> *"My daughter Jovanah was diagnosed with Retts Syndrome. After believing she was autistic for two years, it was hard to accept this. But unlike autism, genetic testing can (and did) confirm the diagnosis.*
>
> *Jovanah was totally addicted to yogurt, milk, and cheese. It was in May of 2000 that I heard about the GF/CF diet and decided to give it a try. Jovanah had a horrible time with this change, screaming for 5 days, and I decided to put her back on milk and gluten. It was only after discovering Karyn Seroussi's Parents Magazine article a few months later, that I understood that Jovanah had experienced a typical withdrawal reaction to the removal of her beloved milk. I again eliminated gluten and casein from her diet, and after a week, she was a different person.*
>
> *Jovanah stopped laughing hysterically all night, and throwing temper tantrums during the day. She started sleeping though the night. She no longer belched constantly, or had gas, and her ear infections cleared up. Other symptoms abated too. Jovanah walked better and stopped staring at lights. Her eyes were no longer crossed, and she started listening to us. She began to emerge from her private world to join ours.*
>
> *Today, Jovanah is nowhere near normal; she is non-verbal, has no use of her hands and still walks with a wide based gait. That said, however, I know that the diet helped her a great deal. Although she cannot speak, she understands us once again. She recognizes her family and schoolmates.*
>
> *Jovanah has gotten past the worst of her syndrome. Girls with Retts are able to learn once they get past the regression stage and level off. I feel Jovanah is leveling off now. She attends a wonderful program, which has really brought out the best in her. She loves school and her friends. Without the help of her teachers, therapist, little school buddies and diet, she would have never come this far. So if anyone wants to know if this diet can help girls with Retts Syndrome, please tell them the answer is a definite yes." -Sandra Leyva*

Sensory Integration Dysfunction: Sensory Integration Dysfunction (SID) is a neurological disorder causing difficulties with processing sensory information, such as vision, smell, hearing, balance, etc., This condition is usually diagnosed by an occupational therapist, and

---

[162] Isaacs, JS, et al. "Eating difficulties in girls with Rett Syndrome compared with other developmental disabilities." *J.Am Diet Assoc.*, Feb 2003; 103(2): 224-30.

[163] Jian L, et al. "Seizures in Rett Syndrome: An overview from a one-year calendar study." *Eur J paediatr Neurol*, Apr 2007.

[164] Reichelt KL, Skjeldal O. "IgA antibodies in Rett Syndrome." *Autism*, 2006 Mar;10(2):189-97.

treatments usually include a type of occupational therapy called sensory integration therapy.

SID can be diagnosed as its own disorder, or a characteristic of other neurological conditions, including autism spectrum disorders, dyslexia, dyspraxia, Tourette's Syndrome, multiple sclerosis, and speech delays. Parents and physical therapists have reported that SID can be greatly alleviated by dietary intervention. Since sensory perception is affected by the abnormal presence of neuropeptides, this lends additional credibility to the theory of OPIOID EXCESS.

Schizophrenia: Schizophrenia is a mental illness characterized by severe deficits in the perception of reality. Symptoms may include auditory hallucinations, paranoid or bizarre delusions, disorganized speech, and social dysfunction.

Robert Cade, at the University of Florida, found that schizophrenics had significantly higher levels of certain urinary peptides (including casomorphin and gluteomorphin) than normal controls.[165]

More schizophrenics than controls show IgA antibody levels above the upper normal limit to gliadin, beta-lactoglobulin, and casein.[166]

A review of the medical literature published by Johns Hopkins in 2006 concluded that a drastic reduction, if not full remission, of schizophrenic symptoms after initiation of gluten withdrawal has been noted in a variety of studies, in a subset of schizophrenic patients.[167]

Therefore, it is logical to conclude that a strict gluten and dairy free diet should be considered as a safe first line of treatment for patients with schizophrenia.

Tuberous Sclerosis: Tuberous Sclerosis is a rare genetic disease that causes benign tumors to grow in the brain and other vital organs. Symptoms may include seizures, developmental delay, and behavioral problems. Although TS is not reversible, it is possible that these symptoms could be addressed by dietary interventions.

"My daughter has tuberous sclerosis and autism. Although I had heard of the diet long ago, I did not believe it would help my daughter because of her TS. We recently started the diet, and I am amazed at how much improved she is." -Lisa Zinn

RESTAURANTS

Special diets don't have to prevent your family from going out to restaurants. The Gluten Intolerance Group has created The Gluten-Free Restaurant Awareness Program (GFRAP), which allows customers to identify restaurants that are willing and able to prepare GF meals in addition to the regular menu.

---

[165] Cade R, Privette M, Fregly M, Rowland N, Sun Z, Zele V, Wagemaker H, Edlestein C. "Autism and schizophrenia: intestinal disorders." *Nutritional Neuroscience* 3: 57-72, 2000.

[166] Reichelt KL, Landmark J. "Specific IgA antibody increases in schizophrenia." *Biol Psychiatry*, 1995 Mar; 15;37(6):410-3.

[167] Kalaydjian AE, Eaton W, Cascella N, Fasano A. "The gluten connection: the association between schizophrenia and celiac disease." *Acta Psychiatr Scand.* 2006 Feb;113(2):82-90.

GFRAP volunteers meet with restaurant owners to explain gluten-free food preparation. Through this comprehensive program, participating restaurants have been provided with specifically designed gluten-free diet reference materials, meal preparation guidelines, employee awareness posters, and sources for gluten-free foods. There is an ongoing liaison between the restaurant and the program volunteers.

The materials in GFRAP have been reviewed for nutritional accuracy by Cynthia Kupper, RD, CD, Executive Director of the Gluten Intolerance Group®, and accurately reflect the current standards of the gluten-free diet, based on the 2000 American Dietetic Association guidelines.

Visit the GFRAP website at www.glutenfreerestaurants.org to locate participating restaurants. While the program focuses specifically on gluten, chefs should be able to provide ingredient information for most of their foods. There are now restaurants listed in several cities, with the promise of more to come.

If you cannot find restaurants in your area that are participating in this program, consider sending them the following letter, contributed by Christie Atkins of Rome, Georgia:

Dear Restaurant Owner or Manager:

I am the mother of a little boy with a gluten and dairy intolerance. This has affected my entire family's social life, since few eateries can guarantee the complete absence of gluten (wheat, rye, barley, oats) and casein (from dairy) in their foods. Socializing is difficult—especially for the siblings of an allergic child, who can become resentful.

It would be extremely helpful to those of us on this commonly-observed diet to know exactly what foods, if any, you could guarantee to be gluten/dairy free on your menu. We would be especially grateful if you could identify the exact ingredients in these foods, such as cooking oils and canned broth. It is imperative that the cooking utensils and griddles used for gluten-free foods are not in contact with other foods being prepared, and that gluten-free foods do not use the same cooking oil vats as those used for breaded fried foods such as french fries, cheese sticks and fried chicken. A crumb of the wrong food could lead to illness.

This is a common medical condition, but there is very little public awareness about gluten and dairy intolerance. I am a member of an extensive support group, including celiacs, people with allergies, people with autism, and others who avoid gluten. I would love to share a list of eateries that are sensitive to this issue and can offer a few safe foods, or perhaps even create a gluten-free menu.

Thank you for your help. You have the opportunity to offer a great service to our community, and you are likely to see our families much more often!

Often, ethnic foods are not wheat-based, and can be a good option. Here are some possibilities:

Asian Food: Chinese and other Asian restaurants are a popular option for dining out, and can be an excellent choice when traveling. You can order as you normally would for the rest of the family and ask for a steamed entrée without sauce for your child. Most Asian restaurants use a rice steamer to make rice (ingredients: rice, water) so there is virtually no risk of contamination. Many have one or two dishes made with rice noodles.

Potential Problems: Typically, the thickener used in commercial woks is corn starch, but unless your child is extremely sensitive, this may not create a problem. Since soy sauce contains wheat, anything cooked in or served with a brown sauce is probably unsuitable for anyone avoiding gluten or wheat. Wheat free soy sauces such as Tamari* can be purchased from the supermarket or natural foods store; you can take some with you to the restaurant, or bring a sauce from home (see below). Many Asian restaurants make liberal use of MSG in their sauces and soups. If they cannot assure you that your food will be MSG free, order steamed dishes only.

At the Restaurant: If you have a favorite, family-owned Asian restaurant nearby, ask the owners what is used in the white sauce. Ingredients such as chicken broth, garlic, salt, and corn starch, rice wine vinegar or cooking sherry should be safe. However, ask if the broth is homemade or store-bought, since canned chicken broth is rarely gluten-free. If the waiters speak English, you can probably have them discuss your gluten problem with the cook. You can bring your local restaurant a few cans of GF chicken broth and ask them to store it for future orders.

Though most corn sensitive children tolerate cornstarch, you may want to provide an alternative if your child is especially sensitive or has reacted to cornstarch in the past. You can fill a food storage container with arrowroot powder, label it clearly with your last name and phone number, and write: "ARROWROOT POWDER - USE LIKE CORNSTARCH." Identify yourself and ask them to please use your canned broth and arrowroot powder for the sauce. Most restaurants will also cook with wheat free tamari if you provide it — just be sure that they clean the wok before preparing your child's food.

Explain that if they can do this, you will be bringing them your business regularly.

Homemade: If you cannot find a local restaurant that will comply, it is easy to make an Asian stir-fry at home. Combine a half-cup of cold chicken broth, some minced garlic, a teaspoon of arrowroot powder or cornstarch (if tolerated), and a pinch of salt or a tablespoon of wheat-free tamari.

Preheat some vegetable oil (to which you have added a few drops of sesame oil) in a wok or heavy skillet and sauté thinly sliced beef or chicken until cooked through. Add pre-sliced, bite-sized vegetables such as broccoli, snow peas, water chestnuts, sliced carrots, etc., along with ¼ cup of water, and stir-fry until the vegetables are tender but firm, and the water has evaporated. Stir in your sauce at the very end and bring to bubbling. The arrowroot or corn starch will cause the sauce to thicken quickly. If it doesn't, add more starch to a small bowl of cold water and add slowly to wok until mixture thickens.

Serve with rice and watch for your family's smiles of surprise.

Note, not all Tamari is wheat-free. Be sure to read the labels carefully. If you cannot find wheat-free Tamari at your market, check the health food store or a local Asian market. If a yeast-free regimen compels you to avoid fermented foods, try Bragg Liquid Aminos. This non-fermented gluten-free product is very similar to soy sauce in taste and appearance.

Indian Food: Indian cuisine also includes many dishes that are either grain free, or can be easily modified. Instead of naan or puri (common breads) you can order pappadum, which are are thin crunchy Indian crackers made of lentil flour. Many Indian dishes contain no dairy or grains, and they often have unusual meats that may work for children with multiple sensitivities. Try a smaller restaurant, where you can discuss the menu options with a manager or cook.

Italian Food: Again, the best choice is a small, family owned restaurant where you can speak with the cook or a manager. A simple meal like broiled chicken and vegetables on seasoned rice (instead of pasta) is delicious when made by an experienced chef. A few pizza restaurants now offer gluten-free crusts, so you can ask for a topping of olive oil, vegetables, meat and sauce (ask to see the ingredients of the crust - some contain corn, soy, and in Europe, wheat starch). Smaller restaurants may let you provide an appropriate crust, and use toppings you specify. Though you are actually providing most of the ingredients, it is still "eating out" to your child.

RETT SYNDROME (See RELATED AND CO-EXISTING DISORDERS)

RICE

If grains are allowed on your child's diet, rice is filling and easy to make. It contains niacin, selenium, and thiamine. If tolerated, rice will contribute to a huge variety of baking and cooking combinations. Brown rice is higher in nutrients and fiber. White rice is higher in starch, but lower in oxalates.

For some, rice triggers as severe reaction as gluten, soy or corn. This may be due to an allergy to the rice protein, worsened by an over-reliance on rice when other foods have been removed from the diet. In other cases it may be due to the similarity between rice and gluten proteins. Dr. Braley from Immunolabs writes, *"Wheat glutenin, cross-reacted with antibody raised against rice globulin, suggests that rice C globulin, which is an antibody found in all rice, represents a protein similar to wheat C glutenin. If you are allergic to one, you may be allergic to the other ... and the reason we may not be picking up on it is because we are not testing the right subfractions."*

Recently, it has been found that some different types of rice grown in different parts of the world contain amounts of arsenic above the level considered safe. Of the types tested, brown rice tended to contain slightly higher amounts than white, while basmati rice from India or Egypt were among the safest varieties. If testing indicates that your arsenic levels are high, this might be something worth investigating.

ROTATION DIETS (See also ALLERGIES & INTOLERANCES, ELIMINATION
   DIETS)

Premise: Intolerance to any food may become more severe if that food is consumed daily. However, if a food is avoided for several weeks, and then re-introduced, the reaction may be more noticeable than ever before. If you rotate the foods in the diet (typically every four days, but that could vary), you may be less likely to worsen matters, and allow a sensitive person to eat a greater variety of foods without putting too much stress on his immune system.

How-to: To keep track of the rotation schedule, it is best to use a food diary, a chart such as the one below, or an inexpensive appointment book, to record the allowed foods for each day. This can be done at the beginning of each month, or every few days.

If you decide to do a rotation diet, you will need to develop your planning skills, and to remember to pack meals whenever you will be going out of the house. However, the odd slip-up or improvisation should not make a huge difference, as long as you return to your schedule as soon as possible.

After several weeks, you may choose to try rotating in foods previously known to cause *very mild* reactions, such as stomach ache, red ears, itchy skin, etc., then wait four days, and decide whether they can be added to the rotation schedule.

There are several ways to rotate foods.

Some people rotate all foods, including those that seem to be well-tolerated, to prevent new sensitivities from developing.

Some have found it easier to rotate only those foods that are known culprits, while using "safe" foods throughout the rotation period.

*Caution: Do not attempt to use any foods that cause hives, swelling, breathing problems or other severe reactions. These should be tested **only** under a doctor's supervision.*

You will have to use your judgement about which type of rotation diet to start out with.

First: Make a "safe" list of all foods your child tolerated well, or reasonably well. This list may be quite short, if your child is very sensitive. Then list foods that are "questionable," or which have shown up as a mild positive on IgG allergy tests. Other foods, known to be problematic, can be added later.

Many families have had good results with a four-day rotation schedule. Start with four days of only the "safe" foods. Then begin rotating in the "questionable" foods: a new one every four days. In your food diary, note any changes, including sleep irregularities, skin, bowels or behavior problems. Trust your intuition and observations, and remove anything you feel is not working.

Typically, grains are amongst the most problematic for sensitive people. Therefore, people commonly rotate GF grains like corn, millet, quinoa, buckwheat, teff, sorghum and amaranth, as well as soy flour, bean flours or grain-free starchy flours such as tapioca, potato, yam, and white sweet potato. Some specialty companies carry rare, exotic root flours for highly allergic people, but these tend to be expensive.

You may be able to identify problem foods by recording allergic reactions or changes in behavior in your food diary. Reactions can take up to three days to manifest, so in this manner, you can look back over several days to see a pattern.

Note: environmental sensitivities (mold, pollen, smoke, cleaning products, etc.) may also affect behavior, so it could take several trials to be certain that a food is the culprit.

A Simple Rotation Diet: In a simple rotation diet, the days are designated (for example, A, B, C, D; A, B, C, D...etc.). The "A-day" food list might include something like lamb, carrots, potatoes, eggs, buckwheat, tuna, and onions. (Foods served on that day could include buckwheat and egg pancakes, fried eggs, fish or lamb stew with carrots, onions and potatoes, lamb patties with eggs, onions and potato starch, tuna with mayonnaise and onions, carrot sticks, baked potatoes, etc.) There are many possible combinations of these foods, so they can always be served together on A-day, but not on any other days.

Note: this chart is only an example. Your rotation chart should include foods that are tolerated by **your child**.

	DAY A	DAY B	DAY C	DAY D
	lamb, carrot, onion, pear, egg, buckwheat, banana, potato, tuna, zucchini, parsnip	*chicken, tomato, garlic, plum, cashew, beans, spinach, quinoa, rice, corn, avocado*	*beef, broccoli, ginger, soy, pumpkin, cucumber, amaranth, blueberries, honey, sesame seeds*	*pork, sage, shallots, strawberries, tapioca, pineapple, coconut, brown sugar, carob*
Breakfast **Snack 1** **Lunch** **Snack 2** **Dinner**	**Thurs, May 3** buckwheat banana pancakes zucchini-carrot muffin tuna-onion-egg croquettes zucchini-carrot muffin lamb stew, pear sauce	**Fri, May 4** corn flakes w/rice milk rice cakes w/cashew butter chicken-spinach rice bowl guacamole & tortilla chips chicken tacos w/toppings	**Sat, May 5** amaranth flakes - soy milk amaranth-pumpkin muffins hamburger, cucumber blueberries w/soy cream beef broccoli -ginger with gf soy sauce	**Sun, May 6** tapioca bread, tahini, jam coconut-carob cookies pork sausages w/sage strawberries ham-pineapple-coconut milk
Skin (circle one)	very good average poor	very good average poor	very good average poor	very good average poor
Bowels (circle one)	very good average poor	very good average poor	very good average poor	very good average poor
Pupils (circle one)	large normal tiny	large normal tiny	large normal tiny	large normal tiny
Behavior (circle one)	very good average poor	very good average poor	very good average poor	very good average poor
Sleep (circle one)	very good average poor	very good average poor	very good average poor	very good average poor

It can be very practical to make large batches of food (such as lamb stew or hamburgers, muffins or cookies) and freeze single portions in zipper bags, labeling each for day "A," "B," "C" or "D."

Some people like to try to group food families together on each day. For example, A-Day is legumes day (peas, beans, peanuts, etc.), B-Day includes squashes and gourds, C-Day includes brassicas (broccoli, cabbage, brussels sprouts, etc.), and so on.

While most seem to define one day as midnight to midnight (calendar day), you can also use 24-hour segments that go from dinner on one day to late afternoon on the next. This means that you can eat eggs for lunch and then again at breakfast-time the next day, or make a stir-fry for dinner and serve the leftovers at lunchtime. See chart below for an example:

	DAY B
	chicken, tomato, garlic, plum, cashew, beans, spinach, quinoa, rice, corn, avocado
	Fri, May 4 – Sat, May 5
Dinner	chicken tacos w/toppings
Breakfast	corn flakes w/rice milk
Snack 1	rice cakes w/cashew butter
Lunch	Leftover taco meat, rice
Snack 2	guacamole & tortilla chips

Another method is to put each individual food on its own rotation schedule. This is much more complicated when you are rotating several foods, but allows greater freedom to combine them in different ways.

There are several great books available on food intolerance and rotation diets. *The Yeast Connection Cookbook* by William Crook has several simple but inventive recipes that make food rotation easier to implement, while *Is This Your Child* by Doris Rapp is the classic resource for identifying food and environmental sensitivities.

RYE

Rye is a gluten-containing cereal grain which is closely related to barley and wheat. It has a slightly lower gluten content than wheat, and may be better tolerated by those who cannot eat wheat or other grains due to allergy or intolerance, but *it is not suitable for those on a gluten-free diet.*

SACCHARIN (See SUGAR SUBSTITUTES)

SALICYLATES (See also FEINGOLD PROGRAM)

Salicylates are chemicals related to aspirin. There are several kinds of salicylate, which plants manufacture as a natural pesticide. These should be avoided in the first stage of the Feingold program, although at a later stage some may be tolerated.

Salicylates are especially high in many fruits - especially unripened fruit, and are often concentrated just under the skin. High levels of salicyates can also be found in several types of vegetables, red grapes, berries, almonds, candies, honey, most spices, and a number of other foods

For more information, go to www.feingold.org.

SARA'S DIET

In the 1990s, Sandra Desorgher-Johnson noticed that her autistic daughter Sara reacted poorly to colored foods, especially foods high in a compound called LUTEIN. She advocated the removal of such foods from the diet long before there was information about phenols and oxalates, which are also frequently found in brightly-colored fruits and vegetables.

SCD (See SPECIFIC Carbohydrate DIET™)

SCHOOL COMPLIANCE (See COMPLIANCE)

SCHOOL LUNCHES (See also MEALS & SNACKS)

Many schools are attempting to increase nutrition in school lunches and snacks, implementing rules such as "if sugar is in the first three ingredients listed, the food cannot be served at school." Other schools are attempting to get rid of foods containing sugars, colors, preservatives, chemicals, and non-nutritive fillers. Unfortunately, most school systems resist these changes for budgetary reasons, when in fact, school systems that have "junked the junk food" are saving money on food, reducing waste and eliminating behavior and learning problems.

The Feingold Program has put together a slideshow at www.school-lunch.org/SCHOOLS/ intro.html, documenting the problems in "typical" school fare, and showing the benefits that come to students and teachers alike by changing school food. If you can, try to share this slideshow with students, parents, and school administrators in your area. It is true that most children on the autism spectrum will be eating a lunch packed at home, but we must still support the efforts to clean up school lunches - after all, our children have siblings and friends who are eating this food.

Many parents are stymied when it comes to making five sack lunches a week. A school lunch generally includes five elements: a sandwich or hot entrée, a fruit, a salty snack, a drink and a dessert. Although we do not want to send in the same food every day, remember that your child may only pick a few foods out of their lunchbox, and the rest will end up in the trash. The goal is to pack a lunch that is as varied as possible but is still appealing to your child.

Children on special diets may be intrigued by the "Lunchables®" at the supermarket, which are packaged lunches with different foods divided into little compartments. Of course these dietary and environmental horrors are little more than expensive packaging filled with junk food, but children do seem to love them. However, it is easy to make your own "lunchable," using healthy, appropriate ingredients and a reusable divided container. These are easy to find; Tupperware® has a school lunch container called a "Lunch'n Things™" on the home page of their website (www.tupperware.com). Your local dollar store or kitchen/bath outlet might also have something suitable.

If your child likes a sandwich for lunch, you can use a gluten free bread or roll to make a sandwich that fits neatly into the center compartment. For those on more restrictive diets, nut breads or nut waffles will also make good sandwiches. Side compartments could hold fruit, vegetables, a drink and perhaps a dessert. The sandwich section can hold other items too—if you pack rice or nut crackers with some leftover sliced meat, or a bit of nut butter and a plastic knife, and your child can make his own "sandwiches." Since this is the idea behind many of the Lunchables®, this might appeal to the child who wants to be like his peers.

Some children do not care for sandwiches, or simply prefer a hot lunch. The simplest hot lunch is leftover dinner. Make a little extra of something you know your child will enjoy, and set it aside before dinner. To keep the main dish hot, use a glass free Thermos®. You can buy a stainless steel "food jar" directly from the Thermos® website, www.thermos.com for under $20. These food jars are unbreakable, and keep food hot for up to seven hours. You can pack the jar with soup, casseroles, pasta or even chicken nuggets---whatever your child will eat.

If you include an appropriate and tasty dip, many children will eat vegetables with their lunch. Berries, grapes or other "finger sized" fruits can be sent in little bags. There are lots of interesting salty snacks—lunches don't have to have chips every day. If nuts are allowed (many schools prohibit them due to allergies) a small bag of nuts makes a more nutritious snack than chips, and works for most diets.

SCHOOL SUPPLIES

Sometimes teachers are scrupulously careful about foods given to children on special diets, but use school supplies that contain forbidden ingredients. While gluten molecules are too large to transfer through the skin, many children taste their paints, glues and other supplies, or touch their hands to their mouths and ingest them accidentally. Having appropriate school supplies is especially important for younger children, who spend more time using arts and craft materials, and who are more likely to put things in their mouths.

Try to meet with teachers at the start of the school year and get a list of supplies that will be used. If your child's school has a sensory table, you can request that it be filled with rice or dried beans, instead of macaroni or gluten grains. You may want to volunteer to be the "playdough parent" and keep the classroom supplied with a safe version that you don't have to worry about (see PLAYDOUGH).

If the school is unwilling to ensure that all of the supplies they use are safe, you can put together a tub of appropriate items for your child's use. For a list of safe school supplies, visit the TACA website (www.gfcf-diet.talkaboutcuringautism.org), and click on "School Implementation" on the links to the left.

SCIENCE

Some doctors discourage parents from trying dietary intervention on the grounds that its usefulness has not been proven. Double-blind studies have been difficult to maintain for the 28 weeks necessary for a good trial, since people usually know what they are feeding their children. However, there are several peer-reviewed reports that establish the utility of dietary intervention, including a one-year, single-blind study,[168] and the many studies referenced throughout this book. A study design now being attempted includes the use of gluten or dairy "challenge" capsules versus placebos, in children placed on the diet.

---

[168] Ann-Mari Knivsberg, Reichelt, K.L., Høien, Torleiv. "Effect of a Dietary Intervention on Autistic Behavior," *Focus on Autism and Other Developmental Disabilities*, 2003 Vol. 18, No. 4, 248-257.

Thousands of case reports likewise lend credibility to the benefits achieved through dietary changes. Defeat Autism Now! Doctors agree that no other effective treatment has a higher probability of success.

See STUDIES for information on where to find printable lists of studies supporting dietary interventions.

SECRETIN

Secretin is a peptide hormone produced in the duodenum. It has been used, for many years, as a test of pancreatic function (often as part of a routine colonoscopy). In the 1990's, a mother named Victoria Beck noticed a marked improvement in her son following a colonoscopy. There were other reports of children with autism having a favorable response to secretin infusions, but double-blinded, placebo controlled studies did not show a statistically significant response. It is likely that a small percentage of children with autism do show improvement following secretin infusion, but this treatment appears to have limited potential for the autism population at large.

SEEDS

Seeds are the mature, fertilized ovules of the certain flowering plants. Nutrients vary, but all seeds contain protein, minerals, vitamins and unsaturated fats. Most are rich in phosphorus and unhulled sesame seeds are an excellent source of calcium. Most seeds are extremely high in oxalates, and must be avoided in the early stages of the LOD.

- **Flax seeds** also contain essential fatty acids. They are a good source of lignans (phytoestrogens) that have anti-viral, anti-bacterial and anti-fungal properties. Flax seeds also contain lecithin, which emulsifies fat and cholesterol. It is better to purchase whole flax seeds and grind them as needed because ground flax tends to go rancid.

- **Hemp seeds** are a concentrated source of essential fatty acids (EFAs). They are also high in other nutrients such as protein, magnesium, potassium, sulfur, ascorbic acid, beta-carotene, calcium, fiber, iron, potassium, phosphorus, riboflavin, niacin and thiamin. Like sunflower seed butter, hemp seed butter is a nut-butter alternative for people who cannot eat peanuts or tree nuts.

- **Pumpkin seeds** are dark green, with a very nutty flavor. Pumpkin seeds and pumpkin seed oil contain both omega-3 and omega-6 fatty acids. They are a good source of vitamin A, calcium and iron. Raw, shelled pumpkin seeds make an excellent snack or lunch box addition. Do not buy the overly salted, crusted seeds available in convenience stores. Buy them, either in the shell or hulled, at the health food store.

- **Sesame seeds** are 19% protein, and are considered one of the highest sources of calcium in the world when the husk is intact. They are also an excellent source of B vitamins and minerals. Raw sesame seeds are brown, compared with the more common hulled white seeds. They can be sprinkled on just about any food to improve the nutrition and flavor.

- **Sunflower seeds** are delicious and very healthy, containing protein, B vitamins, linoleic acid, potassium, magnesium and iron. There are 174 mg of calcium in a cup of seeds, and their phosphorus helps the body absorb it. Sunflower seed flour is one of the richest sources of iron available. Flour can be made by grinding in a food processor. Take care not to over process, or you will have sunflower butter (which can be a good substitute for peanut butter.)

Sprinkle seeds into nutritionally low foods such as cookies or cereal. Many of them can be blended with a little salt and oil into a delicious, spreadable alternative to peanut butter.

SKEPTICISM FROM DOCTORS AND OTHERS

Dietary and nutritional approaches to healing are relatively new concepts for many people. Education about nutrition is minimal in most medical schools, and some doctors insist that dietary interventions are useless or even potentially dangerous. It is becoming common practice for patients to educate their doctors, printing articles and study abstracts, and bringing them in for discussion. At the very least, a good physician should keep an open mind. If you keep data (see RECORD KEEPING) and can show that diet is well correlated with physical and behavioral improvements, you may convince even the most skeptical.

"I am so angry at myself for listening to others and not trying this eight months ago, when my son was diagnosed. I repeatedly asked professionals along the way and everyone discouraged me, even my sister, who has two autistic boys. I can't help but wonder what my son would be like if I had started it back then. A few days ago he got a hold of two goldfish crackers and we had three days of horrible symptoms return. I now have my son taking a multivitamin, a calcium-magnesium supplement, and Omega 3 supplement. I am thinking of trying the yeast diet too. I am trying to find out what else I need to do.

I am now obsessed with medically treating my child along with continuing his educational training. Thank you for your time and for opening my eyes. I have been obsessed with trying to find ways to help my son compensate for his symptoms and now I am obsessed with helping my son alleviate his symptoms. The diet is really doing amazing things for him!"

-Name withheld by request

Sometimes other parents of autism spectrum children will acknowledge the improvements in a child, but deny that biomedical treatments and diets are responsible.

"My daughter is just over three right now. Around 15-16 months I realized something wasn't quite right. She has a twin brother, so it was easy to see a difference. I work in the field and know all too well what autism looks like. By 2 years old she was most definitely autistic.

I started her on a strict GF/CF diet and supplements after reading success stories online. We noticed immediate results, and one by one her behaviors and sensory issues diminished, then disappeared. We had a thorough evaluation done in October and she does not qualify for a diagnosis of autism or PDD. We have a bit of speech delay, but she's only a few months behind at this point. She's otherwise typical in every other way.

I still attend our local autism support group, but I feel kind of funny about it. I'm the only one who put my child on the diet for any length of time and saw dramatic results. No one in the group currently has their kids on the diet. I almost feel as if they think I made the whole autism story up. I've had numerous people question me after seeing my daughter as to whether or not it was truly autism." -Chris Lamont

The only practical advice is to be patient. Research takes us closer each day to the widespread scientific validation and recognition of the importance of dietary and biomedical interventions. Until then, seek out doctors and others who will be open-minded and supportive of the work that you are doing with your child. See also COMPLIANCE, DOCTORS.

SKIN CARE PRODUCTS

Nicotine patches, birth-control patches and other transdermal applications of medications provide ample proof that the skin absorbs many things and passes them to the bloodstream. It is sometimes said that one should never put anything on one's skin that one wouldn't put in one's mouth.

Luckily, according to dermatologist John Zone, MD,[169] gluten molecules are too large to pass through the skin. Therefore, shampoo, lotions and cosmetics should not be a big concern, unless you have a child who is likely to try to drink them. TOOTHPASTE is an entirely different matter, since some of it is likely to be ingested. The same goes for LIP BALM.

However, problems can occur from hand to mouth: a child wearing gluten-containing sunblock might lick his fingers, which is a good reason to avoid giving children access to anything that might pose a threat.

SLEEP DISORDERS (See also ALLERGIES & INTOLERANCES, MELATONIN)

Many autistic children have trouble sleeping. There has been some emerging data indicating that sleep disorders in autism may have to do with a melatonin deficiency (see MELATONIN), which results in an abnormal circadian rhythm.[170] Several treatments have been suggested, and found to be effective for some children. These include melatonin supplements, epsom salt baths before bedtime, light therapy (including a careful avoidance of light in the evenings), and treatment of any food intolerances, which can also disrupt sleep. It's also important to factor in the use of medications, such as Ritalin, which can cause sleeplessness, as well as any underlying illness, such as undiagnosed bowel disease.

SOCIAL ASPECTS OF THE DIET (See also COMPLIANCE)

Many parents worry that a special diet will draw attention to the differences between a special-needs child and his peers, especially in social situations such as birthday and holiday parties. For the most part, children accept their situation as long as they have access to special treats that resemble those of their friends, and as long as they are not teased.

Victoria West, a mom in New Mexico, provided learning materials to the school for a classroom lesson series on allergies and food safety. She used the book, *The Story of Mr. Allergyhead.*[171] The school already had children with severe peanut and chemical sensitivities, had signs posted at all doors advising of restrictions on campus, and were open to this kind of

---

[169] *Living Without Magazine,* Spring 2003.

[170] Kulman G, Lissoni P, Rovelli F, Roselli MG, Brivio F, Sequeri P. "Evidence of pineal endocrine hypofunction in autistic children." *Neuro Endocrinol Lett.* 2000;21(1):31-34.

[171] For more information, visit www.mrallergyhead.com.

information. Since there were other children with allergies in her son's classroom, he didn't feel singled out. Victoria also made up cookie bags at Christmas for all the children, the teacher, and aides just so they could taste the "special" goodies. This helped prevent incidents of classmates implying her son was deprived of "normal" treats.

If possible, it's important to teach your children to respond simply and politely when somebody offers them food. For example, "no thank you, I have food allergies." If they are asked to which foods, they can say, "lots of foods, but especially milk and wheat." If somebody tells them a food is safe for them, they need to be able to explain that they have to check with their parent before accepting it.

It's harder with teenagers, however, especially those who are relatively high-functioning. There is no point in pretending that special diets will never create a problem in social situations. Make sure they know what they can eat outside of the house, for example, ordering a salad and fries when going out with their friends for pizza. They can always discreetly pop a couple of enzyme tablets to be safe. Luckily, more and more young people have been diagnosed with food allergies, so it's likely that your child is not the only one who will have to politely decline.

"My son (age 13) has the message, loud and clear, that those foods make him sick, and he knows we are 100% committed to making sure that he doesn't accidentally get any. When he says wistfully that fresh-baked bread smells so good, I try to acknowledge his feelings: 'Yeah, you must hate having allergies. I'm really proud of you for dealing with it so bravely.'"

SODIUM BENZOATE (BENZOATE OF SODA, BENZOIC ACID)

Sodium benzoate is a food preservative, found most often in sodas, sugar substitutes, frozen foods and vegetables. It is one of the few additives that has been scientifically proven to be linked to hyperactivity in children (see FOOD ADDITIVES). Benzoate/benzoic acid should never be used by people sensitive to aspirin.

SORBITOL (See SUGAR SUBSTITUTES)

SORGHUM

Grown primarily for animal feed, this gluten free grain is also ground into flour for human use. Commonly used in India, it makes an excellent substitute for wheat in baking, particularly when it is combined with other flours. Sorghum is sometimes called Jowar.

SOY

Most doctors who recommend dietary interventions suggest eliminating soy in addition to gluten, casein and other foods. Soy is known to be a highly allergenic food, and although it is a legume, its protein is structurally similar to that of milk. Soy allergy is common in babies and children with milk allergy. In fact, a report from the Committee on Nutrition at the American Academy of Pediatrics (AAP) states:

Severe gastrointestinal reactions to soy protein formula have been described for greater than 30 years, and encompass the full gamut of disease seen with cow milk protein in infancy: enteropathy, enterocolitis, and proctitis. Small-bowel injury, a reversible celiac-like villus injury that produces an enteropathy with malabsorption, hypoalbuminemia, and failure to thrive, has been documented in at least four studies.

Severe enterocolitis manifested by bloody diarrhea, ulcerations, and histologic features of acute and chronic inflammatory bowel disease also has been well described in infants receiving soy protein-based formulas. ...They respond quickly to elimination of the soy formula and introduction of a hydrolyzed protein formula. Their degree of sensitivity to soy protein during the first few years of age can remain dramatic; thus, casual use of soy-based formula is to be avoided. Most children, but not all, can resume soy protein consumption safely after 5 years of age.

In addition, up to 60% of infants with cow milk protein-induced enterocolitis also will be equally sensitive to soy protein. It is theorized that the intestinal mucosa damaged by cow milk allows increased uptake and, therefore, increased immunologic response to the subsequent antigen soy. Eosinophilic proctocolitis, a more benign variant of enterocolitis, also has been reported in infants receiving soy protein-based formula.

These dietary protein-induced syndromes of enteropathy and enterocolitis, although clearly immunologic in origin, are not immunoglobulin E-mediated, reflecting instead an age-dependent transient soy protein hypersensitivity. Because of the reported high frequency of infants sensitive to both cow milk and soy antigens, soy protein-based formulas are not indicated in the management of documented cow milk protein-induced enteropathy or enterocolitis.[172] [173] [174] [175]

In other words, if milk allergy is a problem, soy allergy is likely to be a problem. And just as milk intolerance may be outgrown after five years of strict avoidance, the same may be true of soy intolerance. However, the question still remains: can soy peptides lead to autistic behaviors?

Some time ago, Dr. Shaw from the Great Plains Laboratory expressed concern about soy because a high percentage of the autistic children that he tested for IgG allergy showed reactivity to soy as well as milk. He also noticed some cross-reactivity in his test for casomorphin. Many parents report that soy seems to affect behavior, and one must ask whether this is due to allergy and discomfort, or to the uptake of "soymorphins."

In October 2007, evidence emerged showing that soy can indeed break down into the same kind of opioid peptides known to be derived from dairy and gluten,[176] creating further reason to try a soy-free trial period for your child.

Soy is high in both OXALATES and PHENOLS, other substances that may be problematic. Like milk, soy is becoming a controversial food. It is an excellent cash crop, a delicious substitute for many dairy products, and a good source of protein, but there are several cautionary tales about soy. Some claim that excessive use of soy results in estrogen dominance,

[172] American Academy Of Pediatrics Committee On Nutrition: "Soy Protein-Based Formulas: Recommendations For Use In Infant Feeding." *Pediatrics* Vol. 101 No. 1 January 1998, Pp. 148-153.

[173] Burks AW, Casteel HB, Fiedorek SC, Williams LW, Pumphrey CL. "Prospective oral food challenge study of two soybean protein isolates in patients with possible milk or soy protein enterocolitis." *Pediatr Allergy Immunol.* 1994;5:40–45.

[174] Eastham EJ. "Soy protein allergy.2 In: Hamburger RN, ed. *Food Intolerance in Infancy: Allergology, Immunology, and Gastroenterology.* Carnation Nutrition Education Series. Vol 1. New York, NY: Raven Press; 1989: 223–236.

[175] Whitington PF, Gibson R. "Soy protein intolerance: four patients with concomitant cow's milk intolerance." *Pediatrics.* 1977;59:730–732.

[176] Ohinata K, Agui S, Yoshikawa M. "Soymorphins, Novel mu Opioid Peptides Derived from Soy beta-Conglycinin beta-Subunit, Have Anxiolytic Activities." *Biosci Biotechnol Biochem.* 2007 Oct 7.

leading to decreased fertility and libido. Many people who use soy experience indigestion and flatulence. Although fermented soy products like tamari and miso may be healthy choices, these products are not always gluten free, so check labels carefully.

Soy is one of the largest GMO and sprayed crops, so if you include some soy in your diet, consider organic, non-GMO sources, which may be less problematic for people with food sensitivities.

Research the soy debate yourself – you can start with a visit to the website for the Food and Drug administration (FDA): www.fda.gov. Type "soy" into the search box to read several articles on the subject.

Foods Containing Soybean Protein: edamame, miso, soy albumin, soy flour, soy nuts, soy protein, soy sauce, tamari, tempeh, textured vegetable protein (TVP) and tofu.

Note that some of these foods (soy sauce, tempeh) may also contain gluten. Ingredients labeled "vegetable broth," "vegetable gum," or "vegetable starch," especially in Asian foods, *may* contain soy protein. Soybean oil and soy lecithin are usually considered safe for those with a soy allergy.

SOYBEAN OIL (See FATS & OILS)

SPASTIC COLON (See IRRITABLE BOWEL SYNDROME)

SPECIFIC CARBOHYDRATE DIET™ (SCD™)

The Specific Carbohydrate Diet™ is a special type of gluten-free diet, developed by Dr. Sidney Valentine Haas and described in his book *The Management of Celiac Disease*. Originally developed to treat Crohn's disease, ulcerative colitis, celiac disease and cystic fibrosis, the SCD™ has also been used successfully for treating severe diarrhea, "failure to thrive," and other gastrointestinal problems.

After her daughter responded to this diet, the late Elaine Gottschall wrote a groundbreaking book on the topic called *Breaking the Vicious Cycle: Intestinal Health Through Diet*. This book inspired many families to find out whether the Specific Carbohydrate Diet™ could be helpful for their autism spectrum children.

Theory: This diet is based on the premise that damaged intestinal walls and bacterial overgrowth from undigested carbohydrates cause immune dysfunction and poor health. Because the bacteria are believed to feed on these complex sugars and starches, restricting them should restore the proper ecology of intestinal flora, and allow the gut to heal. Reducing the immune load on the gut may also greatly reduce food sensitivities: after a year on the diet, some people report that their intolerances have been reduced or resolved. Many children with a history of gastrointestinal problems have greatly benefited from this regimen.

Summary of the diet: The SCD™ limits the diet to monosaccharides, which require minimal digestion and are easily absorbed. That means that it eliminates all starches and most sugars, consisting mainly of meats, fish, eggs, vegetables, fruits, nuts, and seeds (see Part I for a list of "safe foods"). Other potentially problematic foods, such as chocolate and soy, are also removed. Although some types of dairy are allowed on the original version of this diet, casein tends to remain a problem for children on the autism spectrum, so many families opt to do a

> *"Children with autism who are implementing SCD™ are demonstrating remarkable improvements in bowel function, language, eye contact, self-stimulatory behavior, anxiety, and mood. The SCD™, unlike other specialized diets, works by removing the foods that cannot be properly broken down. The vicious cycle of malabsorption, maldigestion, inflammation, and food allergies seen in children with autism can be corrected using this dietary approach, and healthy digestion can begin."*
>
> -Pam Ferro, RN, The Gotschall Autism Center

non-dairy version of the SCD™.

Who might benefit: There are many children who make only minor improvement on a gluten and casein free diet, despite strict adherence. Proponents of the SCD™ suggest that these children cannot implant normal flora even with judicious supplementation. They may also continue to show deficiencies in vitamins, minerals, fatty acids and amino acids. Therefore, those on a gluten and casein free diet who continue have chronic yeast overgrowth, *Clostridia*, gas, bloating, diarrhea or constipation are good candidates.

What to do: For GI disorders like ulcerative colitis and Crohns Disease, strict adherence to the SCD™ is required for healing and the relief of symptoms. SCD™ proponents say that the same rigorous adherence is necessary to achieve full results in the case of autism disorders.

Some parents have noted that cutting a substantial amount of starches and sugars will yield significant benefits, and that the level of adherence can be fine-tuned to meet the needs of the individual and the family. However, it's difficult to say how much is "too much," and words like "limit, restrict, and reduce" can mean very different things to different people. A big advantage of the SCD™ is that its guidelines are an absolute: *monosaccharides only.*

Therefore, if you have decided to reduce the amount of starch and sugar in your child's diet, it makes sense to start with a trial on the SCD™, which is bound to help break your child's addiction to these foods. Follow the guidelines specially designed for ASD children at www.pecanbread.com, and ask for support from experienced parents. Even if you see a pattern of ill health which does not improve and you decide to change tack, your child will probably be eating nutritious foods that you never dreamed would cross his lips.

What to expect: As with other special diets, a regression may occur at the start. It is important to not to become discouraged. Some people recommend a gradual removal of complex carbohydrates and sugars to reduce the severity of a die-off reaction.

The SCD™ is divided into stages, with the first stage consisting of very easily digested foods. As the gut heals and inflammation of the tissue is reduced, more foods are introduced. SCD only allows beans after there has been some gut healing, and then, only if there are no negative reactions. It is important to follow the SCD™ guidelines for introductions of foods, and not proceed too quickly. For example, even if you decide to try the special goat yogurt, you should not do so for at least a month. While digestive enzymes are not required, many have found that they make the SCD™ more effective.

Status: The SCD™ is widely supported by the autism community, and talks on this diet are included in the Defeat Autism Now! Conferences. In addition to the thousands of children following a strict SCD™, there are countless others on a modified version, which could be referred to as a "Restricted Carbohydrate Diet." These modifications may stray from the original principles laid down by Dr. Haas, but when the elimination of complex sugars is the primary principle of a diet, it is widely referred to as "the SCD™."

Concerns: Many children suffer from an increased yeast overgrowth at the outset of the SCD™, because bacterial pathogens are the first to die, leaving room for yeast to grow. Since yeast feeds on starches and sugars, it is best to limit the intake of honey and sweet fruits initially. It is also helpful to lightly cook fruits, causing the breakdown of natural sugars prior to ingestion. Pathogenic bacteria can cause the symptoms of fructose malabsorption,[177] so once the dysbiosis has been addressed, fruit may be slowly added back into the diet.

Some children experience a worsening of constipation when the diet is first started. The Pecanbread website provides a protocol for addressing this.

Another concern is that those with oxalate issues may react poorly if they are eating a significant amount of almonds or other nuts.

Overview of The Specific Carbohydrate Diet™

Gluten-containing grains (wheat, barley, rye, spelt, kamut, and possibly oats)	Not allowed
Millet, Quinoa, Amaranth, Buckwheat	Not allowed
Rice, Corn, Soy	Not allowed
Eggs and Meat (incl. beef, lamb, fish, chicken, turkey)	Allowed if unprocessed
Vegetables	Most allowed, if fresh or frozen. Potatoes, yams, turnips, jerusalem artichoke, parsnips and most other starchy root vegetables not permitted
Fruit	Allowed (peeled, seeded, and cooked in initial stages), not canned
Milk Products (milk, butter, cream, yogurt, cheese, casein, whey, etc.) and ingredients	Not in initial phase, then 24-hour goat yogurt, dry curd cottage cheese, specific cheeses and butter, for those who tolerate dairy
Sweeteners	Honey & saccharin only
Vinegar	White or apple cider
Juice	Limited to those confirmed to be without added sugars or starches (whole fruit juiced at home preferred)
Oils	Unlimited
Condiments	OK if no added sugars, starch or spices
Nuts	Most allowed if ground into flour in initial phase. Peanuts and peanut butter not allowed, check that no "anti-caking agents" have been used
Seeds	Not for first 3 months, then cautiously
Seaweed	Not allowed
Beans	Certain types allowed after 3 months, soaked 12 hours then pre-cooked before added to recipes

---

[177] Born P, Zech J, Lehn H, Classen M, Lorenz R. "Colonic bacterial activity determines the symptoms in people with fructose-malabsorption." *Hepatogastroenterology*. 1995 Nov-Dec;42(6):778-85.

Alcoholic Beverages	Beer not allowed. Occasional use: dry wine, gin, rye, scotch, bourbon, vodka
Coconut Products	Unlimited, fresh only, no young green coconut water. Introduce when nuts are added
Gelatin	Unflavored only
Coffee and Tea	Allowed, weak. Herb tea if it does not induce diarrhea. No decaf. coffee/tea

Any food listed is not allowed if it contains any added starch or sugar. Check with manufacturers.

Supplements: In general, supplements are not recommended until some healing of the gut has taken place. At that time, supplements that contain no "illegal" ingredients may be used (a list of "legal" supplements can be found at www.pecanbread.com). Probiotics, after a week or so on the SCD™, are recommended. Parents are advised to start slowly and increase doses very gradually. A specially prepared goat yogurt is the preferred way to provide probiotics; advocates maintain that after some healing has occurred, the goat yogurt may be tolerated even by those who were sensitive to casein. If a child has a milk allergy, or a parent prefers not to use any dairy products, nut yogurts and other fermented foods can be used.

Support: A great deal of support and information is available at the Pecanbread website. There are also online discussion groups and lists to provide parent-to-parent support, such as www.yahoogroups.com/group/pecanbread.

Marjan Hammink of The Netherlands, had this experience:

"Ever since he was born, my son Nick had chronic diarrhea. Things brightened up a bit on a fermented milk drink with lactobacillus shirota caseii, but the effects tapered off. At the age of 4, we had to find an answer to his constant screaming, night terrors, abnormal pain threshold, and lack of eye contact. Nick went GF/CF and steadily improved. We started ABA, saw play skills emerging and a much healthier-looking child. But in the summer of 2001 he regressed: urine and stool samples showed massive overgrowth of Candida and pathogenic bacteria. By November of 2002, Nick was losing interest in his educational program. He developed sweet-smelling, sometimes bright yellow stools with undigested food, and stopped growing. My Defeat Autism Now! Doctor told me to start Nystatin and cut back on his supplements. Nick was not utilizing them, not even the vitamin C.

I searched the Internet again. Some parents had seen great results with yet another type of diet. Reluctantly I ordered a book: Breaking the Vicious Cycle: Intestinal Health Through Diet, *by Elaine Gottschall. Coming from GF/CF, implementing SCD™ was relatively easy - luckily, Nick eats practically everything we put on his plate. We reserve space in the freezer for pre-cooked food and I schedule one morning of cooking every ten days or so. It's a small task, considering the improvements: perfect stool, weight gain, important milestones reached, and 85% potty trained in the daytime. Nick no longer speaks in single words; he tells us whole stories. Liver spots on his face have vanished.*

Of course there have been infringements. A large sip of tea with regular milk made him foggy at once, and a cookie made his poop turn yellow again. But these minor regressions lasted only hours.

We learned of the healing capacities of the homemade goat's yogurt and fermented food in general, but Nick was too casein-sensitive. After 9 months on SCD™, it seemed to be tolerated, but after 10 heavenly days we saw a clear adverse reaction and had to discontinue. There is simply no way to predict if your child will tolerate dairy sooner or later. Determined to get probiotics into my son, I experimented with nut yogurt at the Pecanbread site, and it is now a cornerstone of his diet."

Restricted Carbohydrate Diets – with multiple food allergies

One concern that many parents have when implementing this diet is that children with nut and egg allergies may have trouble getting adequate nutrition from a wide variety of foods. There is now a special web page with instructions for gaining weight and for tracking the caloric content of the child's diet in order to insure that the child gets an adequate amount of calories; it can be found in the "Overcoming Difficulties" section of the Pecanbread website.

> *"My son Mitchell was put on a GF/CF diet at 15 months, even before his diagnosis. I implemented the SCD™ one month later after reading about it, since it seemed my son could not tolerate rice at all and would pass chunks of undigested food. He now has very few IgG issues but almost twenty IgE allergic reactions including dairy, eggs, peanuts, tree nuts, bananas, beef, & legumes*
>
> *Breakfast, lunch and dinner look pretty much the same. He eats a meat (lamb, veal, chicken, turkey or pork), a fat (coconut oil, ghee or sesame oil), and either a veggie or a fruit at each meal. We rotate his vegetables (carrots, squash, zucchini, and broccoli) and do daily cultured vegetables containing cabbage, kale, and a little carrot. His fruits are pears, mangoes, pineapple, peaches (once a week only), and cranberry juice or grape juice diluted with water."* -Meghan Bramlage

Since Mitchell cannot tolerate yogurt, Meghan later introduced Young Coconut Kefir. Although this is not technically acceptable on the Specific Carbohydrate Diet™ (young coconuts are considered an unripe fruit), his improvement has continued.

Another parent wrote:

> *"We tried the SCD™ with my son, discontinued it for a while, and restarted it over the winter, when testing revealed astronomically high anaerobic gut bacteria levels, and nearly forty IgG intolerances. We are nut, seed, bean and dairy free, with limited eggs, but we can use peanut butter occasionally. We are blessed with a non-picky eater, but we limit seafood for the mercury issues, and honey and fruit preventively against yeast.*
>
> *We rotate foods - each food is served on one day a week. Most meals contain protein, fat, and vegetables. Fruit is a dessert or a treat. For instance, today was bacon and eggs with some sliced (sweet) peppers for breakfast. Lunch at school was a pork chop with garlic, steamed kale, carrots and blueberries. Dinner was a mini quiche —it had a zucchini crust, some crumbled bacon, eggs, tomatoes, leeks and chopped spinach. He had strawberry-rhubarb compote for dessert, and half an apple with PB for snack. The area we are really limited on are snacks with 'travelability' (I'm the mom whose kid is eating that cold spinach souffle at the playground). I am experimenting with dehydrating some acceptable vegetables and making meat jerky, but it's tough.*
>
> *Recipes I really miss are the bean/lentilburgers. You can hide a LOT of things in a 'burger-type' food, and rotate your ingredients like crazy. We used to have different variations several times a week. Worth it, though."*

Although there have been many SCD™ success stories, there are also children who require modifications to a strictly starch-free regimen. It is difficult to know when to persist with a special diet and when to change course, which is why it's so important to get support from those who are experienced with this diet, and to have your child under the supervision of a qualified nutritionist.

SPELT

For those with a wheat allergy *who do tolerate gluten*, spelt may be an acceptable substitute. Spelt more closely resembles the wheat grain that was grown and eaten by our ancestors before the grain was genetically modified to increase yield and pest resistance. It is speculated that these alterations to the original forms of wheat may explain why so many modern people experience wheat allergy. However, spelt is a variety of wheat that contains gluten, and *is not suitable for those on a gluten-free diet.*

SPLENDA® (See SUGAR SUBSTITUTES)

STARCHES & CARBOHYDRATES

Starch is a complex carbohydrate used by plants to store excess glucose. Pure starch is a tasteless white powder: starch from potato, tapioca, corn, and arrowroot is often used as a thickener in cooking, and starch is particularly useful in gluten-free baking because it results in a lighter texture when combined with heavier flours.

Starches feed yeast and bacteria in the gut as simple sugars do, although it takes a bit longer for them to break down into sugars during the digestive process (see SPECIFIC CARBOHYDRATE DIET™). Although a grain and starch free approach has proven to be best for some, others have found that soaked grains add important fiber, help stop cravings for starches, and may provide necessary nutrients for the healthy probiotics struggling to colonize in the body.

Some reasons why a bit of starch in the diet may be helpful:

• According to Dr. Timothy Buie, many autistic children have impaired starch digestion. But since some starch-digesting enzymes stop being produced when they are not needed, there may be a reason to keep some grains in the diet.

• Some parents have reported yeast overgrowth while their children are on a diet free of complex sugars. One theory is that they started out with both yeast and bacteria, which competed for sugar in the gut. If you stop feeding the bacteria with polysaccharides, but continue to feed the yeast with fruit and honey, you may end up with an imbalance.

• Some children become dangerously impacted (constipated) while on a starch and grain-free diet. For these children, one option is to keep starches and sugars to a minimum, but allow some high-fiber grains such as quinoa, millet or amaranth.

• Some nutritional supplements, especially probiotics, are not efficacious or viable without some included sugars, including disaccharides or polysaccharides, in relatively small amounts. Otherwise the probiotics will be 'dead on arrival,' and the bad bugs can take back their territory.

"Approximately 85% of our autistic patients follow a gluten and casein-free diet. We stress the importance of protein and vegetables, and recommend limiting certain carbohydrates. We have had great success with this protocol, but we are always interested in ways to fine-tune it for individual children.

The removal of all complex sugars and starches will result in improvements in children with a high parasitic load. Many of these same benefits will be seen with the removal of corn, potatoes, and soy." -John Hicks, MD, reprinted from The ANDI News

STEVIA

Stevia rebaudiana is a type of herb with sweet-tasting leaves. It can be purchased at health food stores when labeled as a dietary supplement, but it is not approved by the FDA as a food additive. It has a slightly odd flavor that may vary from brand to brand, but most find that it adds a pleasant sweetness to foods and drinks. It is available in liquid and powdered form. Donna Gates, author of *The Body Ecology Diet*, has authored *The Stevia Cookbook*, with sugar-free recipes and information about the best sources of stevia.

STOOLS, ABNORMAL (See also BOWEL DISEASE AND AUTISM, ALLERGIES & INTOLERANCES)

During normal digestion, nutrients are absorbed from the food that we eat. By the time digested food reaches the colon, most of the nutrients have already been absorbed (see DIGESTION). Once there, excess liquid is removed from the contents of the intestines, and the intestinal flora help digest any remaining nutrients. Fiber and water are critical to the formation of stool. Insoluble fiber provides bulk and water keeps the stool soft. Water is also needed to keep the stool soft and to prepare it for elimination. Muscular waves, known as peristalsis, move the stool towards the rectum. Mucus in the colon serves as a lubricant to help move the stool along.

Constipation: Constipation refers to difficult, painful or hard bowel movements. It can cause extreme discomfort, including abdominal pain & bloating, nausea, rectal pain and just generally feeling ill. In severe chronic cases, constipation may lead to fecal impaction. Constipation may be caused by diet, hormones, dehydration, or a side effect of medications. Sometimes the cause is anatomical, or there can be a constriction in the intestine. Treatments include a change in dietary habits, laxatives, fiber therapy, enemas, and occasionally, surgery.

Many children on the autism spectrum appear to have diarrhea, when in fact, constipation is the problem. Despite nearly constant loose stools, abdominal x-rays often reveal a significant impaction. In other words, the liquid stool interpreted as diarrhea was actually seepage that made it past the impaction. In such cases, treatment with a stool softener, followed by laxatives, often relieves some of these children of an astonishing amount of stool. Over a period of days or weeks they may experience a great deal of relief and improved functioning. If you suspect that this might be your child's problem, ask your pediatrician to do an abdominal x-ray to rule out fecal impaction.

> *"My daughter has a lot of loose, poorly digested stools, and a bloated tummy. I never thought of her as "constipated", but a KUB (abdominal x-rays) done on three occasions all showed a prominent amount of stool in her colon). Also, her poops are often quite voluminous, suggesting poor digestion and absorption."*

Constipation can be a vicious cycle - if a child experiences pain when moving his bowels, he may avoid potty visits. The longer the child holds feces in, the harder they become and the more difficult they will be to pass. This can then lead to an even greater aversion to moving the bowels.

There are several remedies for constipation, in four basic categories:

Dietary Changes: The primary improvements in those children with constipation coincide with the removal of all gluten and dairy from the diet. Opiates and opioids are extremely binding; it is well known that constipation is one of the most common side effects of opioid pain medications. If some children are affected by opioid peptides, it should not surprising that they would suffer from constipation. Relief from constipation is one of the early signs that dietary interventions may be useful.

A double-blind, crossover study compared cow's milk with soy milk in sixty-five children with chronic constipation concluded that, in young children, chronic constipation can be a manifestation of intolerance of cow's milk. Casomorphin from dairy has long been known to reduce bowel motility, and milk protein intolerance has been repeatedly shown to be a primary cause of chronic constipation in children. [178] [179] [180] [181]

In people without other medical problems, the main dietary intervention is the increase of fluids (preferably water) and dietary fiber. The latter may be achieved by consuming more vegetables and fruit, whole meal bread and by adding flax seeds to one's diet. Increasing both soluble and insoluble fiber (see FIBER) may lead to significant improvements. For those with more severe, recurring constipation (or alternating constipation and diarrhea), a focus on soluble fiber can stabilize the consistency of the stool, normalizing bowel movements (see IBS). Certain supplements, such as magnesium and aloe vera juice, can also be helpful.

Treating Dysbiosis: Another important approach has turned out to be stabilizing the balance of gut flora with healthy bacteria such as those found in probiotic supplements, cultured vegetables and non-dairy kefir. Healthy intestinal flora is critical for proper digestion and elimination (see GUT FLORA, PROBIOTICS). According to Defeat Autism Now! Doctor Sidney Baker, MD, once constipation has been treated and bowel movements are regular, anti-fungal medications may keep the problem from recurring in some patients.

Laxatives: *Bulk-forming laxatives* are generally derived from natural sources such as agar, psyllium or plant gums. Others are synthetic cellulose products like methylcellulose. Both types work in the same way, dissolving in the intestines and then swelling. They soften the stool and make it easier to pass. Because they are not absorbed from the intestines, this type of laxative is safe for long-term use. Note: psyllium seeds contain about 20% mucilage, which is not allowed on the SCD™.

Osmotic laxatives increase the amount of water in the small intestine and the colon, increasing the size of the stool, making them easier to pass. Milk of magnesium, sorbitol, magnesium

[178] Iacono G, Cavataio F, Montalto G, Florena A, Tumminello M, Soresi M, Notarbartolo A, Carroccio A. "Intolerance of cow's milk and chronic constipation in children." *New England Journal of Medicine* 1998 / 339 (16) / 1100-1104.

[179] Defilippi C, Gomez E, Charlin V, Silva C. "Inhibition of small intestinal motility by casein: a role of beta casomorphins?" *Nutrition.* 1995 Nov-Dec;11(6):751-4.

[180] Daher S, Tahan S, Solé D, Naspitz CK, Da Silva Patrício FR, Neto UF, De Morais MB. "Cow's milk protein intolerance and chronic constipation in children." *Pediatr Allergy Immunol.* 2001 Dec;12(6):339-42.

[181] Turunen S, Karttunen TJ, Kokkonen J. "Lymphoid nodular hyperplasia and cow's milk hypersensitivity in children with chronic constipation." *J Pediatr.* 2004 Nov;145(5):606-11.

citrate and polyethylene glycol-based laxatives (such as Miralax) are examples of osmotic laxatives. Osmotic laxatives can cause diarrhea and dehydration, so they should be taken under the supervision of a doctor.

Stimulant laxatives increase the motor activity of the bowels by stimulating the nerves of the intestinal wall. Stimulant laxatives are generally used only when osmotic laxatives don't work. They are typically used to prepare for colonoscopy or other diagnostic procedures.

Emollient laxatives include mineral oil and stool softeners. Mineral oil coats the inside of the colon, which helps the colon retain water and thus adds moisture and bulk to the stool. It is useful to prevent straining. Stool softeners also promote water retention in the stool; this can be very helpful when the stool is very hard and painful to pass, but can take a few days to work. Stool softeners are usually used together with stimulant laxatives. Try giving a tablespoon of extra-virgin olive oil per day for several days - sometimes that is all it takes to do the trick.

Rectal Suppositories: These are small bullet-shaped tablets containing glycerin or a drug called bisacodyl. When inserted into the rectum and left there for several minutes, they effectively dissolve the hard stool that surrounds them, triggering defecation.

Enemas: An enema is a procedure that is easily done at home with a special enema kit, or with pre-mixed disposable plastic enema bottles (both can be purchased at the pharmacy). A bag of warm fluid, suspended above the patient, flows gently into the large intestine through a nozzle. This stimulates the bowel as it softens the stool, allowing it to be easily passed into the toilet. Enemas are used when constipation is particularly severe and has been resistant to laxatives. Enemas usually contain water, or a combination of water and other ingredients such as baking soda or mild hand soap. Some enemas contain phosphate solutions which are effective but can irritate the bowel. Enemas containing mineral oil are gentler but can be messy.

Colonics: Claims that colonic hydrotherapy promotes good health by removing toxins from the bowel are highly disputed. However, when impaction is so severe that other methods fail, a colonic will almost always clear out the contents of the bowel and provide immediate relief. In this procedure, the patient reclines on a special bed or chair, which is set up with an apparatus that flushes the bowel with warm water, using a tube inserted in the rectum. Obviously, this is not a procedure that will be tolerated by small children, or by those with communication problems. To find a colon therapist in your area, see the International Association for Colon Hydrotherapy website at www.i-act.org.

Bowel impaction is a serious and painful condition. Constipation that resists all the above measures requires physical intervention. Manual disimpaction (the physical removal of impacted stool) can be done under sedation or a general anesthetic—this avoids pain and loosens the anal sphincter.

Constipation is usually easier to prevent than to treat. The relief of constipation should immediately be followed with prevention using increased fiber (fruits and vegetables) and a decreasing nightly dose of osmotic laxative. With continuing narcotic use, nightly doses of osmotic laxatives can be given indefinitely.

Diarrhea: Diarrhea is one of the most common symptoms of illness in children with autism spectrum disorders. In one study, seventeen percent were found to have a history of chronic diarrhea.[182]

There are many references to diarrhea throughout this book, because it can be a symptom of one or many underlying problems often seen in this population. Although brief episodes can be caused by a viral infection or food poisoning, some of these children have diarrhea that has been going on for months or years. Chronic diarrhea leads to insufficient absorption of nutrients, weight loss, dehydration, and ill health.

Sometimes, diarrhea is the result of unhealthy intestinal flora (see DYSBIOSIS) or a *Clostridia* infection. Often, it is a result of food allergy or intolerance. In many cases, it is a combination of both. This is probably why some children with severe, chronic diarrhea have improved greatly from the SCD™ and other programs that limit common allergens and target dysbiosis.

Diarrhea is not healthy, and needs to be addressed. If your child suffers from chronic diarrhea or loose stools, he may not be absorbing enough nutrients from his food, as it passes too quickly through the GI tract.*

As noted above, many children on the autism spectrum appear to have diarrhea, when in fact, constipation is the problem, and the liquid stools are actually seepage that made it past an impaction. Another concern is that some of these children may be suffering from intestinal inflammation caused by years of untreated food allergy. Even when the foods are removed, the inflammation may cause the diarrhea to persist. It is very important that autistic children with chronic gastrointestinal problems or abnormal stools be investigated promptly by a knowledgeable pediatric gastroenterologist (see BOWEL DISEASE AND AUTISM, COLONOSCOPY).

Note: If your child has large particles of undigested food in his stools, DIGESTIVE ENZYME TABLETS may be helpful.

STOPPING DIETARY INTERVENTION IN A "NON-RESPONDER"

It is clear that not every child will respond to dietary intervention. If a dietary regimen has been strictly followed for a reasonable period (at least three months and preferably six) and there is no noticeable improvement, it is reasonable to assume that diet will not be an important intervention for your child. However, many parents do not observe an effect, and then see a marked regression when "normal" foods are re-introduced (this is more common children over the age of five). This probably means that the diet was helping, but the changes were gradual rather than dramatic. If you see a regression within a few weeks of stopping the diet, it would obviously be wise to reinstate it. Before you decide that dietary intervention is not working, be certain that there has been 100% compliance. Even traces of gluten, casein, soy or other restricted foods can confound your results. Be sure you have given dietary intervention a fair trial before moving on.

STOPPING DIETARY INTERVENTION IN A "DIET RESPONDER"

Parents who see great changes may decide to revert to a non-restricted diet after some healing has taken place. For certain children (for example, some of those who were successfully chelated) stopping the diet has not been followed by regression. However, for some, as in celiac disease, a gluten-free diet may have to be considered as a lifelong regimen for some children

---

[182] Molloy CA, Manning-Courtney P. Prevalence of chronic gastrointestinal symptoms in children with autism and autistic spectrum disorders. *Autism*. 2003 Jun;7(2):165-71.

who have reacted poorly to it in the past.

> *"Nicholas (age 6) has been on a gluten and casein free diet for over 2 years. I recently saw a NAET type doctor/chiropractor who told me my son was no longer allergic to dairy and that he needed the essential fatty acids in milk for his brain. I decided to put him back on dairy (it's been about 2 months), and he is now a mess! As you know, life would be so much easier if he didn't need the diet anymore, and since for Nicholas it wasn't a cure (I always maintained that it significantly decreased his stims), I thought that I would try dairy again to see if perhaps his reduction of stims was a coincidence (as many of the diet's critics have told me).*
>
> *Anyway, Nicholas is now spinning in circles, and is very sensitive to sound. His sensory needs in general have increased significantly, and his teachers have all commented on how fidgety he is now - 'jumping out of his chair.' He is now waking up and staying up at 3:00 am and all hours of the night.*
>
> *Is there a way to 'purge' his system to speed up the recovery process? Have parents ever seen permanent regression from cheating? I am anxiously awaiting your response!" -Amy (Last name withheld by request)*

In this type of situation, there is little that can be done other than removing dairy again and waiting for the renewed behaviors to pass. When gluten is returned to the diet, it can take longer for it to leave the system. See INFRACTIONS for help combating occasional diet infractions.

Sometimes the response to reinstatement of a "normal" diet can be severe. The following letter to *The ANDI News* was sent by a mother in Massachusetts who did not wish to be named:

> *"Four years ago I helped to start a support group in my area for parents doing the diet, and I was adamant that this was a lifetime treatment plan, with no excuses for "cheating" or giving up as long as the child was improving and doing well. My son responded extremely well to the removal of gluten and casein at age five, and by age nine, he had lost his diagnosis of autism and had done wonderfully in a regular third-grade classroom without supports.*
>
> *In years past, any trace of contamination led to diarrhea, screaming, return of autistic behaviors, and multiple other problems, so we were very careful not to re-introduce those foods. However, last June my son ate some regular pizza and, presto, nothing happened. Had his gut healed? Had his immune system kicked in and repaired the root of the problem?*
>
> *At that point, it seemed unfair to keep a healthy child on such a restricted diet, so we let him have ice cream, bread, cereal, the works. For at least a month, we congratulated ourselves on "fixing" the problem. But then things began to fall apart. My son started complaining that he was seeing things, and then that he was hearing voices in his head. By August, he had been hospitalized twice for violence and delusional behavior, and he was diagnosed with schizophrenia.*
>
> *As you can imagine, we put him back on the diet, and he is slowly returning to normal. But he was unable to attend fourth grade with his friends, and he has been set back by many months."*

Fortunately, regressions are not usually so severe. The alarming behavior typically begins gradually, and the child is put back on the diet before symptoms grow worse (see REGRESSION).

There are certainly several subtypes of this disorder, and some children may be able to return to somewhat regular eating patterns after some period of time. One theory of this phenomenon is that the gut does indeed "heal," keeping undigested gluten and dairy peptides out of the bloodstream, should they be re-introduced. However, a theoretical concern is that if the child still has high IgG or IgA titers to gluten, he could experience an autoimmune reaction similar to that in celiac disease, and before long it could re-damage the lining of the gut wall. If something else is damaging the gut wall, a return to a normal diet might also mean a return to the leaky gut syndrome and the problems associated with it (see DYSBIOSIS, ALLERGIES & INTOLERANCES).

A qualified autism-biomedical practitioner may be able to do some testing to determine whether re-introducing certain foods could be a safe experiment. If you do not have a doctor who can do testing, it is probably best to err on the side of caution, and continue dietary intervention until more is known about the disorder, and about the long-term consequences of stopping the diet.

Should you decide to stop the diet you may want to follow these steps to reduce the risk of regression:

- Do a baseline report at www.autism.com/ari/atec, and make no other changes to your child's treatment protocol. Introduce a small amount of milk (such as a teaspoon), and wait a week before proceeding. If the child becomes sick or regresses for any reason during that week, wait until he is back at "baseline" and begin again.

- If there is no reaction, increase the "dosage" to about ¼ cup and wait another week. Then begin giving that amount on a four-day rotation. After a month, if no regression is seen, increase the dosage to ½ cup, but remain on a four-day rotation, keeping notes about behavior and health on days 1, 2, 3, and 4.

- After two months, introduce gluten in the same quantities, on the same schedule as dairy, above. A month later, regardless of positive, negative, or no result, do a follow-up report at www.autism.com/ari/atec.

Note: Never challenge with a substance that has been known or suspected to cause anaphylaxis or breathing problems without competent medical supervision.

STUDIES

There are a number of scientific studies supporting dietary interventions for the treatment of autism and related disorders, many of which are referenced throughout this book. For extensive lists of studies relating to autism and diet, autism and immune dysfunction, and autism and gastrointestinal issues, visit www.autismndi.com (click on "Studies" on the bar at the top). There is also an excellent list of studies addressing food and behavioral problems compiled by the Feingold Association, at www.feingold.org (click on "Scientific Studies" at left).

SUCRALOSE (See SUGAR SUBSTITUTES)

SUGAR

The food industry has discovered that adding sugar to packaged food makes people buy more, and eat more. However, foods high in sugar are often called "empty calories" because they provide so little nutrition along with the caloric intake. In addition, sugar contributes to weight gain and tooth delay. It causes a spike in blood sugar that triggers the release of insulin, which will generally send the blood sugar level lower than normal (see BLOOD SUGAR).

Many believe that fruit or fruit juice can be a healthy substitute for sugar between meals, but fructose has a similar effect on the body, and orange juice contains almost as many grams of sugar as cola. A recent study found that consumption of 12 fluid ounces a day of fruit juice by children is associated with short stature and with obesity.[183]

Apart from concerns about nutrition, tooth decay and blood sugar, sugars are generally limited for those on special diets because they feed excess of yeast and bacteria in the GI tract. This has been of great concern in the autism population for many years, and it is important to understand and address this problem (see DYSBIOSIS).

Corn syrup has been implicated due its sulfur content (see CORN SYRUP), and many sugary foods contain artificial colors or a sodium benzoate preservative (or both), which have been shown to result in increased hyperactivity in children in the general population (see FOOD ADDITIVES). But whether plain table sugar (sucrose) can cause hyperactivity in children is unlikely. A healthy child should be able to eat a small amount of sugar without ill effects (see NUTRITION).

SUGAR SUBSTITUTES

There are several sugar alternatives on the market today, usually found as ingredients in diet soda, sugar free gum and candy, and other diet foods. They may be used alone or in conjunction with other sweeteners, to balance out qualities like shelf life and flavor. All are gluten and dairy free.

The most common artificial sweeteners are aspartame (Equal®, NutraSweet®), acesulfame potassium (Sweet One®, Sunette®), sucralose (Splenda®), and saccharin (Sweet 'N Low®). Sugar alcohols, also called polyols, are forms of natural sugars that include sorbitol, mannitol, erythritol, and xylitol.

Stevia, a natural sweetener derived from an herb called *stevia rebaudiana*, is not approved by the FDA as a food additive, but can be purchased at natural food markets, when labeled as a dietary supplement (see STEVIA).

The excessive use of sugar in children with autism and related disorders, who often have impaired carbohydrate digestion and abnormal intestinal flora, is discouraged. Therefore, artificial sweeteners that could be appropriate substitutes would be a welcome addition to the diets of children on the autism spectrum. However, concerns have been raised about several of the commonly used sweeteners:

• Although these sweeteners have been approved by the FDA, some consumer groups question their safety, and saccharin is listed by the FDA as a "weak carcinogen" as a result of conflicting studies on laboratory animals. It is unclear how many of these concerns are justified, since lobbyists in the sugar industry and in the alternative sweetener industry, all with powerful conflicts of interest, have been fiercely driving the debate.

---

[183] Dennison BA, et al. "Excess fruit juice consumption by preschool-aged children is associated with short stature and obesity." *Pediatrics*, 1997 Jan;99(1):15-22.

- Some argue that potentially harmful effects are unlikely, because these are so much sweeter than sugar, and only small amounts are required. Neotame, an artificial sweetener made by NutraSweet® and chemically similar to aspartame, is between 8,000 and 13,000 times sweeter than sucrose (table sugar) and thus can be used in trace amounts. However, some substances are highly neurotoxic even in tiny amounts. Since the FDA does not require labels to include ingredients that comprise less than one percent of the product, it's possible that a potent sweetener like neotame could be used in foods without having to be listed on the label, and those with sensitivities would be unknowingly exposed.

- Aspartame is broken down into aspartic acid, which is a known neurotoxin (see EXCITOTOXICITY). A series of studies have linked aspartame to multiple serious health problems (see ASPARTAME).

- There are some concerns about the lack of independent research, since many or most of the product safety studies are funded by the manufacturer. The non-profit group, Truth in Labeling, writes, "At the time of our review of Monsanto's application, three human studies on the safety of neotame were presented. The studies had few subjects, all of whom were employees of the company. Some of the subjects reported headaches after ingesting neotame, but the researchers concluded that the headaches were not related to neotame ingestion. Not mentioned in the studies was the fact that migraine headache is, by far, the most commonly reported adverse reaction to aspartame in the files of the FDA."

- Some sweeteners, including sucralose and most sugar alcohols, are not fully absorbed through the gastrointestinal wall, which can result in intestinal discomfort, gas, bloating, and diarrhea. Those with any sort of gastrointestinal problem should avoid them entirely. An exception to this may be a new sweetener called "Lakanto," which is a combination of erythritol and a Chinese fruit called luo han guo. Distibutors claim that it does not cause diarrhea, gas or bloating, perhaps because Lakanto is made by fermentation while other sugar alcohols are made from hydrogenation. Lakanto seems promising, since it tastes good, can be used for baking, and can be substituted one-for-one for regular sugar. However, it is currently very expensive. See the online store at www.bodyecologydiet.com for more information.

As with every aspect of dietary intervention, it is important to balance your child's needs by choosing the diet that will create the best overall results. In the absence of concrete data, this balancing act requires research, intuition, moderation, and a great deal of common sense.

SULFATION (See also METHYLATION)

Sulfation is the process whereby a chemical compound called sulfate is attached to other chemicals in the body, in order to regulate or eliminate them. Those with sulfation defects will have trouble metabolizing phenolic foods such as dairy products, chocolates, wheat, corn sugar, apples, and bananas (see PHENOLS). Deficiency of the enzyme called phenol sulfur transferase leads to impaired sulfation, which disrupts other metabolic pathways, including those needed for detoxification (see PHENOL SULFUR TRANSFERASE DEFICIENCY).

SUNETTE® (See SUGAR SUBSTITUTES)

SUPPLEMENTS (See also NUTRITION)

Children on the autism spectrum rarely eat a balanced diet. Even those who are not on a restricted diet typically eat a narrow range of foods. That these children need dietary supplements has been confirmed by a double-blind, placebo-controlled studies (see NUTRITION). One study found that a strong, balanced multi-vitamin/mineral supplement resulted in improvements in children with autism in sleep and gut function, and possibly in other areas.[184]

When you further restrict the diets, for example by removing dairy, then you must also add calcium, magnesium and vitamin D from other food sources and usually, from supplements. Children on the autism spectrum may need to take more supplements than a typical child. Your doctor will want to run blood tests to measure vitamin and mineral levels (see TESTING) and look for other deficiencies. Some may need to take B vitamins in doses above the RDA (recommended daily allowance).[185] Many children on the autism spectrum are deficient in vitamins A, C, D, zinc and folic acid. Some may need to take other supplements too, such as amino acid formulations (see AMINO ACID DEFICIENCIES).

Vitamins are nutrients we need to stay alive. They are essential for our bodies to function normally and many must be supplied because the body does not make them. Along with other nutrients (proteins, fats, carbohydrates, and minerals) they are required for children to grow and for all humans to live. All essential vitamins must be supplied by the diet or supplemented in order for a person to be healthy. *Please keep in mind that you should not exceed the recommended maximum dose of any vitamin unless your doctor has determined that this is appropriate for your child.*

Vitamins that May Be Deficient in Those with Autism Disorders:

Vitamin A is a fat soluble nutrient, often called beta carotene on food labels. Vitamin A exists in two forms, retinol and carotene. Retinol is found only in foods of animal origin. Carotene can be found in both animal and plant foods. Beta carotene is the most common form found in multivitamins. Vitamin A is important for eye health and builds resistance to respiratory infections. Non-dairy food sources include egg yolks, sweet potatoes, winter squash and cantaloupe. Vitamin A works best when taken with B complex, vitamin D, vitamin E, calcium, phosphorus and zinc.

Vitamin B$_1$ is also called thiamine. It is water soluble so any excess is excreted. Thiamine promotes normal appetite and aids digestion (especially of carbohydrates). It should be taken with other B vitamins. For children on restricted diets, there are not many appropriate foods sources other than legumes and peanuts. This vitamin is destroyed by heat and oxidation.

Vitamin B$_2$ is also called riboflavin. It is not destroyed by heat but by light (especially ultraviolet light). Riboflavin is important for growth and healthy skin, hair and nails. Food sources include leafy green vegetables and fish.

Vitamin B$_5$ is also called pantothenic acid. It can be made in the body. It is important for the function of the adrenal glands, and needed for the conversion of fat and sugar to energy. It is

---

[184] Adams JB, Holloway C. "Pilot study of a moderate dose multivitamin/mineral supplement for children with autistic spectrum disorder." *J. Altern Complement Med.* 2004 Dec;10(6):1033-9.

[185] Kuriyama, S., Kamiyama, M., Watanabe, M., & Tamahashi, S. "Pyridoxine treatment in a subgroup of children with pervasive developmental disorders." *Developmental Medicine & Child Neurology,* 2002;44, 284-286.

needed to make infection fighting antibodies. Dietary sources include meats, egg yolk, nuts, chicken and green vegetables.

Vitamin B₆ is also called pyridoxine. This vitamin is needed for the production of red blood cells and antibodies. It is essential for the proper absorption of other B vitamins. B₆ is actually a group of nutrients (pyridoxine, pyridoxinal and pyridoxamine) that function together and are required for the production of some digestive enzymes and for protein metabolism. B₆ is important for the nervous system, and helps to assimilate protein and fat. Most of the multivitamins formulated for children on the autism spectrum include fairly large doses of B₆. Dietary sources include meat, poultry, fish, shellfish, cabbage and cantaloupe.

In autism, it has been reported that B₆ is most effective when taken with magnesium, which will usually counteract any hyperactivity that arises from the B₆. According to more than 5000 parent responses on the ARI Treatment Checklist, nearly one half of autistic patients benefit from the combination of B₆ plus magnesium.

Vitamin B₁₂ is also called cobalamin. Important for growth, concentration, memory and balance, cobalamin also forms and regenerates red blood cells. It is important for a healthy nervous system. It can be found in beef, pork, fish, shellfish and eggs. In 2002, Defeat Autism Now! Doctor James Neubrander made the discovery that the type of B₁₂ called methyl-cobalamin was very helpful to children on the autism spectrum; methyl-cobalamin is closely allied with the folic acid biochemical pathway and is necessary for detoxification. For autistic children with a deficiency in this enzyme, supplementing with methyl-cobalamin improves detoxification. The most effective method of administration is by injection, using a very thin needle tolerated well by most children. Compounding pharmacists are able to preload the single dose syringes and parents inject their children on a schedule determined by their doctor. Dr. Neubrander and others have reported huge gains in language, socialization and behavior.

Biotin is another member of the B-complex family of vitamins. It is important for metabolism. It is said to help alleviate eczema and other skin problems. Dietary biotin can be found in egg yolks, unpolished rice, nut and fruits. Biotin is one of the few vitamins that can be synthesized in the body by intestinal bacteria.

Choline and inositol are B-complex members that work together to use fats and cholesterol. Combined they form lecithin. Choline is one of the few substances known to cross the blood-brain barrier. It helps memory, has a soothing effect, and assists in detoxification. Dietary sources include egg yolks and green leafy vegetables. Wheat is one of the main sources, so children using any dietary intervention may be deficient. Most multivitamins contain approximately 50 mg of choline and inositol; these two nutrients are always kept in balance.

Vitamin C is also called ascorbic acid. This water-soluble vitamin is usually supplied by citrus fruits and juices, but it also in strawberries, green and leafy vegetables, potatoes, sweet potatoes and cantaloupe. It is important in the formation of collagen, a component of bones and cartilage, and for the absorption of iron. A potent antioxidant, vitamin C is said to help prevent viral and bacterial infections, and reduce the effects of some allergens. For those reducing oxalates, vitamin C should be limited to no more than 250 mg per day.

Vitamin D is also called calciferol. It is a fat-soluble vitamin normally acquired through diet and exposure to sunlight. Vitamin D promotes strong bones and teeth by enabling the proper absorption of calcium and phosphorus (this is why milk is usually fortified with vitamin D). Non-dairy sources include salmon, tuna, egg yolk, fish oils and oily fish like sardines and herring. Most people in northern climates, especially those with medium to dark skin, do not get sufficient vitamin D from sunlight. However, even in sunny climates, some people may be chronically deficient. Defeat Autism Now! Doctors report that low levels of vitamin D are almost universal in their autistic patients, which means that they are not benefiting from the considerable anti-inflammatory properties of this vitamin. A childhood deficiency of vitamin D has also been linked with the onset of multiple sclerosis in adulthood,[186] further emphasizing the need for adequate supplementation.

Vitamin E is also called tocopherol. Unlike other fat-soluble vitamins, very little vitamin E is stored in the body, with approximately 65% of the daily dose being excreted in the stool. Vitamin E is an important antioxidant, preventing oxidation of fat compounds, vitamins A and C and some amino acids. it is important for healing and to prevent cell damage. Dietary sources include vegetable oils, broccoli, brussels sprouts, eggs, spinach and soybeans.

Folates and folic acid are forms of water-soluble B vitamins. Folic acid refers to the synthetic vitamin used in supplements, while folates, including folinic acid, are the form found in foods. Critical for the proper development and maintenance of cells, especially during times of rapid cell division such as fetal development and childhood, it was discovered several years ago to be critically important for preventing neural tube birth defects, and pregnant women were advised to take a daily supplement of folic acid. Folate deficiency is believed to be the most common vitamin deficiency in the world due to food processing, food selection and intestinal disorders. People with food sensitivities and environmental illnesses who are deficient in B vitamins may see some clear improvements from supplementation.

Minerals that May Be Deficient in Those with Autism Disorders:

Calcium (see also CALCIUM) works with phosphorus to build healthy bones and teeth. It also helps the body use iron, helps nutrients pass through cell walls, keeps the heart beating regularly, and metabolizes iron. There must be sufficient vitamin D for calcium to be absorbed. Proper absorption of calcium can be inhibited by large amounts of fat, oxalic acid (see LOD) and PHYTIC ACID. Those on dairy free diets need to monitor their overall calcium intake. *Note: Calcium can cause or worsen constipation. Adequate doses of magnesium may counteract that effect.*

Copper is required for converting iron into hemoglobin. It is also important for the utilization of vitamin C. However, too much copper can cause sleep disturbances and other problems. Dr. William Walsh of the Pfeiffer Institute reports that the test results of children on the autism spectrum typically show abnormalities in the ratio of copper to zinc, which can be corrected with supplementation.

Iron is a critically important mineral, essential for the production of hemoglobin, myoglobin (red pigment in muscles) and some enzymes. It is also important for the metabolism of the various B vitamins. Iron is important for growth and prevents anemia and fatigue. The best dietary sources are meat, clams, egg yolks, nuts and molasses.

---

[186] Munger KL, Levin LI, Hollis BW, Howard NS, Ascherio A . "Serum 25-hydroxyvitamin D levels and risk of multiple sclerosis." *JAMA 2006;*296 (23): 2832-8.

Magnesium is sometimes called the serenity mineral, because it can be calming and improves mood and appetite. In many cases, it can help relieve or reduce constipation. Magnesium is required for calcium and vitamin C metabolism and is essential for nerve and muscle function. Dietary sources include figs, grapefruit, lemons, corn, almonds, nuts, seeds and dark green vegetables. It has been reported that magnesium is most effective for those with autism when taken with vitamin B$_6$.

Phosphorus is involved in every physiological chemical reaction. It is needed for normal heart and kidney function. It is found in fish, poultry, meat, eggs, nuts and seeds. Calcium and vitamin D are necessary for proper phosphorus function.

Zinc is often found to be low in children on the autism spectrum (with corresponding high levels of copper). Zinc is a very important mineral, involved in the maintenance of enzyme systems. It helps form insulin and is essential for protein metabolism. It helps maintain the acid-alkaline balance and is important to brain function. It promotes growth and increases mental alertness. Because it naturally stimulates appetite, some doctors recommend zinc supplementation when a child will not eat enough. Although there are many dietary sources of zinc, most of it is destroyed in processing. Many plants are also lower in zinc than they used to be, because of soil that has been depleted of nutrients.

Some signs of zinc deficiency are impairment of taste, a poor immune response and skin problems. Other symptoms of zinc deficiency can include hair loss, diarrhea, fatigue, delayed wound healing, and decreased growth rate and mental development in infants. It is thought that zinc supplementation can help skin conditions such as acne and eczema, prostate problems and anorexia nervosa. White spots on the fingernails can also indicate a zinc deficiency.

This mineral is highly recommended for those on the autism spectrum, and their families. According to Defeat Autism Now! Co-founder Dr. Sidney Baker, the serum zinc level in his autistic patients is usually marginal or sub-normal.

Other Supplements:

Taurine is a sulfur-containing amino acid found in the tissues of the central nervous system, and needed for a variety of biological functions. Acting as a neurotransmitter, it appears to neutralize the negative effects of glutamate, and has been documented to reduce seizures in some types of epilepsy.[187][188]

Those lacking certain enzymes may become deficient in taurine, as well as those on limited diets. Taurine deficiency can be measured with lab tests, and should be corrected with supplementation. Defeat Autism Now! Doctor Sidney Baker, in 2002, analyzed 61 urine amino acid tests done on autistic children, and found that 62% were deficient in taurine, so this might be an important thing to discuss with your child's doctor (see AMINO ACID DEFICIENCIES).

---

[187] Airakseinen EM, et al. "Effects of taurine treatment on epileptic patients." *Prog Clin Biol Res.* 1980;39:157-66.

[188] Fukuyama Y, Ochiai Y. "Therapeutic trial by taurine for intractable childhood epilepsies." *Brain Dev.* 1982;4(1): 63-9.

See also DI-METHYL GLYCINE (DMG).

How do you get your child to take supplements?

There are companies, such as Kirkman Laboratories, that have developed supplement formulations to suit the special needs of the autism spectrum population. These are usually available in liquids or powders that can be mixed into food or drinks. Some supplements, such as calcium powder, are heat stable, and can be baked into muffins or stirred into sauces.

Although some children are quite orally defensive, it is actually fairly easy to teach most young children to swallow pills, once you know the trick. This works best for children who tolerate a small amount of sugar, but once they have learned how to swallow the pills, you can phase it out.

You will need a box of tiny candies (such as white peppermint Tic Tacs™), a glass of something thick and a little sweet (such as chocolate DariFree™) and a straw. Have the child sit up straight with his chin tilted slightly down. Have him place the candy on his tongue, then take a big swig from the straw. He may master this on the first or second try, but if not, he probably won't mind trying again. Accidentally biting into a Tic Tac™ is a lot more pleasant than chomping down on an enzyme capsule. The key is in learning how to temporarily suppress the gag reflex, and once you get it, you've got it. Have him do this for several days in a row, applauding him each time. Then you can ask him to try two candies at once, and then three. At this point, he should be able to manage a larger pill.

SUPPORT GROUPS

If you are new to dietary interventions, you will find that joining a support group will be a valuable use of your time. There may be one in your area, but if not, there are some wonderful groups online. Those who have never been on an online support group will be amazed at how quickly their questions can be answered, and at the quality of support they can get from others who are more experienced.

Here's how it works: The person who starts a group is called the *Listowner.* Some groups are moderated (the posts need to be approved) by the listowner, or by an appointed moderator. When a new member joins the group, they can join in on the conversation, and ask or answer questions. Each group has its own rules, or "netiquette," which will be sent to you when you join. These rules govern such things as the scope of the list, the format that postings should take, what is and isn't allowed (for example, advertising is generally prohibited), and whether or not controversial issues ("hot topics") may be posted.

Remember to keep your posts short and to the point, and if you post something that is "off topic," put "OT" in the subject heading (*"OT: Need sympathetic neurologist in FL."*) Unless you are a doctor (and even if you are one), try to avoid giving medical advice online - remember, every child is different, and what worked for your child may not work for all.

Lists have archives of past postings, some of which go back several years. You can often find the answer you are looking for without even posting the question. If you type some keywords into the archive search box, and you may find that many of your questions have already been answered.

Some of the most popular autism-diet groups include:

Gluten-Free/Casein-Free Diet (GF/CF): www.yahoogroups.com/group/gfcfkids

The Specific Carbohydrate Diet (SCD): www.yahoogroups.com/group/pecanbread

The Low Oxalate Diet (LOD): www.yahoogroups.com/group/Trying_Low_Oxalates

The Feingold Diet: www.yahoogroups.com/group/Feingold-Program4us

The Body Ecology Diet: www.bedrokcommunity.org

SWEET 'N LOW® (See SUGAR SUBSTITUTES)

SWEET ONE® (See SUGAR SUBSTITUTES)

TAHINI

Sometimes called sesame paste or tahini butter, this thick paste is made from puréed sesame seeds. Although it can have a slightly bitter flavor, tahini is richer in protein than milk, yogurt, almonds, cashews, hazel nuts, walnuts, soy, sunflower, wheat germ, legumes and pecans. Tahini contains potassium, phosphorus, magnesium, vitamin A, B, and E, and natural lecithin, which reduces blood fat levels and provides protection from environmental pollutants. It is one of the best sources of methionine, an essential amino acid, and calcium, which is great for non-milk drinking children.

Tahini is easily digested, enabling a quick supply of essential nutrients, and adds nutrition and texture to baked goods. For children who are allergic to nuts, or attend a school with a "no peanut" policy, tahini makes a great "TB & J" sandwich. Tahini is traditionally used in middle eastern foods such as hummus and baba ghanoush. Many children will eat these spreads on crackers or as a "dipping sauce" for vegetables. As with other products made from seeds, tahini is very high in oxalates.

TEFF

Teff is a cereal crop (grain) originating in Ethiopia. It is ground into a dark, almost bluish flour. It is sometimes eaten as a breakfast porridge, and is most commonly used in an Ethiopian flatbread called injera. It is gluten free and can be used for baking, especially when blended with other flours.

TESTING (LABORATORY TESTING)

Parents and medical professionals can easily be confused by the array of tests available, and how to determine which tests are most likely to identify problems in people on the autism spectrum. Running all of these tests can be expensive, so you may have to prioritize the tests with your doctor based on likely benefit and cost.

The following are tests recommended by Sidney Baker, MD, and Jon Pangborn, Ph.D., Co-Founders of Defeat Autism Now! Detailed information about understanding and interpreting the results of these tests can be found in their book, *Autism: Effective Biomedical Treatments.*

- Blood Chemistry and CBC Analysis
- Comprehensive Stool Analysis
- Ammonia
- Genetic Testing
- Intestinal Permeability (See LEAKY GUT)
- Celiac Disease (See CELIAC DISEASE)
- Allergy Testing for Food / Inhalants (See ALLERGY TESTING)
- Organic Acids Analysis (See ORGANIC ACIDS TEST)
- Fatty Acids Analysis (See OMEGA-3 and OMEGA-6 FATTY ACIDS)
- Element Analysis and Metallothionein Assessments (See PFEIFFER TREATMENT CENTER)
- Immune Testing (See IMMUNE SYSTEM ABNORMALITIES)
- Urinary Peptide Analysis (See OPIOID EXCESS)
- Testing for Toxic Levels of Mercury and other Heavy Metals (see CHELATION THERAPY)

In addition, make sure your doctor helps you identify and address any nutritional deficiencies, and follow up with further tests if necessary.

If you are concerned about your child's reaction to having blood drawn, ask your doctor for a prescription for "EMLA Cream" before the test. It numbs the skin so he won't feel the needle. Slather some on both of his inner arms about an hour before your appointment and wrap some plastic wrap loosely around them to keep it from wiping off before the blood draw. If you distract your child when the needle is inserted, it should go fairly smoothly.

THANKSGIVING (See HOLIDAYS)

THICKENERS

Thickeners are often used in cooking, to thicken sauces, gravies, stews puddings and pie fillings.

The following are gluten free, but inappropriate for those avoiding starches. To use, mix the starch with an equal amount of *cold* liquid until it forms a paste, then whisk it into the liquid you are thickening. Take care not to overcook.

- **Arrowroot starch (AKA arrowroot powder or arrowroot flour)** With its neutral flavor, arrowroot is a good thickener for delicately flavored sauces. It also works at lower temperatures, and tolerates acidic ingredients and prolonged cooking. Sauces made with arrowroot can be frozen and thawed with no degradation of flavor or texture, which is not true of all thickeners. One tablespoon thickens one cup of liquid.

- **Cornstarch** is the most commonly used starch thickener. Whether or not children who are sensitive to corn can tolerate it is unclear. If you use it and notice a reaction, it is obvious that another starch should be chosen. One tablespoon thickens one cup of liquid.

202

- **Clearjel®** is a modified cornstarch used by professional bakers to thicken fruit fillings. It thickens without cooking, tolerates high temperatures and can be frozen.

- **Instant or quick cooking tapioca** is derived from the manioc (a root vegetable, sometimes called cassava). These small, starchy granules are used to make tapioca pudding and to thicken pie fillings. Because the grains don't dissolve, little gelatinous balls remain. If you want to use tapioca but do not want this texture, you can use **tapioca starch**.

- **Kudzu** is made from the tuber of the kudzu vine, imported from Asia and now growing out of control over the southern US. It comes in small chunks which must be crushed into a powder before use.

- **Potato starch** can also be used as a thickener in baking, but should not be boiled. Because it is permitted during Passover, most stores with a good kosher section will carry it.

- **Sweet rice flour** (also called mochi flour, glutinous rice flour and sweet glutinous rice flour) is another thickener that is stable when frozen. This is not the same as rice flour.

THIMEROSAL (See VACCINES)

TITANIUM DIOXIDE

Titanium dioxide is a finely ground inert mineral, similar to white sand. It should not be digested or absorbed by the body at all, but passed through and excreted in the stools. (Many children on the diet have light-colored stools, but titanium dioxide probably explains why those who use DariFree™ (a milk alternative) sometimes have stools that actually appear *white*).

Titanium dioxide is not a toxic mineral. It is an inert mineral and should not be confused with titanium, which is a metal that can be detected with a toxicity level test. Food-grade titanium dioxide is commonly used in many consumer products including pharmaceuticals, icing, candy, milk, cheeses, many non-dairy and fat-free foods, toothpaste, sunscreen, soap, shampoo, cosmetics (including products commonly used around the eyes), vitamins, and nutritional supplements. Although it is not absorbed, you could think of titanium dioxide as a very fine grit that is passing through the intestines. If there are issues of intestinal permeability, it is possible that the presence of any gritty matter could slow down the gut healing process. Recent studies have found that while normal subjects are known to experience no ill effects from the mineral, some subjects with Crohn's Disease experienced remission or reduced disease activity after implementing a diet free of inorganic microparticles such as titanium dioxide.[189] [190]

Concerns about this possibility may be outweighed by the need for appetizing foods that your child will accept, at least during the early weeks of the diet. As always, you should balance instinct, judgment, and the information at hand to decide which products to use in order to best keep your children happy and healthy and on their diet.

---

[189] Lomer MC, Thompson RP, Powell JJ. "Fine and ultrafine particles of the diet: influence on the mucosal immune response and association with Crohn's disease." *Proc Nutr Soc.* 2002 Feb;61(1):123-30.

[190] Powell JJ, Thoree V, Pele LC. "Dietary microparticles and their impact on tolerance and immune responsiveness of the gastrointestinal tract." *Br J Nutr.* 2007 Oct;98 Suppl 1:S59-63.

TOE WALKING

Walking on tip-toes has long been accepted as a "soft" neurological symptom of autism. It may be a sensory problem, specifically in the vestibular system. Some have suggested that it is related to gastrointestinal discomfort.

TOOTHPASTE

Many popular brands of toothpaste contain gluten, and some children tend to swallow quite a bit. Check with the manufacturer to be sure; there are some "natural" brands that contain no gluten or other unwanted additives, such as Tom's of Maine.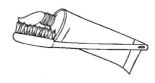

Note: Since dental work can be traumatic for children with communication disorders, always supervise toothbrushing, and make sure it is done thoroughly and daily.

TOPICAL CREAMS (See SKIN CARE PRODUCTS)

TRAVELING WITH SPECIAL DIETS

Below are some tips from Peg Tipton, who has mastered the art of packing food for her son Matt when away from home (see also CAMP, SLEEPAWAY).

The Hotel: We look for hotels with an efficiency kitchen, but most hotels will provide guests with a small refrigerator and even a microwave. Call ahead to arrange for these items to be in your room when you check in.

I cook food before the trip, freeze it, and travel with it frozen, but cooking pasta and rice fresh, as well as fresh boneless chicken or hamburgers, makes your child's vacation more special. Sometimes, on a weekend vacation, we pack Matt's toaster oven in the car.

The Flight - Checked Baggage: We pack a large cooler bag with perishables, with a blue freezer block to keep our items cool. The frozen items stay pretty frozen. The last time we traveled, up to 5 lbs. of blue ice packs and dry ice were allowed in checked baggage.

The Flight - Carry-on Baggage: Blue Ice is allowed for medicines and baby formula, but other than that you will need a doctor's note saying that you need to keep your child's food with ice packs. Dry ice is allowed in carry-on luggage---up to 4.4 lbs.---but you wouldn't use it for a day's travel. I always call the Transportation Security Administration (TSA) at 866-289-9673 to check on the current rules.

Eating Out: We usually try to feed Matt before we go to the restaurant, so he isn't hungry while we wait for the food. I bring his dessert or snacks for him to eat while the rest of us eat our dinner (check with the restaurant before being seated, to make sure this is okay).

Items We Pack:

• Supplements in plastic day of week pill carriers (keep these in a cool, dark place).

• Grill covers from Home Depot (if you will have access to a grill)

• Cutting board (thin, lightweight)

• Plastic zipper bags – freezer and sandwich size

You can find the location of natural foods shops before your trip. Get directions from the hotel using Mapquest (www.mapquest.com) or a similar online service.

When we first get to our destination we make a trip to Wal-Mart and pick up a skillet, baking pan, cutting board—whatever we couldn't bring. We leave these items in the hotel room. Within 48 hours we get to a grocery store to buy the groceries we need.

Foods We Bring on the Plane:

- 2 filled lunch boxes, including wet cloths in plastic bags
- Pumpkin muffins and cookies
- Other snacks

Groceries We Pack:

- Frozen bread
- Frozen Chicken for 2 dinners
- Rice Cereal – 2 boxes
- Small container of Jelly
- 3 Bags Rice Pasta
- Chicken Coating Mix (2 bags) for cooking chicken
- Prunes, individually wrapped

Groceries at Destination:

- Organic Meats: Chicken, Chicken Wings, Hamburger, Steak, Pork Chops
- Bacon
- Cascadian Farms French Fries
- Organic Spinach Leaves, Broccoli, Celery, Cucumber, Fruit
- Olive Oil, Rice Milk, Organic Juice
- Aluminum foil

> *Don't be fooled by airline promises of gluten free meals. One dad reported that he was thrilled when he found that "gluten free" was one of the menu choices, and ordered the special meal for his son. He laughed at his wife for filling a carry-on suitcase with GF/CF food "just in case." The "gluten-free" meal turned out to be a wheat flour tortilla wrapped around a decidedly suspicious looking filling. The moral of the story: pack food and snacks for any trip you are planning, and carry plenty of extras in case of unexpected delays. (A few packs of GF gum or low-sugar lollipops are also helpful for takeoff and landing.)*

The Gluten Intolerance Group® (www.glutenfreerestaurants.org) sponsors a website that lists restaurants that can accommodate special diets. You may also enjoy the following books:

Waiter, Is there Wheat in My Soup? The Official Guide on Dining Out, Shopping and Traveling Gluten-Free and Allergen-free by LynnRae Ries

Let's Eat Out!: Your Passport to Living Gluten And Allergy Free by Kim Koeller and Robert La France.

NOTE: *When traveling in Europe, be aware that in some countries, a product can be labeled "Gluten Free" even if it has wheat starch, which can contain up to .3% gluten. Be sure to check the ingredients.*

TRITICALE

Triticale is a gluten-containing grain that is a hybrid of wheat and rye. It is often well-tolerated by those who cannot eat wheat or other grains due to allergy or intolerance, *but it is not suitable for those on a gluten-free diet.*

TUBEROUS SCLEROSIS (See RELATED AND CO-EXISTING DISORDERS)

ULCERATIVE COLITIS

Ulcerative colitis is an inflammatory bowel disease (IBD) affecting the large intestine, and causing intestinal inflammation, pain and diarrhea. Ulcerative colitis is typically treated with drugs to suppress the body's immune response and inhibit the inflammatory response. However, symptoms may be relieved to some extent by addressing intestinal permeability (see LEAKY GUT) and food sensitivities. Other nutritional approaches, including the Specific Carbohydrate Diet™ have been helpful for many patients. Long-term systemic effects can include skin, eye, mouth, immune system, joint or liver diseases as well as an increased risk of colon cancer.

VACCINES

Although this is a book about dietary intervention, the subject of vaccines needs to be addressed. Many families using dietary interventions believe that vaccines triggered, at least in part, gastrointestinal illness in their children.

Mercury: There has been a lot of publicity about the possible involvement of mercury toxicity as a cause of autism (see MERCURY). This may be medically plausible, and is not controversial in itself, but has become a "hot topic." This is because a child can be exposed to mercury from different sources, but one of them is in the form of a vaccine preservative called thimerosal. The concern is that exposure to mercury can lead to immune and metabolic instability, which could possibly set a child up for a regression into autism when other factors are present.

MMR (Measles-Mumps-Rubella): Another theory about why some of our children have ended up autistic is that gut damage resulted from a measles infection in the gastrointestinal (GI) tract. Pediatric gastroenterologist Dr. Andrew Wakefield, while at the Royal Free Hospital in London, biopsied tissue from infected sites in the large intestine of autistic children (referred to him for abdominal issues), and claimed to have found evidence of vaccine-strain measles virus in these sites, in significantly higher prevalence than in developmentally normal pediatric controls (see BOWEL DISEASE AND AUTISM). These findings are under investigation.

Controversy: The medical establishment accuses parents of casting about wildly for a someone to blame, and parents accuse the medical establishment of a "conflict of interest" at best, and a "cover-up" at worst. Parents who report that their autistic children reacted poorly or regressed after their shots are labeled "anti-vaccine." Studies meant to resolve the issue are criticized for poor design. Parents of small children fear autism, the medical community fears an epidemic of deadly childhood diseases. Both fears are founded.

Emotions run high when it comes to what causes a child's autism, and the unassailability of the vaccination program. It has been difficult for all parties involved to objectively evaluate this "hot potato" issue. As one doctor testified in a hearing in Washington, "autism could not be caused by vaccines because of the possible consequences of such a finding." By this, he most likely means that there might be a decrease in public confidence in the vaccination program, leading to a resurgence of several dangerous, and even deadly, diseases. But the deeper implication is chilling: *"Regardless of whether vaccines cause autism, vaccines can't cause autism."*

Many parents report that their child had adverse reactions to early vaccinations, but became autistic after the MMR. This could imply that heavy metal toxicity compromised their ability to handle the MMR, or that the MMR tipped the scales for a child who was already vulnerable. According to Lyn Redwood, Co-founder and board member of SafeMinds and the National Autism Association: "Mercury is documented to cause immune system impairment, which reduces the body's ability to fight off infections. When an infant with a damaged immune system is injected with a live virus like measles, the infection can become chronic."

In March, 2008, the U.S. federal government agreed to award damages to the family of a girl who developed autism after receiving nine vaccines in a single day. Their conclusion was that specific kinds of "rare, previously-existing conditions" might set a child up for problems with vaccination. The questions remain: how rare are these problems, and what causes them to be "previously-existing?"

A study in May, 2008 found that children given acetaminophen (Tylenol) after their MMR vaccine were significantly more likely to develop autism,[191] which opens up some new and challenging questions about the cause and effect.

"When I said that my child had been normal and became autistic after a vaccine, I was told I didn't know what I saw. When I said I thought the shots were to blame, I was told I was a desperate parent, looking for a scapegoat. When I said I wanted safer vaccines, I was called 'anti-vaccine,' and shown pictures of children suffering from the measles."

From the perspective of gut damage and the need for dietary intervention, anything that interferes with the production of digestive enzymes and causes gut permeability is going to create a problem - whether is be a vaccine, a virus, or a microbial overgrowth in the GI tract.

Autism rates in industrialized countries appear to be increasing dramatically. Further studies are needed to resolve this complicated issue. Large epidemiological studies may not prove be as useful as physically examining the affected children for signs of viral infection or the inability to excrete toxic metals. There are probably even faster and less expensive ways to get answers, such as doing a retrospective study of the prevalence of autism in the vaccinated and unvaccinated younger siblings of affected children.

VINEGAR

In the last five years, celiac societies have come to accept the judgement of grain scientists, that "grain" vinegar is indeed gluten free. According to Dr. Don Kasarda, a respected U.S. grain chemist who has provided research-based information to celiac groups for many years:

[191] Schultz ST, Klonoff-Cohen HS, Wingard DL, Akshoomoff NA, Macera CA, Ming Ji. "Acetaminophen (paracetamol) use, measles-mumps-rubella vaccination, and autistic disorder: The results of a parent survey." *Autism.* 2008 May;12(3):293-307.

"Amino acids, peptides and proteins are of such low volatility compared to the high volatility of ethyl alcohol that they should not be found in the distilled alcohol. There is no scientific evidence for gluten peptides in alcohol or vinegar that I am aware of. I have never encountered a single chemist who thinks there are gluten peptides in distilled alcohol from wheat grain. I have not personally researched this matter because it is such an unlikely possibility and to prove the absence of gluten peptides that might be present in minute amounts is likely to be a major, costly undertaking and not at all easy. I realize that some celiac patients may have a disagreeable digestive response to white vinegar…but if it doesn't bother you don't worry about it. If it does bother you, don't ingest it. Malt vinegar is the only vinegar that I think might contain harmful peptides."

Aside from the gluten question, there are other controversies about vinegar. Most of the anti-yeast diets suggest avoiding vinegar, while some suggest it as a beneficial supplement and yeast-killer. The acetic acid in vinegar is thought to slow starch digestion and reduce the glycemic index of starchy foods, and apple cider vinegar may lower the post-meal rise in glucose. Raw, unrefined apple cider vinegar is recommended on the BED and some other programs, because despite being an acidic solution, it is said to have an alkalinizing effect on the body.

VITAMINS (See SUPPLEMENTS)

VOCAL CORD DYSFUNCTION

Sometimes seen in those with autism, Vocal Cord Dysfunction (VCD) is a surprisingly common condition of throat closure or a choking sensation that can cause sudden, severe episodes of breathing difficulty, including wheezing. VCD can feel like straining to breathe through a straw. These episodes can include high pitched, whistling, or gasping sounds. Panic from the feeling of not getting in enough air can lead to repeated emergency room visits or hospitalizations. VCD is usually misdiagnosed as asthma, anaphylaxis, or hysteria. According to gastroenterologist Dr. Kenneth Fine, gluten sensitivity can cause reflux, which in turn can lead to VCD.

WATER

Nutritionists suggest that parents accustom their children to quenching their thirst with a glass of water instead of with sugary drinks or fruit juice. This is excellent advice, but be aware that there are increasing concerns about tap water safety on several fronts.

A five-month investigation by the Associated Press, found that antibiotics, sex hormones, and other prescription drugs contaminate the drinking water supplies of at least 41 million Americans. How did the drugs get there? When people take pills, their bodies absorb some of the medication, but the rest of it is flushed down the toilet. Water treatment plants aren't designed to remove pharmaceutical residues, so they stay in the water.

The Environmental Working Group (www.ewg.org) suggests that you:

- Find out what it is in your water in their "Tap Water Database:" Enter your US Zip Code at www.ewg.org/sites/tapwater.

- Use a reverse osmosis filtration system, which will remove many chemicals (although not all)

- Contact your Senators and Representatives to demand stricter oversight

See the Environmental Working Group's summary of the report at www.ewg.org/node/26128

WESTON A. PRICE FOUNDATION (See also FATS & OILS, NOURISHING TRADITIONS)

Dr. Weston A. Price was a dentist who studied the diets of isolated, non-industrialized cultures. Their diets included fish, eggs, shellfish, organ meats and butter from pasture fed cows. His research led to a theory that humans can achieve good health only when they eat nutrient-dense whole food, including animal fats. Price analyzed the diets of the people in these cultures and found that they were far richer in water-soluble vitamins, calcium and other minerals. They also contained ten times the fat-soluble vitamins such as vitamins A and D than the typical American diet. Price also discovered a new fat-soluble vitamin that he called "Activator X," now believed to be vitamin K2.

In addition to spreading information about diet, the Foundation supports organic and biodynamic farming, pasture feeding of livestock and community supported farms. They also believe that the benefits of raw milk (unpasteurized) are substantial, and support organizations working towards universal access to clean, certified raw milk (see RAW MILK).

The Weston A. Price Foundation is a non-profit organization that publishes a quarterly journal called *"Wise Traditions in Food, Farming and the Healing Arts,"* which focuses on scientific validation of dietary, agricultural and medical traditions worldwide.

"The book Nourishing Traditions, by Sally Fallon, covers and explains all of Weston's principles and helped me incorporate Price's principles into my family's diet. It even includes a cookbook to help you make these changes in your diet.

My concern with many of the diets out there is that the children aren't getting enough saturated fats and minerals. Grass-fed lamb, beef, organ meats, shellfish, salmon, halibut, pastured turkey and chicken are all great sources of vitamins and minerals and are rarely allergenic. More and more parents of autistic children are successfully using raw milk. Our children are starving for healthy saturated fats and minerals; this supplies both. We use raw goats milk.

Many of the food intolerances seen in these children has to do with the way the animal ate, how it was cooked and prepared, etc., and not the actual protein. And every kid needs cod liver oil, across the board, unless they are eating wild game and salmon 3 times a week. (Magnesium seems to be necessary to supplement, and the B's because we don't all soak our grains and make homemade breads.) I realize these meats are not cheap, but neither are all the supplements we buy for our children. With the right food perhaps supplementation won't be needed.

I make beef and chicken stocks weekly, from bones which boil for over 24 hours and are loaded with all the minerals we need, using a little added vinegar to pull them out. My kids love the soups made from them. I believe so strongly in all of the above that we are selling our house in the suburbs and buying a small farm, with goats, chickens, etc. I have seen the healing in my own body. So worth it all, in my opinion." -Juliann Rank

WHEAT (See also GRAINS)

Wheat is the most commonly cultivated cereal crop in the world. Comprised of the kernel (wheatberry) endosperm, bran and germ, it is used for bread, pasta, bagels, crackers, cakes, muffins and countless other foods. All forms of wheat must be avoided by those on gluten free diets.

WHEATGRASS

Wheat grass refers to the young grass of the wheat family. Although it is part of the wheat plant, it is considered a vegetable because it is cut before the plant forms an actual grain (wheat berry). Therefore, pure wheatgrass is probably gluten free.

Some people maintain that wheat grass is a healthy supplement, providing chlorophyll, amino acids, minerals vitamins and enzymes. It is generally taken juiced or as a powder.

WHEY (See also MILK)

Whey is the liquid that remains after milk has been curdled and strained. It is used in different forms as an additive in many processed foods, some of which would otherwise be dairy free. Whey is not recommended on a casein free diet because it contains lactose (milk sugar), and may contain traces of casein.

WITHDRAWAL (See also "DIE-OFF REACTIONS," OPIOID EXCESS)

Behavioral regressions following removal of gluten and casein can be severe, and often there are physical symptoms. Parents have reported fevers, diarrhea and vomiting when the children have gone "cold turkey." Even with a gradual removal of these proteins, parents often report an immediate improvement for a few days, followed by a very difficult period. In very young children the negative effects usually pass within a week or two. For older children and adults, withdrawal can last from ten days to three weeks, or longer. But they do pass, and with them, the addiction to these foods.

> *"Austin was spacey and hard to reach, still scripting and echoing. The next thing we decided to try was the gluten and casein free diet. His response to the diet was frightening, because he got so much worse! He went through a severe withdrawal, but luckily I heard Paul Shattock speak about the diet that very week. After his presentation, I talked to him about our situation. He told me "usually, the worse the withdrawal, the better the outcome." We stuck with the diet and Austin just kept getting better and better."* -Jane Steele

XANTHAN GUM

Xanthan gum is a powder produced by fermenting corn sugar with a microorganism called *xanthomonas campestris*. It acts as a gluten substitute, giving structure to gluten free baked goods (see COOKING & BAKING). Because it contains no corn protein, it is generally tolerated by people who do not tolerate corn, but if a product causes a reaction, this ingredient may be the cause. Xanthan gum is generally chosen over other gums (e.g. guar gum), which tend to have laxative effects. As with other gums, it is not appropriate for use on the SCD™.

XYLITOL (See SUGAR SUBSTITUTES)

YCK (See YOUNG COCONUT KEFIR)

YEAST & FUNGUS (See also DYSBIOSIS, GUT FLORA)

Yeasts are small organisms classified as fungi. Various species of yeast exist everywhere in our environment, including in and around our bodies. Although not particularly dangerous in small amounts, they can be of concern when the intestinal microflora has been thrown off-balance, and they are allowed to proliferate. *Candida Albicans* is an opportunistic yeast that causes such infections, especially in individuals with improperly-functioning immune systems, or those who have been exposed to antibiotics. (There are other species of pathogenic yeast that can cause infection, such as *Cryptococcus neoformans*, however, the most common type of pathogenic yeasts are those in the *Candida* family.)

"Classic" symptoms of those suffering from candidiasis (yeast infection) include fatigue, sugar cravings, food intolerance, skin problems, loss of libido, muscle weakness, muscle spasms, insomnia, numbness or tingling in the hands and feet. *Candida* is also frequently associated with fibromyalgia and chronic fatigue syndrome.

Other concerns are that *Candida* could interfere with the absorption of vitamins and minerals and the production of digestive enzymes, leading to malnutrition and poor digestion. This could further weaken the immune system, allowing *Candida* and other pathogens to establish themselves in the intestines.

Depending on the tissues affected, infections can be very localized. A *Candida* infection of the mouth, called "thrush," is common in infants, possibly transmitted from the mother through the birth canal during delivery. (It has been proposed that these children are more likely to have ongoing or future problems with candidiasis.) Other examples of localized infections are vaginal yeast infections or a yeasty diaper rash.

Candida, when allowed to flourish, grows root-like structures called "rhizoids," which are said to penetrate the gut wall, allowing it to establish colonies outside the gut (this is called a "systemic infection"). Since it thrives in anaerobic conditions (low or no oxygen) it may end up in the joints, sinuses, muscles and other organs, resulting in joint pain, sinus problems, muscle aches and headaches.

The question of whether candidiasis can be responsible for mental problems has been a subject of debate. Sufferers report an improvement in several areas when treated for *Candida*, such as poor memory, confusion, apathy, attention problems, developmental disabilities, and eating disorders.

Systemic infection with *Candida* is suspected in children with autism, ADHD and other disorders for three reasons. The first has to do with test results. Yeasts tend to colonize the intestinal tract in clusters, or in folds or pockets of the intestine, so they may not always be evident during an endoscopy (examination with a tiny camera inserted in the intestinal tract). However, excess amounts of certain "metabolites" (waste products) of yeast have been identified in the urine of these children using an ORGANIC ACIDS TEST.

The second reason is that some of these children show signs of candidiasis, such as gas and bloating resulting from the fermentation of yeast and sugars in the gut, or "drunken" behavior such as an uneven gait or inappropriate laughter. These may initially become worse when antifungal treatment begins (see DIE-OFF REACTIONS).

The third reason, and perhaps the most important, is anecdotal: treatment with anti-fungal medication has led to great improvement in thousands of children with autism spectrum disorders.

Yeast in Food: Lots of people on an "anti-yeast" regimen wonder about limiting nutritional yeast and the yeast used for baking. These may or may not be problematic. One concern is that those who have had the ongoing presence of yeast in the body may develop a sensitivity to it, just as they might to foods or other antigens (see MOLDY FOODS).

Beneficial Yeast: Some probiotic supplements contain "beneficial yeasts" such as *Saccharomyces boulardii.* Several studies have shown this to be effective at treating dysbiosis, and fighting infections of a dangerous bacterium called *Clostridium difficile* (see ANAEROBIC BACTERIA). The yeasts found in kefir starters are sources of beneficial yeasts.

Treatment: When antibiotics were first developed and prescribed, *Candida* infection was a known concern, and doctors were advised to include nystatin, an anti-fungal drug, concurrently. That information has now been all but lost, even though all doctors know that antibiotics can cause yeast infections, and that the probiotics found in yogurt can help treat or prevent them. A small number of gynecologists do routinely prescribe anti-fungal medication for patients who must take antibiotics.

The following are two of the treatments most commonly recommended by doctors for treating yeast and fungal overgrowth:

Nystatin is a prescription antifungal drug. Because it is not absorbed through skin or mucous membranes, it is considered a relatively safe drug for treating oral or gastrointestinal fungal infections, and can be used over longer periods of time. Liquid nystatin preparations often contain sugar; if the nystatin available at your local pharmacy has sugar, you may want to have the prescription filled at a compounding pharmacy.

Diflucan is a prescription medication with anti-fungal properties, used for yeast or fungal infections in various parts of the body.

Because the action of drugs like Diflucan is systemic (circulating in the bloodstream and working throughout the body), they carry a higher risk of affecting liver function. Whenever possible they are prescribed for short periods. When longer treatment is necessary, the patient's liver enzymes are carefully monitored.

Natural treatments include garlic extract, grapefruit seed, caprylic acid, lemon grass and coconut oil. Adding zinc and selenium to the diet may also be helpful.

In addition to using anti-fungal treatments, it is usually recommended to "re-inoculate" the gut with healthy flora, which will help prevent re-colonization by harmful microbes (see PROBIOTICS). Since yeast feeds on sugar, it is also advisable to remove as much sugar as possible from the diet. Most anti-yeast regimens restrict refined sugars, limit natural sugars such as fruit, and cut down on carbohydrates, which break down into sugars when digested. The SCD™, BED, "Feast Without Yeast," and "The Yeast Connection" programs were developed with these issues in mind.

THE YEAST CONNECTION

Dr. William G. Crook, after many years as a general practitioner, observed that yeast infections, especially candidiasis, were responsible for a host of health problems in his patients. In 1985 he published a landmark book called *The Yeast Connection,* which brought widespread attention to this problem.

YEAST DIE-OFF (See DIE-OFF REACTIONS)

YOGURT & KEFIR (See also PROBIOTICS, CULTURED FOODS, YOUNG
  COCONUT KEFIR)

The main benefits of fermented dairy products come from the high quality and quantity of probiotics contained within. Not only are these associated with ridding the body of excessive amounts of harmful microflora, but recent scientific research has shown that certain strains of microflora in fermented milk can actually reduce or prevent allergies.[192] One type of kefir displayed anti-inflammatory and anti-allergic effects in mice with bronchial asthma.[193] Another study found that giving certain strains of probiotics to infants in the first six months of life decreased the risk of allergy by half, and adults treated with special strains of bacteria in yogurt experienced relief from severe atopic dermatitis (eczema).[194]

There is little doubt that these healthy flora are important, but is it safe to feed yogurt to children who must avoid casein? Some people contend that the fermentation process denatures casein and makes it safe for those avoiding casomorphin. Unfortunately, research by dairy scientists does not support this. One study confirmed that "peptides displaying opioid, mineral binding, cytomodulatory and hypotensive activities have been identified in cheese and yogurt."[195]

However, some children have been reported to be able to tolerate the amount of casein in the carefully-prepared goat yogurt recommended on the SCD™, so it's an individual choice as to whether to try it. It has been suggested that it's better to wait until the gut is presumed to be healing before introducing yogurt or raw butter, but in any event, casein does not stay in a child's system for long, and is unlikely to cause a lengthy regression after it is removed.

Do not give milk products in any form to children with a known milk allergy.

If introducing dairy is out of the question for your child, you can reap the considerable benefits of fermented food while still avoiding casein. Probiotics can come in the form of YOUNG COCONUT KEFIR or CULTURED VEGETABLES. Yogurt may be made from nut milk (see NUT YOGURT). And probiotics can be found in high-quality dairy-free capsules and powders.

---

[192] Enomoto T, Shimizu K, Shimazu S. "Suppression of allergy development by habitual intake of fermented milk foods, evidence from an epidemiological study." Arerugi. 2006 Nov;55(11):1394-9.

[193] Lee MY, Ahn KS, Kwon OK, Kim MJ, Kim MK, Lee IY, Oh SR, Lee HK. "Anti-inflammatory and anti-allergic effects of kefir in a mouse asthma model." Immunobiology. 2007;212(8):647-54.

[194] Matsumoto M, Aranami A, Ishige A, Watanabe K, Benno Y. "LKM512 yogurt consumption improves the intestinal environment and induces the T-helper type 1 cytokine in adult patients with intractable atopic dermatitis." Clin Exp Allergy. 2007 Mar;37(3):358-70.

[195] Fitzgerald, Richard J, Murray, Brian"Bioactive peptides and lactic fermentations." (2006) *International Journal of Dairy Technology* 59 (2) , 118–125

YOUNG COCONUT KEFIR (YCK) (See also BODY ECOLOGY DIET, PROBIOTICS, YOGURT & KEFIR)

Many people would like to give their children the benefits of yogurt or kefir, which are rich in probiotic microflora, but know that they cannot tolerate dairy products. Donna Gates (author of *The Body Ecology Diet*) has come up with this solution: young green coconuts. Young green coconuts are high in minerals and have the right amount of natural sugar to feed and culture probiotics. They are valued in Eastern medicine for their healing properties, and are readily available in most ethnic markets. Fortunately, they are very well tolerated by most people.

Young coconut kefir is made using the clear juice of the young coconut (not to be confused with coconut milk, which comes from a mature coconut and is nutritionally different). This juice is then fermented with a powdered preparation of beneficial bacteria and beneficial yeast. The fermentation process eats up the natural sugars in the juice, makes the minerals in the juice much more bioavailable, and creates a drink filled with probiotic organisms and cleansing substances. The probiotic yeast in the kefir starter, is much hardier than the bacterial species, and is said to be effective at ridding the body of detrimental yeast. The minerals are then made available to the body to help start the healing process, and the good bacteria can gain a foothold in the gut.

When you buy these, they will often come with the green outer shell removed. The hard brown inner shell is coated with a white spongy material, and they are shaped like small primitive huts with pointy tops. A case of 9 should cost under $15.

Using a hammer and an awl (or screwdriver), poke a hole in the pointy end. You can also use a drill, which may be easier when the green husk is still attached. Enlarge the hole to about 1/4 to 1/2" thick. Turn it upside-down onto a clean glass jar and poke another hole on the back until a clear liquid drains out. These immature coconuts have a lot of liquid, and very little meat. The meat is very tasty – you can crack open the shell and scoop it out after draining the juice. If the meat and liquid are pink, do not use it -- it has spoiled.

Add one packet of kefir starter powder to the liquid from approximately 9 coconuts. Pour it into clean jars, leaving about 1" or so head space for expansion. Screw the lids on tightly and shake the jars. Let the jars stand for 24 to 36 hours to ferment at room temperature (if it is cool indoors, let them stand for two days). (The starter can be ordered from www.bodyecologydiet.com, or by calling 1-800-511-2660.)

The slightly fizzy drink tastes somewhat odd; it is a little tangy, but not unpleasant. Serve a glass with meals, and at bedtime, with a few drops of stevia and some black currant juice, if desired. After use, save about 1/3 cup per jar to use as a starter for the next batch. You can recycle the products of one kefir packet 6-7 times. Wash the jars thoroughly before starting each new batch.

YCK is technically not allowed on the Specific Carbohydrate Diet™ because young coconuts are considered unripe fruit. This has been debated, since the natural sugars should be broken down when the juice is kefired. Just keep in mind that because YCK is so rich in probiotics, it should be started in very small doses to avoid a die-off (see "DIE-OFF" REACTIONS).

Afterword

Back in 1996, the first public meeting of Defeat Autism Now! in Chicago was abuzz with excitement over some new ideas, and there were far more questions than answers. Is autism an immune-mediated disorder? Is yeast or bacteria somehow involved? Can diet or vitamin therapies lead to improvements?

At that time, many people still did not have Internet access or email, and we hoped that our books and *The ANDI News* would help get the message out to the public: that autism in its many forms is *treatable*.

More than a decade later, we have many new questions, but we also have some answers. We know that many autistic children have an excellent chance at responding favorably to changes in diet, vitamins & supplements, anti-fungal therapies, immune therapies, heavy metal detoxification, omega-3 fatty acids, investigation and treatment for bowel disease, and other interventions. Tragically, this knowledge has come partly because of the dramatic increase in the number of autism cases around the world, which has opened several painful and controversial cans of worms.

This is a tense and exciting time for all of us who have been following the story of the biomedical treatment of autism. The sense of urgency we share gives it a kind of meaning that other people rarely understand, as each piece of the story unfolds and each revelation gives hope and new possibilities to our families.

Providing support to parents and caregivers has been a fulfilling endeavor for us; we feel we have learned more than we have taught and we have gained more than we have given. Thanks to the many excellent websites and discussion groups on the Web, more information than ever before is available to parents using biomedical and dietary interventions for their children.

Thank you for sharing your stories and insights with us, and a special thanks to our many readers and supporters—some of you have been with us since the beginning. We look forward to continuing to hear from you and meet you at conferences. We know that, like us, you will continue to search for answers.

With our very best wishes,

Lisa Lewis and Karyn Seroussi

Appendix A: Diet Overview

Overview of Restricted Foods on the Gluten-Free, Casein-Free Diet, Specific Carbohydrate Diet™, and Body Ecology Diet

Food	GF/CF*	SCD™**	BED***
Gluten-containing grains (wheat, barley, rye, spelt, kamut, and possibly oats)	Not allowed	Not allowed	Not Recommended
Rice	Individual	Not allowed	Not Recommended
Corn	May be problematic	Not allowed	Some OK if tolerated
Soy	May be problematic	Not allowed	Not allowed unless fermented (miso, tempeh)
Millet, Quinoa, Amaranth, Buckwheat	Individual	Not allowed	Unlimited (80/20 rule), pre-soaked
Eggs and Meat (incl. beef, lamb, fish, chicken, turkey)	Individual	Allowed if unprocessed	Recommended; organic free range/wild caught preferred; use 80/20 rule
Vegetables	Individual	Most allowed, if fresh or frozen. Potatoes, yams, turnips, jerusalem artichoke, parsnips and most other starchy root vegetables not permitted	Unlimited and recommended to be 80% of the diet. Fermented vegetables are highly recommended and should be consumed regularly
Fruit	Individual	Allowed (peeled, seeded, and cooked in initial stages), not canned	Not recommended except lemon, lime, cranberry or black currant. Tomatoes not recommended.
Milk Products (milk, butter, cream, yogurt, cheese, casein, whey, etc.) and ingredients	Not allowed	Not in initial phase, then 24-hour goat yogurt, dry curd cottage cheese, specific cheeses and butter, for those who tolerate dairy	Raw butter and cream immediately, kefir after about a month. ("ghee" may be used for people with extreme casein sensitivities)
Sweeteners	Individual	Honey & saccharin only	Stevia & Lakanto only
Vinegar	Individual	White or apple cider	Raw apple cider only- foods pickled in vinegar not recommended
Juice	Individual	Limited to those confirmed to be without added sugars or starches (whole fruit juiced at home preferred)	None except pure cranberry, black currant, lemon or lime
Oils	Individual	Unlimited	Olive, coconut and pumpkin seed recommended
Condiments	Individual	OK if no added sugars, starch or spices	Limited to wheat-free tamari, herbs and spices, Celtic sea salt

Nuts	Individual	Most allowed if ground into flour in initial phase. Peanuts and peanut butter not allowed, check that no "anti-caking agents" have been used	Prefer raw and soaked for 12 hours
Seeds	Individual	Not for first 3 months, then cautiously	Prefer raw and soaked for 12 hours. Pumpkin seeds recommended
Seaweed	Individual	Not allowed	Highly recommended
Beans	Individual	Certain types allowed after 3 months, soaked 12 hours then pre-cooked before added to recipes	Not recommended- soak 12 hours if used. Adzuki beans preferred
Alcoholic Beverages	Beer not allowed	Beer not allowed. Occasional use: dry wine, gin, rye, scotch, bourbon, vodka	Not recommended
Coconut Products	Individual	Unlimited, fresh only, no young green coconut water. Introduce when nuts are added	Young Coconut Kefir, coconut oil, and raw coconut meat recommended (cultured preferred), unsweetened flake coconut for occasional use
Gelatin	Individual	Unflavored only	Not recommended, substitute agar agar
Coffee and Tea	Individual	Allowed, weak. Herb tea if it does not induce diarrhea. No decaf. coffee/tea	Not recommended, herb/green tea OK

Table notes:

(GF/CF): All gluten and casein free foods are allowed. Other foods should be restricted based on individual intolerance. Certain *brands of foods* or *ingredients* are not allowed if they contain any amount of gluten or casein.

(SCD™): Any food listed is *not allowed* if it contains any added starch or sugar. Check with manufacturers.

(BED): This is not an exclusionary diet, so nothing is "illegal" with the exception of sugars and sugary foods and hydrogenated oils; certain foods are recommended as particularly healing and followers of the BED are advised to eat them preferentially over other foods. The 80/20 rule indicates that grains or meat should be only 20% of a meal that is also 80% vegetable.

For a list of restricted foods on the Low Oxalate Diet, see **LOW OXALATE DIET.**

Appendix B: Resources & Support

Recommended Reading

Allergy Busters: A Story for Children with Autism or Related Spectrum Disorders Struggling with Allergies by Kathleen A. Chara, Paul J., Jr. Chara, Karston J. Chara, Angela Litzinger

Biological Treatments for Autism and PDD by William Shaw

The Body Ecology Diet by Donna Gates

Breaking the Vicious Cycle: Intestinal Health Through Diet by Elaine Gottschall

Children with Starving Brains by Jacquelyn McCandless

Diet Intervention and Autism: Implementing a Gluten Free and Casein Free Diet for Autistic Children and Adults by Marilyn Le Breton. (British)

Enzymes for Autism and other Neurological Conditions. Karen L. DeFelice

Feast Without Yeast: 4 Stages to Better Health : A Complete Guide to Implementing Yeast Free, Wheat (Gluten) Free and Milk (Casein) Free Living by Bruce Semon, Lori Kornblum

Just Take a Bite by Lori Ernsperger by Tania Stegen-Hanson (Author)

The Kid-Friendly ADHD and Autism Cookbook: The Ultimate Guide to the Gluten-Free, Casein-Free Diet by Pamela Compart, Dana Laake

Nourishing Hope by Julie Matthews

Gluten-Free Quick & Easy: From Prep to Plate Without the Fuss - 200+ Recipes for People with Food Sensitivities by Carol Fenster

Gluten-Free Cooking For Dummies by Danna Korn (Author), Connie Sarros

The Gluten-free Gourmet, Second Edition: Living Well Without Wheat by Bette Hagman

The Gluten-Free Gourmet Cooks Fast and Healthy: Wheat-Free and Gluten-Free with Less Fuss and Less Fat by Bette Hagman

Recipes for the Specific Carbohydrate Diet: The Grain-Free, Lactose-Free, Sugar-Free Solution to IBD, Celiac Disease, Autism, Cystic Fibrosis, and Other Health Conditions by Raman Prasad

Special Diet Celebrations by Carol Fenster

Special Diets for Special Kids by Lisa Lewis

Special Diets for Special Kids II by Lisa Lewis

Unraveling the Mystery of Autism and Pervasive Developmental Disorder: A Mother's Story of Research & Recovery by Karyn Seroussi

Online Food Retailers

Allergy Grocer (Grocery specific to all food allergies, intolerances)
www.allergygrocer.com

Aunt Candice Foods (Bread, Cookie, Pancake Mixes, Bars)
www.auntcandicefoods.com

Autism Network for Dietary Intervention (ANDI Bars, Links to other food & resources)
www.autismndi.com

Enjoy Life Foods (Cookies, Bagels, Bars)
www.enjoylifefoods.com

Gluten Solutions (Wide selection of GF groceries)
www.glutensolutions.com

Glutino (Wide assortment of GF foods)
www.glutenfree.com

Josef's Gluten Free Bakery (Breads and other baked goods)
www.josefsglutenfree.com

Kinnikinnick Foods (Waffles, Pancake & Bread Mixes, Doughnuts)
www.kinnikinnick.com

Vance's Foods (DariFree)
www.vancesfoods.com

Supplements and Digestive Enzymes

Houston Nutraceuticals
PO Box 6331, Siloam Springs, AR 72761-6331
Phone: 1-866-757-8627, 1-479-549-4536, Fax 1-479-549-4540
info@houstonni.com, www.houstonni.com

Kirkman Labs

6400 SW Rosewood Street, Lake Oswego, OR 97035
1-800-245-8282, 1-503-694-1600, Fax 1-503-682-0838
www.kirkmanlabs.com

Klaire Labs® A Division of ProThera, Inc.

10439 Double R Blvd, Reno, NV 89521
Phone 1-888-488-2488, 1-775-850-8800, Fax 775-850-8810
www.klairelabs.com

Personal Nutrition Counselors

Charlie Erica Fall, Hopewell, NJ
cefall@comcast.net
609-466-8393

Nadine Gilder, Toms River, NJ
Autism Educational Services
732-473-9482 ngilder@att.net

Betsy Prohaska Hicks, Delavan, WI
Pathways Medical
betsy@pathwaysmed.com

Julie Matthews, San Francisco, CA
www.nourishinghope.com
415-437-6807

Laboratories (see TESTING)

Alletess Medical

216 Pleasant Street, Rockland, MA 02370
Phone: 1-781-871-4426, Toll free: 1-800-225-5404, Fax: 1-781-871-4182
nutritionist@foodallergy.com, alletess@foodallergy.com, www.foodallergy.com

Doctor's Data, Inc.

3755 Illinois Avenue, St. Charles, IL 60174-2420
Phone: 1-630-377-8139 Toll-free: 1-800-323-2784, Fax: 630.587.7860
inquiries@doctorsdata.com, www.doctorsdata.com

Enterolab

10875 Plano Rd., Suite 123, Dallas, TX 75238
Phone: 1-972-686-6869
www.enterolab.com

Genova Diagnostics

63 Zillicoa Street, Asheville, NC 28801
Phone: 1-828-253-0621, Toll-free 1-800-522-4762
www.genovadiagnostics.com

The Great Plains Laboratory

11813 W. 77th St., Lenexa, KS 66214 USA

Phone: 1-913-341-8949, Toll Free: 1-800-288-0383, Fax: 1-913-341-6207

gpl4u@aol.com, www.greatplainslaboratory.com

IBT Laboratories

11274 Renner Boulevard, Lenexa, KS 66219

Phone 1-913-492-2224, Toll-free 1-800-637-0370, Fax 1-913-492-7145

www.ibtlabs.com

ImmunoLabs

1620 West OaklandPark Blvd., Fort Lauderdale, FL 33311

Phone 1-800-231-9197 ext. 6555

www.immunolabs.com

Metametrix Clinical Laboratory

3425 Corporate Way, Duluth, GA 30096

Phone 1-770-446-5483, Toll-free 1-800-221-4640, Fax 1-770-441-2237

inquiries@metametrix.com, www.metametrix.com

NeuroScience Inc.

373 280th St., Osceola, WI 54020

Phone 1-715-294-2144, Toll-free 888-342-7272, Fax: 1-715-294-3921

https://www.neurorelief.com/

Nordic Laboratories

Nygade 6, 3.sal, 1164 Copenhagen K, Denmark

Phone: +45 33 75 1000, Fax: +45 33 75 10 09

Email: cm@nordic-labs.com, www.nordicclinic.dk

Optimum Health Resource Laboratories, Inc.

2700 North 29th Avenue, Suite # 205, Hollywood, Florida 33020 USA

Toll Free: 1-888-751-3388, Local: 1-954-920-3728, Fax: 1-954-920-3729

info@optimumhealthresource.com, www.optimumhealthresource.com

Sage Medical Laboratory

1400 Hand Avenue, Suite L, Ormond Beach, FL 32174

Phone 1-877-SAGELAB (1-877-724-3522), Fax: 1-386-615-2027

www.foodallergytest.com

Quest Diagnostics

3 Giralda Farms. Madison, NJ 07940

800-222-0446

www.questdiagnostics.com

US Biotek

13500 Linden Ave North, Seattle, WA 98133

Phone: 1.877.318.8728, Fax: 206.363.8790

www.usbiotek.com

Compounding Pharmacies:

Hopewell Pharmacy & Compounding Center

1 West Broad Street, Hopewell, NJ 08525
Phone: 1-800-792-6670, 609-466-1960, Fax: 1-800-417-3864, 1-609-466-8222
www.hopewellrx.com

Lee Silsby Compounding Pharmacy
3216 Silsby Rd, Cleveland Hts, OH 44118
Phone: 1-800-918-8831, 1-216-321-4300
www.leesilsby.com
Lee Silsby carries Glutathione Cream (by prescription)

Wellness Pharmacy®

3401 Independence Drive, Suite 231, Birmingham, Alabama 35209
Phone: (205-879-6551, Toll Free: 1-800-227-2627, Fax: 1-205-871-2568/1-800-369-0302
www.wellnesshealth.com
Wellness carries the single dose vials of the Measles, Mumps and Rubella vaccine.

Additional Web Resources

www.gfcfdiet.com
www.autism.com
www.autismone.org
www.autismndi.com